ALL OUR RELATIONS

GENDER RELATIONS
IN THE AMERICAN EXPERIENCE

Joan E. Cashin
Ronald G. Walters
SERIES EDITORS

Angel Kwolek-Folland, *Engendering Business: Men and Women in the Corporate Office, 1870–1930*

Margaret Creighton and Lisa Norling, eds., *Iron Men, Wooden Women: Gender and Seafaring in the Atlantic World, 1700–1920*

Stephen M. Frank, *Life with Father: Parenthood and Masculinity in the Nineteenth-Century American North*

Anya Jabour, *Marriage in the Early Republic: Elizabeth and William Wirt and the Companionate Ideal*

Catherine Gilbert Murdock, *Domesticating Drink: Women, Men, and Alcohol in America, 1870–1940*

Lorri Glover, *All Our Relations: Blood Ties and Emotional Bonds among the Early South Carolina Gentry*

All Our Relations

Blood Ties and Emotional Bonds among
the Early South Carolina Gentry

Lorri Glover

The Johns Hopkins University Press | Baltimore and London

© 2000 The Johns Hopkins University Press
All rights reserved. Published 2000
Printed in the United States of America on acid-free paper

2 4 6 8 9 7 5 3 1

The Johns Hopkins University Press
2715 North Charles Street
Baltimore, Maryland 21218-4363
www.press.jhu.edu

Library of Congress Cataloging-in-Publication Data
will be found at the end of this book.
A catalog record for this book is available from the British Library.

ISBN 0-8018-6474-7

CONTENTS

Acknowledgments vii
Introduction ix

CHAPTER ONE
"An Earthly Paradise" or "A Damned Fraud":
The First Generation of Colonists   1

CHAPTER TWO
"A First, & Dear Connection": Sibling Bonds and Kinship
Networks across the Life Course   23

CHAPTER THREE
Sibling Ties and Gender Values   59

CHAPTER FOUR
Making Money, Making Class   87

CHAPTER FIVE
"The Long and Steady Attachment": Politics and Kinship   113

Conclusion   140

APPENDIXES
1. Estate Dispersal Patterns and Sibling and Kin Connections   149
2. Most Powerful Members of the South Carolina
   Assembly, 1730–1775   151
3. Longest-Serving Members of the South Carolina
   Assembly, 1730–1775   153
4. Biographical Sketches of Key Figures   155

Notes   159
Index   201

ACKNOWLEDGMENTS

As I reflect on my research, I feel a bit like my subjects. As a professor, of course, I will never enjoy any wealth or power. But, like the men and women I have studied, I have been ushered along, protected, and counseled by a wide array of kindred spirits who made possible any success I have. Lawrence Nelson first inspired me, through his passion for history and his gift for teaching, to become a historian. I would have never imagined the power of the past or known the joys of academic life had he not been my teacher. Theda Perdue was a mentor to me in the fullest sense of the word. With wisdom and humor she helped shape my research and provided a model for my career. Joan Cashin has been an unfailing friend of this project throughout the entire writing and publication process. She believed in the value of my study, read the entire manuscript twice, and helped me to sharpen my analysis and writing style. Susan Becker and Steve Ash, in their advice and from their example, have helped me to become a better teacher-scholar.

The head of the history department at the University of Tennessee, J. B. Finger, supported me at every turn, providing personal encouragement and funding for travel and research. Ron Walters, Susan Becker, and Wayne Bodle read the manuscript in its entirety. Their suggestions strengthened the arguments and limited the flaws in the book. Eric Schramm, who copyedited the manuscript, taught me a great deal about language and saved me from a number of embarrassing mistakes. Henry Fulmer and the staff of the South Caroliniana Library, along with Walter Edgar and the Institute for Southern Studies, offered much-appreciated support while I conducted research in Columbia. I also benefited from the advice of archivists at the Southern Historical Collection, the Duke University Library, and the South Carolina Historical Society. James Barkley at the South Carolina State Archives helped me acquire and understand Charlestonians' wills. Kent Dollar was the hardworking research assistant who took time away from his own work to do the quantitative analysis of those wills. I received support for the project from the University of Kentucky, Otterbein College, and especially the University of Tennessee. My research benefited from public presentations, particularly at the Southern Historical Association and the Omohundro Institute of Early American History and Culture. I am grateful to Robert J. Brugger, the staff at the Johns Hopkins University Press, and the anonymous reader of the manuscript for their advice.

My friends Matt Schoenbachler, Craig Friend, and Debbie Blackwell did the impossible by making graduate school bearable and sometimes even fun. Steve Ash, Bruce Wheeler, Kurt Piehler, Beth Haiken, Penny Hamilton, and Kim Harrison made it a joy to come to work at UT. My family supported me when everyone in our hometown kept wondering when I was ever going to "finish school." And Dan Smith was there all the way. He talked about Charleston's planter-merchants for endless hours, read countless drafts, and helped me think through my ideas even when they conflicted with his own work. I remember each of the thousand times he told me that it was all going to be okay. And I have every intention, eventually, of believing him. Finally, my sister, Jerolyn Lier, who is the very best person I know, deserves special thanks for this project, since she first impressed upon me the power of the bond between siblings. In retrospect, I know that our connection inspired me to explore this subject.

INTRODUCTION

In the 1740s, after several years of experimentation on her plantations, Eliza Lucas struck gold with an indigo plant. The economic impact of indigo on the lowcountry and the copious records Eliza left concerning her agricultural endeavors made her South Carolina's most famous female planter. Eliza, however, showed more concern about the family relationships she cultivated—especially with her brothers, Thomas and George, and her sister, Polly—than the crops she grew. After her father had sent Thomas and George abroad, Eliza longed to be reunited with them and wrote often, advising them on their character and their careers. Afraid of being separated from Polly as well, Eliza convinced her father that she could oversee her younger sister's education. Eliza Lucas loved her siblings, and she insisted that they should take responsibility for and find comfort in one another. They were, she explained, bound "by blood as well as friendship."[1]

When I first read Eliza's description of the bonds she shared with her siblings, it surprised and intrigued me. I had gone to the archives hoping to understand the attitudes and values that prominent colonists embraced as they constructed family dynasties. As a young woman, Eliza Lucas kept meticulous accountings of the three lowcountry plantations she oversaw for her father. Her letterbook, I hoped, would open an important window into father-daughter relationships and dynastic financial strategies and therefore enable me to see how the Lucas family expanded their wealth and power across the generations. But interwoven with Eliza's letters to her father was this correspondence concerning Polly, Thomas, and George. The Lucas sibling letters suggested to me another, powerful dimension to family life.[2]

The further I waded into the documents, the more often I heard women and men echo Eliza's sentiments about these intragenerational bonds of blood and friendship. Eventually their words convinced me that the more revealing story—indeed, the key to understanding elite culture in South Carolina—lay not in "vertical" family dynasties, but rather in the "horizontal" ties between siblings and kin. I moved toward an entirely different set of questions about family life: Why did siblings and kin matter so much to early Carolinians? Did these bonds transcend childhood, and with what consequences? What values and assumptions governed these relationships? What impact did they have within the patriarchal household?[3] Did these bonds matter only in a familial context, or did they also influence eighteenth-century society and culture?

In time, Eliza Lucas and her contemporaries revealed a much broader definition of family than I had imagined. Myriad references to sororal and fraternal bonds, some explicit, others subtle, indicated that siblings and kin exercised a profound influence over one another. Brothers and sisters frequently had more in common than did other family members, and their connections lasted longer than their ties to parents or spouses. Kin similarly pervaded Carolinians' lives, and along with siblings gave their relatives emotional and practical support and a sense of belonging and personal identity. Much of the time, sisters and brothers acted as if they were equal partners in family matters. They cooperated on such diverse matters as child rearing, trading, courtship, and politics. Sisters advised brothers on military service, and brothers counseled sisters about nursing newborns. The lines between men and women shifted and blurred, and scant attention was granted to gender. Siblings and a wide array of kin willingly and eagerly cooperated with one another and paid little heed to deference and hierarchy in their interactions. Instead, they chose to build their relationships on an ethos of cooperation and mutuality.[4]

As I expanded my own definition of family and my perceptions of how eighteenth-century families were supposed to operate, I saw the cohesiveness of their world. Public and private intertwined and often seemed as one.[5] Elites in the lowcountry were, in the first place, hopelessly intermarried. They honored a very narrow definition of incest and regularly married cousins and other kin. Furthermore, this interrelated elite controlled most of the shipping and mercantile firms in Charleston and monopolized political offices in the colony.[6] They conducted business in their firms and in the government using the same attitudes they embraced in their private lives. Little competition took place between businesses, and virtually no factionalism divided political life. Instead, these interrelated elites agreed to set prices, invested together, and passed legislation as a block—all aimed at promoting their agenda to amass more and more power, but achieved through cooperation and interdependence.

These feelings and actions seemed to contradict what I thought I knew about the hierarchical, deferential nature of colonial society. And sibling relationships clearly diverged from the power-based relationships within the patriarchal household. In the eighteenth century, parent-child and husband-wife relationships, according to religion, custom, and often law, upheld an unwavering commitment to hierarchy and subordination. And colonial America was a world in which prominent whites (the self-appointed "better sort") worked, with no small measure of success, to institute a rigid social order based on race, class, and gender. Thus, both the relationships within the conjugal household and the underlying structure of early American society hung on inequality and patriarchalism. Despite this familial and societal commitment to place and power, siblings and kin in the lowcountry—and in time, the whole class of interrelated elites in Charleston—constructed relationships based on mutuality, cooperation, and interdependence.

The two sets of values, deference and patriarchal power on the one hand, mutual aid and egalitarianism on the other, existed alongside each other and often collided. Women, for instance, while acting as partners with brothers, were still required to defer to their husbands. Parents sometimes clashed with kin over educating children. And testators struggled to balance competing family obligations. Ultimately, lowcountry elites used one set of values (patriarchy and deference) to ensure their dominance over poor whites, Indians, and slaves, while embracing another (cooperation and equity) within their own kin universe and class. The result, I discovered, was something both more and less than the hierarchy and patriarchalism we often associate with early America.

The values expressed and the behaviors exhibited by siblings and kin provide new insights into the creation of class, the power of patriarchy, the subordination of women, and the pervasiveness of deference. By looking at early American life experiences through this prism, one sees that sibling and kin ties played at least as great a role as wealth in constructing class identity; that siblings created relationships that ignored and even challenged the dictates of patriarchy; that sisters operated as partners in most family matters; and that women and men cultivated an ethos of cooperation in their kin networks and their class. This broader definition of family, then, offers a deeper understanding not only of eighteenth-century family values but also of the impact of those values on early American society.

Ironically, this revealing dimension of family life has been largely hidden in the historical record. To begin with, kinship is more difficult to investigate than conjugal connections. Kin ties stretch beyond the household, are unique to each individual, and change over the life span. Typically, neither laws nor religious codes dictated the nature of kin and sibling ties. Instead, they existed because of the perceptions and actions of individuals. The difficulty of uncovering these ties in the historical record has been compounded by early American family historians' propensity to focus attention on the shifting balance between patriarchal power and individual autonomy within the household.[7] The horizontal connections between siblings and kin, characterized by egalitarianism and interdependence, do not easily fit into these debates about power and autonomy. More generally, family historians have tended to apply contemporary idealizations of the family (that is, private nuclear households) to their analyses of the past. When scholars define family essentially as the conjugal household, relationships that transcend the household appear less important and attract less attention.[8] In most scholarship, then, siblings and kin constitute a "hidden family," occasionally invoked but rarely analyzed by historians and difficult to track in the sources.

The value of these relationships was most decidedly not, however, hidden to eighteenth-century Carolinians. From the point of colonization throughout the eighteenth century, Carolinians self-consciously identified with their siblings and kin and worked hard to cement their bonds to one another. As evidenced in Chapter One, many of the first migrants into the lowcountry came as emissaries for Barbadian and English relatives hoping to expand their family empires into mainland British North America. The colony began as a commercial enterprise, and the personal nature of early modern business required extensive kin ties. The initial intentions of using kin networks to promote business interests intensified after colonists arrived to find the lowcountry a virtual death trap. High mortality rates, frequent out-migration, and the general precariousness of life all conspired to enhance colonists' reliance on siblings and kin.

Chapter Two traces the emotional attachments between siblings and kin over the life course. The letters, daybooks, and wills of prominent Carolinians demonstrate that these women and men recognized siblings (step, half, and full varieties), aunts and uncles, nieces and nephews, cousins, and in-laws as integral members of their families and as key players in their emotional lives. From birthing children to laying the dead to rest, the kin group intersected with the patriarchal family, and the contradictory values of the two systems clashed. In particular, the cooperation and mutuality that characterized these life-long attachments provided an alternative pattern of gender relations.

Chapter Three explores the meaning of gender within the intragenerational families of elites and proves that subordination did not define the familial experiences of lowcountry women. Rather, as sisters and kinswomen, women acted as equal partners in many family matters and in the construction of class identity. As the century progressed, elites used their intragenerational connections to monopolize economic and political power within the colony and to create a self-conscious interrelated ruling class.

Chapter Four investigates the intermingling of economics and family ties to acquire wealth, while Chapter Five unravels the connections between kinship and political authority. In both cases siblings and kin provided the motive, the means, and the value system for amassing power. Borrowing the styles of siblings and kin, the planter-merchants thwarted the challenges of unrelated merchants and backcountry rivals and even weathered the democratizing impulses of the American Revolution. By persistently and aggressively cooperating with one another, they forestalled the collapse of their power nexus until after the turn of the nineteenth century.

This did not occur without complications. While most Charlestonians enjoyed equitable, cooperative sibling and kin ties, exceptions to the general pattern existed. Age and stage of life, for example, sometimes altered the mutuality of sibling relationships. When siblings found themselves separated by significant age differences, or when one sibling became better educated than the others, their relationship could grow tense or indifferent. In many cases, age gaps caused elder siblings to treat younger siblings more like children than partners: that is, the relationships took on a style more akin to parental models. Although sisters and brothers ignored many of the gendered norms of the patriarchal household, their interactions always took place within the context of a society committed to female subordination. Brothers and sisters could operate as partners on some matters, like education and child rearing, but others, such as business ownership and political participation, remained beyond the scope of possibilities within eighteenth-century America. Some sibling sets failed to develop close attachments to one another, while a few individuals rejected their siblings outright. Sibling ties, after all, came about by the accident of birth. Not surprisingly, the connections between siblings could be complicated, indifferent, even estranged. But the complexity of sibling ties in the lowcountry did not grow out of any inherent sibling rivalry or birth order struggles.[9] Rather, the circumstances of their lives—age, experiences, and personality—strengthened or weakened their relationships. Despite these complications, most did enjoy close bonds. Those who ignored or rejected their siblings found themselves in the distinct minority.

Even fewer talked openly about problems within the kin group. The gentry worked hard to keep family conflicts to a minimum, and the letter-writing style of eighteenth-century elites complemented this demand for harmony. Writing served as an outward manifestation of class identity, and elites corresponded with an eye toward a wide readership.[10] Always aware of the implications of their words, lowcountry elites thus rarely mentioned conflicts in their personal writings. This covert tendency to keep family feuds quiet cannot, however, invalidate the overt actions of siblings and kin that clearly attested to their affection for and reliance on one another. While the documentary silence on the issue of family feuds raised my suspicions, I concluded that the obvious determination of elites to downplay conflict was actually further evidence of the importance of these intragenerational relationships. Sibship and kinship simply mattered too much to risk losing over petty differences. Only the most egregious misconduct—overt betrayals, for example, or squandering an estate—could lead to a severing of family ties. To an interrelated class of people who almost singlemindedly pursued a quest for wealth and power, and who depended on their relatives to succeed, few other issues seemed worth the risk to their happiness and status.

The protection and cooperation that elites enjoyed in their own circle stood in direct opposition to the turbulent, racially conflicted world they inhabited. And their commitment to egalitarianism within their own ranks contradicted their treatment of unrelated settlers, enslaved Africans (who endured the most brutal slave system on the mainland), and displaced Indians. The gentry rigidly ranked and grossly exploited those outside their race and class. Their cohesiveness grew out of their interrelatedness and the application of hidden family values to the other dimensions of their lives. That intense class cohesion and cooperation allowed elites to devote their undivided attention to pursuing their own interests at the expense of the other members of society. In the end, the hidden family of siblings and kin supplied these elites with both the personal values and the strategic means to build what they called their "earthly paradise" in the tumultuous Carolina lowcountry.

ALTHOUGH THIS STUDY focuses on the planter-merchant class in the lowcountry, their experiences were not unique, either in South Carolina or in early America. The dearth of evidence precluded studying kinship among South Carolina's poorer whites or "black majority" in the same kind of intensive, personal way as was done with the gentry. However, the sparse evidence from the eighteenth century and the expansive literature on the nineteenth century suggests that kinship, both biological and fictive, enabled African Americans to transcend the brutality of slavery and carve out autonomous communities and cultures.[11] Scattered evidence from middling farm families and artisans indicate that they, too, engaged in similar behaviors as the gentry. Although the evidentiary base is weak, elites seem to have shared with poorer whites and enslaved Africans in South Carolina a clear identification with and reliance on intragenerational family ties. Elites alone, however, maintained elaborate records of their experiences. Their routines, their passions, their loyalties are all there in the archives. We can get beyond occasional anecdotes and conjecture and inside the intimate parts of their lives in ways impossible for other Carolinians.

While the gentry shared with slaves and poorer whites emotional attachments to kin, they embraced a distinct class agenda in their family ties. This determination to use kin to secure status and power linked South Carolinians to elites in other regions. In fact, the South Carolina lowcountry offers an ideal setting for a case study of the interplay between kinship and elite culture in the eighteenth century. Although often lumped together with their more frequently studied neighbors in the Chesapeake, Charleston's elites had as much in common with merchant families in cities like Philadelphia and Boston as they did with Virginia planters.[12] In all these regions, family played a pivotal role in the creation of an elite culture and provided the means to maintain wealth and prominence. Charlestonians' class identity and commitment to protecting class interests ran deeper and their control over their city was stronger largely because they enjoyed more extensive and intensive kin connections and greater cultural cohesion. In other words, South Carolinians stood out from elites in these other parts of eighteenth-century America primarily because of their success, and not because they created unique family systems. Moreover, only by looking at elites' hidden family connections and values can we see precisely how they came to dominate eighteenth-century society.

Ultimately, I suspect that siblings and kin represented a crucial part of Americans' emotional lives and social worlds far beyond the borders of South Carolina and well past the eighteenth century. Critical regional variations notwithstanding, early American white families had several key things in common. To begin, siblings were a nearly universal experience. The relative absence of birth control and the economic responsibilities that children fulfilled in most families made childless couples and only children rare, even in demographically unstable areas like the seventeenth-century Chesapeake, the early-eighteenth-century lowcountry, and the southern backcountry. Furthermore, family was not an isolated, privatized institution in early America. Instead, family functioned as both an emotional and an economic entity: individuals, irrespective of region, depended on their relatives for their livelihood as well as for personal needs. Finally, family meant not simply parents and children but also siblings, in-laws, cousins, and other kinfolk. And these extensive family connections could inform everything from personal identity to political behavior. Scholars studying topics as diverse as military service, politics, religion, and African-American culture have, usually inadvertently, hinted at the power of siblings and kin throughout the eighteenth and nineteenth centuries.[13] But the full force of siblings and kin in other regions and among other peoples remains to be seen. I hope that this case study will encourage historians to think more broadly about what family meant in the past and to seek to reveal, in other locales, the nature and significance of these hidden family ties.

ALL OUR RELATIONS

CHAPTER ONE

"An Earthly Paradise" or "A Damned Fraud"
The First Generation of Colonists

In the spring of 1670, the first group of permanent English settlers arrived on the shores of what is today Charleston, South Carolina. Stephen Bull, a member of an established, wealthy English family, sailed with those first ninety-odd immigrants. As the *Carolina* approached the bay, he saw stretched before him potentially limitless opportunities. Carolina offered a relatively temperate climate, a long growing season, good rivers, rich soil, and free land. When Bull arrived on the shores of Carolina he brought with him nine servants and the Bull family name. For the former he received 1,050 acres of rich land along the Ashley River, but the latter proved far more lucrative.[1] Bull's relatives financed his settlement in Carolina and eagerly anticipated his success there. All the Bull family resources stood ready to ensure that this came to pass. Further, his familial connections earned him the favor of the lord proprietors and an appointment as proprietary deputy on the Grand Council. Bull and his descendants numbered among South Carolina's wealthiest and most politically influential families from the late seventeenth century until the American Revolution. By the mid-eighteenth century, the Bulls stood, along with other kin groups including the Draytons, Rutledges, Middletons, Pinckneys, Manigaults, and Izards, at the center of political, economic, and social power in the Carolina lowcountry.[2]

Edward Hyrne, conversely, spent his years in the lowcountry barely eking out an existence. In early 1700 Edward and his wife, Elizabeth, fled England, Edward's creditors, and the disapproval of their families and determined to start again in Carolina. Ill-prepared to deal with the lowcountry environment, alone in a new place, and impoverished, the Hyrnes found "our necessities are very great and pressing." Lacking both the financial and familial connections necessary to succeed, Edward and Elizabeth watched again and again as their dreams of prospering in Carolina died. Around 1706 Edward reluctantly traveled to England and issued a desperate appeal to Elizabeth's brother for financial support. While Edward's brother-in-law begrudgingly agreed to provide some money for his sister and nephews, he assured Edward that only a court order could make him acquiesce to all the Hyrne's financial appeals. The trip a failure, Edward attempted a return to Charleston. But before he could board the next ship, he was arrested and thrown into debtor's prison.[3]

Bull and Hyrne, like most other early Carolinians, did not rise or fall solely—or even primarily—on their own merit. Ambition, wealth, and chance all contributed to a successful Carolina venture, but the single most important determinant in the fate of the earliest colonists was familial connections. Bull went to Carolina not as an individual entrepreneur, but rather as an emissary of the Bull clan. Edward Hyrne, on the other hand, fled to Carolina to escape his creditors and the disdain of his wife's family. While Bull enjoyed the support of his kin abroad and parlayed his family name into political appointments, social status, and economic gain, the Hyrnes remained alone, estranged from their relatives, bereft of a kinship network either in England or in the colony. Bull prospered beyond his own grand dreams. Halfway through the winter of 1700–1701, Edward Hyrne reported that only the kindness of strangers kept him and his family from starving to death.[4]

When one understands the nature of Carolina settlement, it is not at all surprising that Bull spent his last days on South Carolina's Grand Council and Hyrne spent his in debtor's prison.

SETTLING SOUTH CAROLINA was, from the beginning, a family affair. The free white men and women who first came to colonial South Carolina did so primarily with the endorsement and encouragement, and in some cases at the behest, of their families. Indeed, many migrated as emissaries for relatives in Europe or the West Indies with the intention of expanding established family empires along the Carolina coastline.[5]

Lowcountry immigrants were hardly alone in this initial reliance on kin. Indeed, family and kin were essential to European colonization throughout early America. From the "little commonwealths" of Puritan New England to the ethnic enclaves of New York and Philadelphia to the Calvert dynasty in Maryland, family—in all its myriad forms—lay at the heart of most colonization efforts. Even early Virginians, long accused of only "looking out for number one," apparently joined together in elaborate familial and neighborhood networks.[6]

Although most early British-Americans depended on family during initial migration, their commitment to transatlantic kin often waned over time. Subsistence farmers and planters could afford to sever Old World connections and seek personal and familial independence because they saw little long-term need for extended family ties. They sold their goods in local markets or bartered with neighbors for the things they could not produce themselves. For many, extended family could seem more like a burden than a blessing. In fact, the quest for autonomy sometimes drove private households away from extensive kinship networks.[7]

South Carolina elites, on the other hand, carried their reliance on kin far beyond the initial period of settlement. From the beginning, Charleston was planned as a center for transatlantic businesses. Because they migrated expressly to build international family empires, Charleston's businessmen needed their relatives abroad to provide financial assistance and serve as liaisons in their trading ventures far longer than many other British-Americans.[8] That, after all, was what drove seventeenth- and eighteenth-century businesses. Furthermore, throughout the colonial era, lowcountry elites remained both more interrelated and more homogeneous than the gentry in any other city in British North America. Philadelphia, Boston, and New York developed over time into larger, more heterogeneous urban centers. They remained far less intimately connected to slaveholding than Charleston and maintained far more diverse populations. Charleston, conversely, fell under the control of a uniquely homogeneous, insular, cooperative, interrelated ruling class, much like their neighbors in Barbados.

Colony of a Colony

So many of South Carolina's earliest merchants and planters came from the overcrowded islands of the British West Indies that Carolina is sometimes called a colony of a colony.[9] A contingent of Barbadians, led by Sir John Yeamens, first commissioned William Hilton's exploration of coastal Carolina in the mid-seventeenth century. A Barbadian planter, Sir John Colleton, urged Sir Anthony Ashley Cooper, the brothers John and William Berkeley, and several other wealthy Englishmen to seek land from Charles II, who eventually granted them a tract extending from present-day North Carolina to Spanish Florida and the "South Seas." Most importantly, a large majority of the first generation of South Carolinians traced their roots to Europe through the West Indies. In the last decades of the seventeenth century thousands of West Indian colonists left the islands for other areas of British North America. While immigrants came to Carolina from Bermuda, the Bahamas, and Jamaica, the largest contingent came from Barbados. In fact, half of the 684 settlers who came to Carolina between 1670 and 1680 whose place of origin can be determined came from Barbados.[10]

Scholars generally understand the ties between the West Indies and Carolina, but they underestimate the role family played in this connection. In an essay on South Carolina and the Caribbean, Jack Greene argued that one of the more important connections between the two areas was the inhabitants' disregard for the development of family.[11] Greene based his assertion on the paucity of patriarchal family systems rather than any thorough investigation of the possibility of differing family patterns.

In fact, intragenerational family ties played a crucial role in the English-Barbadian colonization of South Carolina. Most migrants came from the rich sugar plantations of Barbados to the unknown environment of the lowcountry because of familial concerns. By the late seventeenth century, land had grown scarce on the tiny island, the political and economic autonomy of the planter class had waned, sugar estates had consolidated, and the avenues for advancement had become narrow and guarded. Consequently, many Caribbean planters looked elsewhere for profits and the expansion of familial influence. South Carolina provided a likely setting for these family empires. Beginning in the 1670s, members of the Barbadian elite class sent younger brothers and kin up to South Carolina to establish plantations and counting houses. These Barbadian immigrants brought with them a strong sense of family responsibility, a passion for wealth and status, and a desire to advance their family's economic and political power quickly and by almost any means.

They also imported their particular brand of slavery. Among the mainland colonies, only South Carolina introduced slavery at the beginning of European settlement. By the early eighteenth century the ratio of blacks to whites was roughly four to one, although in some areas it ran as high as seven to one. These ratios mirrored those in Barbados. Barbadian settlers in Carolina also brought along their slave code, which Carolinians largely copied and adopted in 1696. Thus, these Barbadian migrants constructed in the lowcountry a slave-based plantation society remarkably similar to the one they left behind.[12]

As in Barbados, a small family-based planter elite emerged in the Carolina lowcountry and exercised tremendous political, social, and economic influence. But South Carolina was not just a mirror of Barbados; it also provided an extension of Barbadian elite power. Between 1669 and 1737, eleven of the twenty-three governors of South Carolina migrated from the West Indies or had close kin in the islands. In the late seventeenth and early eighteenth centuries, Barbadian immigrants, including John Colleton, brothers Arthur and Edward Middleton, and George Lucas, congregated in the Goose Creek area of the lowcountry. These "Goose Creek" men formed economic alliances and a political faction that enabled them to shape public life in the first generation of colonization. It was, in fact, the Goose Creek men who eventually broke the power of the proprietors.[13]

It took a while for these transatlantic family empires to come to fruition. Plans stalled as immigrants got more than they bargained for in Carolina.

Dying to Be in Paradise

These well-laid plans for expanding family empires ran afoul of the harsh lowcountry environment, and siblings and kin took on even greater weight when colonists realized their "earthly paradise" was a death trap. Among the first generation of colonists, demographic and social instability in Carolina extended their initial reliance on relatives abroad. At the same time, short life expectancy coupled with the preponderance of disease and frequent emigration necessitated an even deeper dependence on intragenerational kin within the colony.

It took only a few years after the founding of Charleston for the word to spread from Europe to the West Indies to the northern and mid-Atlantic colonies: "Those who wish to die quickly, go to Carolina." Dysentery, malaria, smallpox, "bloody flux," and a host of other debilitating, often deadly diseases plagued early lowcountry settlers. Epidemics of yellow fever, mumps, measles, and whooping cough swept the colony in wave after wave. In the summertime, residents often complained that the smells of death filled the streets. The subtropical climate and disease-carrying mosquitoes would have brought trouble enough on their own. But Carolinians drank dangerously contaminated water and fought year after year with Native Americans, which heightened the general precariousness of life in the lowcountry.

Colonial South Carolinians died at alarming rates and at unusually early ages. Between 1680 and 1720 almost half the men residing in St. John's parish who survived childhood died before they reached their fiftieth birthday. Another 37 percent died in their fifties. During that same period in neighboring Christ Church Parish, 73 percent of men who lived to age twenty died before age fifty. Between 1721 and 1760 that figure rose to 85 percent. Women fared no better. In St. John's between 1680 and 1720, 55 percent of women reaching adulthood never saw their fiftieth birthday. Both women and men considered themselves old—and lucky—if they survived more than fifty years.[14] Mortality rates did not stabilize until the last third of the eighteenth century, and even then South Carolina remained a hotbed of diseases. When he arrived in Charleston in 1757, James Glen informed his brother-in-law that he and his companions had "been seized by Fluxes, Vomiting, and all the Symptoms which attend intermitting Fevers . . . and Am told that this Disorder is a Tribute paid by most Strangers upon their arrival here."[15]

Young Carolinians grew up in a society pervaded by parental sickness and death. Most children of the first generation of colonists could expect to lose one or both of their biological parents. Ann Clark and her sister lived with their late mother's former husband and his new wife because both biological parents had died when the sisters were young girls. Mary Smith raised Ann Smith Waring, the orphaned daughter of Mary's stepdaughter and stepson-in-law. Sarah Amory went to live with her mother's friend, Sarah Rhett, after Amory's father, mother, sister, and brother all died in the yellow fever epidemic of 1699–1700.[16] Orphaned children like these often found themselves turning to siblings and kin to fill the emotional and practical roles of dead parents.

In time, the prevalence of parental sickness and death helped transform the emotional context of family life.[17] Surrounded by death, lowcountry colonists clung all the more fiercely to members of their intragenerational family, particularly their siblings. Individually and collectively, Carolinians came to focus increasing attention on relatives within their own generation. Intragenerational kin—always more extensive than parent-child bonds—also became more intensive.

Somewhat surprisingly, this turbulent social and familial environment did not derail colonization efforts. Despite the harsh climate and the tremendous potential for failure, each passing year more and more immigrants traveled to the lowcountry. In 1672 fewer than 400 whites lived in South Carolina. By the middle of the eighteenth century, 25,000 whites called the colony home. They lived alongside nearly 40,000 blacks who had been stolen from their homes in west Africa and were forced to toil in the shipyards and rice fields that formed the foundation of South Carolina's wealth.[18]

Given Carolina's well-earned deadly reputation, it is hard to imagine why so many free immigrants took so great a gamble. Some, no doubt, were ignorant of the realities, while others were misled by propaganda. For many, religious toleration offered the greatest incentive. In 1680 the proprietors began a vigorous campaign to recruit French Huguenots and English dissenters. By the beginning of the eighteenth century, more than 500 Huguenots had answered the call. Families of English dissenters soon followed. Even after the establishment of the Church of England in 1706, the lowcountry remained religiously diverse and tolerant. For other settlers, adventure, not religion, provided the allure. When asked about his daughter's move to Carolina in the 1720s, one father explained that she "has a rambling Head and a Mind to see strange places." And some, like Edward Hyrne, fled to Carolina hoping to escape the disapproval of their families.[19]

More than anything else, however, land and the potential wealth and power that accompanied landownership drew people to the Carolina lowcountry. For women and men living in England and the overpopulated islands of the West Indies, the lure of land seemed too compelling to ignore. Affra Harleston and John Coming rolled the dice in the late seventeenth century. Shortly after marrying, they moved to Carolina intent on starting a family dynasty. But they remained childless, and their hopes floundered. John and Affra decided to ask his nephew Elias Ball and her nephew John Harleston to come live with them and eventually inherit the Coming lands. Both nephews balked at the offer, and a disappointed John Coming changed his will and left everything to Affra. She did not long survive as an isolated widow, and upon her death left all her worldly goods to the two nephews. Eventually the two young men, along with John Harleston's sister, decided to try the family luck again. With the bequest from their aunt and their mutual cooperation, they succeeded where Affra had failed. In fact they founded one of Carolina's oldest, most powerful families—the Balls.[20] Their experience illustrates that although land lured people to Carolina, family connections allowed them to thrive.

A Transformed Familial World

Most migrants left England and the Caribbean for the turbulent but alluring Carolina lowcountry imagining that they would conserve British familial and cultural practices. Transplanted Carolinians, whether they originated in England or the West Indies, envisioned themselves primarily as Britons, so British values were the ones they sought to emulate. But, in reality, their drive to acquire wealth sometimes overrode their desire to replicate traditions. In some cases, Carolinians adopted kin strategies that diverged from English standards because these tactics advanced their economic standing in the colony. Demographic factors disrupted relationships within the patriarchal family and forced Carolinians to abandon other English traditions and deepen their reliance on siblings and kin. Finally, the widespread availability of rich land contributed to Carolinians' reassessment of family relationships. Demographic instability, land acquisition, and business agendas collectively produced a system of family relationships and functions that differed significantly from early modern English traditions. Some changes grew out of conscious kin-strategies; others resulted from unavoidable differences in climate and geography. But in both cases, the changes that Carolina society underwent encouraged colonists' identification with extended kin and put them on a path that increasingly diverged from the world they had left behind.

For example, in the late seventeenth and early eighteenth centuries, while English men and women increasingly entered into marriages based on mutual affection, South Carolina elites revivified the traditional connections between marriage and money.[21] Marriage remained far more financially focused for a far longer time in Carolina than it did in other parts of the British empire. Visitors to the lowcountry from England as well as from other colonies regularly criticized Carolinians for pursuing economically advantageous marriages and talking openly about their choices.

Carolinians cast off other English practices as well. Remarriage, for instance, became far more acceptable and commonplace among Carolinians. English communities frowned on remarriage after the death of a spouse. Extended family members and potential heirs worried about the dispersal of estates when second wives and new children entered the picture. Moreover, relatives feared that a young child who lost one parent might be forced into a blended household with a distracted parent, an unloving stepparent, and contentious half or step-siblings. The potentially negative emotional and financial ramifications of remarriage and the skepticism of family members persuaded most widowed people to remain single. From the sixteenth through the nineteenth centuries England experienced a continuous decline in the number of widowed spouses who remarried. In the seventeenth century only 22 percent of widows and widowers chose to remarry, and by the eighteenth century that figure had fallen to 16 percent.[22] Not surprisingly, those few who chose to remarry tended to be fairly young people without children. The brevity of their marriages meant that the bonds to their late spouses' families were not so deeply rooted. And the absence of children erased concerns about creating stepfamilies and complicating estate dispersals. Of course, Britons could afford to embrace such marital views because they enjoyed a relatively stable mortality rate and thus produced few young widows or widowers.

South Carolinians, inhabiting a demographically unstable region and greedy for wealth and power, formed a different opinion on the subject of remarriage. Economic agendas and high death rates pushed early settlers toward remarrying more often than their British contemporaries. Aware of the fiscal and physical necessity of kin ties, Carolinians eagerly and quickly remarried after the death of a spouse. Charles Pinckney's first wife died in January 1744, and by May his second wife was drafting thank-you notes for wedding gifts. Like Charles Pinckney, Thomas Dale remarried less than six months after his wife died. He then begged his friends in England to "prey keep the Secret for some time because it does not look very decent with you tho' we do not mind it here."[23]

Thomas rightly suspected that Britons would look with dismay and disdain at the speed with which he and other Carolinians replaced dead spouses. Seventeenth- and eighteenth-century English men and women, unlike their Carolina contemporaries, maintained strict criteria concerning the grieving process, and they considered it highly indecent to mourn a deceased mate less than one year. Anyone who dishonored the tradition by marrying within the mourning period faced the rebuke of his or her family.[24] Again, cultural values and demographic factors influenced the differing perspectives of Carolinians and Britons. High mortality rates in South Carolina made preserving marital attachments nearly impossible. And it ran counter to the business objectives of most colonists to grieve too long after death fractured these bonds.

As Carolinians remarried more often and more quickly than their English kinsmen, they also narrowed the definition of incest and chose close kin as spouses. Cousin and exchange marriages (between sets of siblings from two different families) pervaded the family trees of South Carolinians throughout the colonial era. The first generations of colonists employed these practices, hoping to extend and intensify kin ties and to protect family estates from fragmentation. In subsequent generations, elites used these kin-based unions as a critical component in the construction of their powerful interrelated class. The determination to enter into such marriages, however, diverged from the standards set by English elites. Indeed, while Carolinians looked first to cousin and exchange marriages as a potential solution to the emotional and financial fragmentation of their families and later as the building blocks for class identity, English gentry repudiated such unions. One study that sampled families from the eighteenth-century House of Lords found that these elites married their cousins and in-laws very rarely. Between 1720 and 1780 cousin marriage took place in less than 1 percent of cases. Exchange marriages happened even more infrequently.[25]

Carolinians' choice to take kinfolk as mates, despite British aversion to the practice, grew out of their redefinition of incest.[26] Britons observed stricter codes against sex and marriage—disallowing a wider array of consanguineous and affinal kin—than did Carolinians. As with remarriage customs, both the precariousness of life and the acquisitiveness of colonists contributed to this divergence in incest taboos. Survival and economic advancement mattered more to the first generations of colonists than honoring religious dictates. Kin-based unions enhanced emotional ties within the family and simultaneously diminished the dilution of family holdings. Once Carolinians got around the moral dilemmas posed by marrying certain relatives—an easily accomplished task given the essentially irreligious nature of the colonial population—narrowing the incest taboo appeared practical and profitable and thus justifiable.

Just as Carolinians' circumscription of marriage prohibitions distinguished them from their mother country, so too did their abandonment of primogeniture. English families engaged in primogeniture throughout the early modern era because they needed to protect family resources, particularly land, across the generations. The limited availability of land and the necessity of land holding for financial stability led English fathers to bequeath the family patrimony to the eldest son. But in South Carolina the perceived widespread availability of land (actually the property of local Yamassee and other Indian nations) and the diminished intergenerational concerns of colonists made primogeniture unnecessary. In its place, colonists adopted a system of partible inheritance.[27]

The supersedure of primogeniture with partible inheritance transformed the nature of sibling ties and relationships within the intragenerational family. By limiting inheritance to first-born sons, primogeniture imposed a rigid age and gender ranking among siblings. This ranking tended to exacerbate sibling tensions and rivalry since it led siblings to see one another more as competitors than as allies. The success of one sibling at the expense of the others could also provoke resentment within the sibling group. And the privileging of age and gender over ability imperiled family holdings and caused tensions. Indeed, the vast majority of conflicts within English families in the colonial era arose over property disputes.[28] Ne'er-do-well heirs, remarried beneficiaries, and imprudent financial decisions took on even greater weight in families in which one person maintained control over the patrimony. Although this system of distributing property did allow English families to avoid the fragmentation of their estates across the generations, within any particular generation it tended to increase sibling conflict and resentment.

Conversely, partible inheritance encouraged cooperation and egalitarianism within generations but complicated estate planning across generations.[29] The abandonment of primogeniture democratized economic relationships among sons (and to a lesser degree, daughters) who all shared in family holdings. It thus had the unintended effect of alleviating some of the sibling resentment that often accompanied the system of primogeniture. Age and gender no longer rigidly dictated place in the family. The eradication of the economic need to rank children diminished conflicts between siblings, who learned that they should share and expand family holdings rather than compete over them. Thus, the decision of Carolinians to divide real and personal estates among a broader array of kin, while driven primarily by the greater availability of land within the colony, demonstrated the growing tendency of colonists to focus on intragenerational considerations.

Carolinians' rejection of primogeniture and extended mourning periods, their redefinition of remarriage and incest taboos, and their proclivity for financially influenced and kin-based marriages—much like their business practices and their emotional attachments—reflected their growing reliance on intragenerational kin ties. The acquisitiveness of the business-focused colonists, the widespread availability of land, and demographic instability fueled this dramatic shift in family life. These three factors made extended, intensive kin ties more necessary and productive than they had been in England. In order to survive in the harsh lowcountry environment and thrive in the transatlantic mercantile community, colonists needed to extend their attachments to family members within their own generation. And while these factors intensified colonial reliance on siblings and kin, they also helped diminish the tensions and rivalries that could arise in those relationships. As these intragenerational ties played a greater and greater role in economic and practical matters within lowcountry society, cooperating to enhance family holdings and to promote family interests came to matter more than advancing individually.

Overall, the intragenerational focus that imbued family life in the lowcountry differed markedly from the private lives of English gentry. There, the growing importance of affective, nuclear families, the commitment to primogeniture, and relative demographic stability meant that kin did not play as powerful a role as they did in colonial South Carolina. Indeed, many scholars argue that kin mattered little in seventeenth- and eighteenth-century England and that Britons recognized few if any relatives beyond the nuclear family.[30]

The evidence from Carolina, while clearly demonstrating that colonists relied on kin more than did Britons, nonetheless complicates this vision of English kinfolk. English families—at least the colonizing, business-focused families that formed connections to Carolina—did offer aid and comfort to their lowcountry kindred. Carolina and English relatives corresponded with one another, shipped goods across the Atlantic, and cooperated to set up markets in the lowcountry. Their cooperativeness seems to have been rooted in large measure in the economic interests of colonizers and colonials. Carolina began as a business venture, and within the Atlantic world business was both familial and financial. Kin formed the basis of most business activities and provided the keys to financial success.[31] Thus, Carolinians followed the kin strategies of a unique group within England: business families who, unlike most other people in their society, consciously arranged themselves into what one scholar called "a bilaterally extended, dense tribalistic network" of kin.[32]

While Carolinians adopted the English business practice of intermingling kinship and finances, they also expanded their reliance on kin beyond the strictly economically utilitarian—thus creating an exaggerated version of a common experience in certain English families. The interweaving of family and finances and the importance of extensive kin networks came to pervade the lowcountry, influencing social and cultural developments far beyond mere business interests. In time, the world of trustworthy, responsive kin essential to early modern businesses came to form the core around which Carolinians built their physical and psychological lives.

"What a Sad Thing Is Solitude"

When Carolinians applied the business lessons they learned from their English kindred to the demographically unstable lowcountry, they created a culture in which people depended primarily on siblings and kin for many of their practical and emotional needs. Among other things, as colonists spread throughout the lowcountry they congregated in family-based neighborhoods just as the Goose Creek families did in the seventeenth century. After Gabriel Manigault married Anne Ashby in 1730, they bought Silkhope plantation so that she could be near her brothers and sisters. Eliza Lucas bragged that she settled near six other families "with whom we live in great harmony." Eventually lowcountry elites grew so accustomed to living surrounded by kin that they saw isolation and independence as troubling. When Peter Manigault left Charleston to study in

England, he lamented the separation from his relatives and friends. Years later his son similarly complained, "What a sad thing is solitude."[33]

While they created emotionally salient kin connections within the colony, early Carolinians continued to work hard to maintain the kinship networks that linked Charleston to Europe and the West Indies. For their part, family members abroad welcomed the opportunity to aid their Carolina kin. In most cases, European and West Indian families saw colonial South Carolina as a place to expand familial holdings and power. Others, simply wanting to see their kin advance, happily assisted in any way they could.

Charlestonians needed their kin abroad to supply them with both necessities and luxuries unavailable in their new homeland. Upon immigrating to Charleston in 1700, Elizabeth Massingberd Hyrne repeatedly asked her family in Lincolnshire for items that could not be found in Charleston. Elizabeth asked for the things she needed to survive (tools and cloth) as well as things she needed to recreate the world she had left behind (brass pots and books).[34]

On the most basic level, new settlers needed provisions to survive and emotional encouragement to withstand the lowcountry. Judith Manigault, for instance, immigrated to Charleston in 1685 with her brother and husband. Her sojourn into paradise turned out to be a terrible ordeal. Judith endured recurrent illnesses, her beloved brother died, and despite all her hard work she rarely had enough to eat. Judith's other brother, in Europe, willingly provided her with whatever money and provisions he could spare. Equally important, he sympathized with her plight in Carolina and gave much-needed emotional support.[35]

The deprivations and instability that required Carolinians to rely more and longer on intragenerational kin also forced them to shift their perceptions of gender. Many women like Judith Manigault found themselves filling familial and work roles they had never imagined possible. Women not only directed the household economy and cared for families but also herded livestock, tended fields, operated businesses, and served as surrogate planters and traders when their husbands died. While widowed men often hired housekeepers to do their late wives' work, women merely added their husbands' responsibilities to their own. Affra Harleston worked alongside her husband until he died and then maintained their farm alone until her own death in 1699. After her father returned to their native Antigua, Eliza Lucas assumed responsibility for the family businesses. At age sixteen, she ran three plantations.[36] In the tumultuous Carolina lowcountry, colonists could no more hold onto their gendered ideals than their patriarchal households. As family lines extended and blurred, so too did the divisions between women and men.

All the while, elites never lost sight of their original intentions. Their families were changing, but their economic and political goals were not. By turning to family abroad and intragenerational kin in Carolina, elites slowly built the empires they had originally envisioned. But these empires took on an unexpected intragenerational focus.

Horizontal family connections, particularly those between siblings, formed the basis for financial and logistical aid in early colonization. Some of the most influential families in Charleston traced their roots to the migration of siblings. Brothers often moved to Charleston together, and once in residence provided one another with political alliances, economic support, and sometimes served as surrogate parents. In the 1670s, for example, brothers Edward and Arthur Middleton came to Carolina to expand the family's wealth and influence, while the oldest Middleton brother, Benjamin, remained in Barbados and oversaw the family holding there. The Colleton brothers, Peter, Thomas, and James, similarly cooperated in both personal and public matters after their father, John, died. Peter, the eldest brother, served as one of the eight lord proprietors of Carolina and controlled the family's chief plantation in Barbados. In 1681 he retired to England and his younger brother Thomas assumed control of the Barbadian wing of the family empire. Peter and Thomas sent the third and youngest brother, James, to Carolina in 1686. Like many of the first generation of white immigrants, James acted as emissary for his siblings. His brothers financed his Carolina venture, and their continued financial and political support advanced James's career. James's success, in turn, advanced his brothers' status, so everyone in the family benefited from the arrangement.[37]

Many of the people who controlled political systems and economic life in the early colonial period did so by utilizing their sibling connections. The brothers Charles, Thomas, and William Pinckney built an extremely powerful kin network by relying on one another. Their father, Thomas Pinckney, a younger son of English gentry, came to the New World (first to Jamaica and then Charleston) hoping to make a name for himself and a great deal of money before returning home. His mission accomplished, he went back to England in 1697. But his three young sons stayed behind in South Carolina. For them, the colony became much more than a temporary business venture. Together they worked to make Charleston their home. When their father died within a few years of leaving the colony, the Pinckney brothers were left to fend for themselves. They turned a necessity into a virtue and eventually created one of the most powerful family networks in colonial South Carolina.[38] The Rutledge family developed in a similar manner. Andrew Rutledge and his brother John migrated to South Carolina around 1730. Alone in the lowcountry, the brothers relied heavily on one another, lived in close proximity, and served as elected members of the general assembly for Christ Church Parish.[39] By the close of the eighteenth century, the Rutledges had built a family empire that matched the Pinckneys' in wealth and political influence.

Less powerful sets of siblings followed this lead. Up-and-coming merchants and farmers did all they could to advance the interests of their kinsmen and secure connections for them. When Richard Hughes traveled to Charleston in 1711, his brother Pryce financed Richard's trip, acted as his agent in Wales, and urged his friend Thomas Nairne, a South Carolina Indian Agent, to befriend Richard. After Richard succumbed to the Carolina environment in 1713, Pryce traveled to Charleston. While living in the colony, Pryce asked his sister Mary and brother-in-law John Jones to conduct his affairs abroad. Similarly, when Englishman Thomas Dale, supported by his father and his close friend Thomas Birch, first moved to South Carolina in 1731, he found Charleston welcoming and lucrative. Having relied on his family to aid in his establishment there, Dale welcomed the opportunity to help his younger brother: "I have met with very great Encouragement and my Business engrosses dayly so that I design to take my Brother to be my Journeyman."[40] Hughes and Dale knew that connections abroad and locally were key factors in individual success or failure in Charleston. They probably did not realize that by the 1730s, kinship networks were beginning to control virtually every facet of public life in the colony.

Kin and Community Building

Siblings and kin groups not only contributed to the success and persistence of particular colonists but also dramatically shaped economic and political life in South Carolina. Kin support proved essential to the development of early merchant firms, businesses, and plantations in and around Charleston. Not surprisingly, the colony's counting houses and plantations operated as family businesses—partnerships between brothers, cousins, uncles, and nephews. With the aid of their kin, early lowcountry elites laid the foundation for future family interests. In the late seventeenth century, Stephen Bull and his brother John, a London merchant, helped establish the lucrative deerskin trade in Carolina. Another London merchant, William Wragg, financed his nephews' move to South Carolina. With the aid of their wealthy and well-connected uncle,

Samuel and Joseph Wragg built the largest slave-trading business in early-eighteenth-century South Carolina. In many cases, family connections made all the difference in colonial business ventures. As one early Carolinian explained, "The connexions, capital, & application to Business, those Younger Gentlemen together with the aid of their Fathers & other able friends will give them an Ascendent over other Houses."[41]

Although relatives abroad expected a return on their investment in Carolina, their willingness to aid kin in Charleston was not strictly contingent upon financial restitution. Families and kin recognized the great risk associated with loaning money to Carolinians and anticipated the inability of their kin to repay their debts. Elias Ball assured his nephew and namesake in Charleston that he trusted the younger Elias would *want* to honor his debts, but feared he would never be able to repay a loan. Still, the elder Elias loaned his nephew money—not only for the initial venture, but also for many years after.[42]

Relatives did demand family allegiance in return for their financial backing. Since for both Britons and Carolinians family was as much an economic as an emotional institution, restitution and respect became interwoven. When the two Elias Balls did disagree, the conflict arose not over the younger Elias's ability to repay debts to his English kinsman, but over a perceived lack of respect for the sacrifice the elder Elias had made. In the end, the two men reconciled their differences and made promises of lifelong friendship because they believed that cooperating together was the lucrative and the right thing to do.[43]

Elias Ball and others like him appeared to be motivated by a sense of cooperation that superseded individual interests. A desire for extensive family prosperity, not simply personal gain, governed their behavior. Siblings and close kin frequently collaborated to advance their collective status. Brothers coordinated the migration of younger siblings or moved to Charleston together. They also worked hard to maintain connections to relatives abroad, which brought access to markets and credit while simultaneously diminishing the risk of individual failure. Carolina remained, in the truest sense of the phrase, a family affair. Lowcountry elites' focus lay more in the extension of family influence abroad and within the colony than on individual aggrandizement.

The commitment to aid kin and the quest for family power influenced politics as well as business. Early Charlestonians frequently called on their siblings and kinsmen for the political connections needed for financial and social success. While Peter Colleton lived in South Carolina in the late seventeenth century, he asked his London nephew John More to use his power as a magistrate to advance Colleton's agenda. When Colleton and other early immigrants experienced a growing problem with privateers, he encouraged his nephew to lobby for the passage of a parliamentary act against such activities. Colleton further urged More to "doe you your selfe put the law in Execution as far as you have power as you are a Magistrate by Imprisoning any that are going into the Service of forraigne princes or that you Suspect are of themselves going upon any pyraticall Designe . . . & by seizing any prize brought in that land." Although himself a financial failure, Charles Lowndes left his two youngest sons, Rawlins and Charles, something more valuable than money: a legacy of important friendships and familial connections in England, the Islands, and South Carolina. The Lowndes brothers successfully parlayed those connections into respected careers in public office.[44]

By the third decade of the eighteenth century, the foundation of powerful kin-based economic and political coalitions was firmly in place. Early elites built their long-desired family empires by adapting their original intentions to match the reality of life in the lowcountry. The rest of the eighteenth century was given over to extending and protecting this dominance of public life.

"It Is Well If Many People Come Together"

Sibling and kin ties not only determined who would succeed and who would fail—they also enriched people's private lives. Most people who lived in early South Carolina found that being surrounded by wide webs of kin and friends both enhanced their chance at success and made them happier. Eliza Lucas quickly fell in love with Carolina after her move from Antigua, and she praised her "hospitable and honest" neighbors.[45] Writing to his brother in Switzerland in 1733, Anthony Gondy likewise raved about his new home. According to Anthony, life was peaceful, leisurely, and prosperous. He found the colony "quite an earthly paradise." Gondy had traveled to Carolina with a large group of family, friends, and neighbors from his native Switzerland. In one letter he discussed attending the wedding of a favorite cousin, Marianne, and hunting with another cousin, Albert. He also assured his brother that all thirteen single women in the group had entered into advantageous marriages. Immersed in a broad kin group, Anthony wanted to share his success with relatives abroad: "In short, it is incredible; wherefore I ask all our friends and relatives who are not of great means that they may please join us here."[46]

Another migrant, Samuel Dyssli, shared little of Anthony Gondy's enthusiasm for Charleston. In a letter to his relatives abroad, Samuel warned them: "Let nobody hanker to come to this country!" Carolina, according to Samuel, was "a damned fraud." Samuel never found the wealth and opportunity that the lowcountry supposedly offered. Instead, he insisted that for every successful man, a thousand suffered. Financial ruin was not even the greatest threat: "Diseases here have too much sway, and people have died in masses. . . . Moreover, the children soon go [to work] the one here and the other there, and are treated like slaves and brought up in ignorance." During his short, lonely stay in Carolina he contracted a fever that lasted three months and endured a six-month recurrent bout of bloody flux. Ultimately, Dyssli attributed much of his misery in the lowcountry not to illness or poverty, but to his solitude, and advised that "it is well if many people come together."[47]

Those who failed to secure the aid of family members in their Carolina venture ran a high risk of personal unhappiness and financial failure. John Jenny went back to his native Barbados in 1680 after experiencing one failure upon another in Charleston. His brother, who had remained in Barbados, explained that John returned "in such a weak condition and so discouraged, that he thinks he shall never see that place again."[48]

Many traveling alone to South Carolina shared similar disappointments. In the early eighteenth century, Edmund Brailsford, after marrying a woman his family regarded as unsuitable, left his native England for Charleston. Consequently, he found himself estranged from his father, four brothers, and other family members. He hoped for a new start in the Carolina lowcountry, but his experiences never matched his expectations. After a few years in Charleston, his situation grew so desperate that he could not get anyone to ship him goods from abroad or trade with him in the colony. Despite these hardships, his family in London refused to come to his aid. Broke and desperate, he eventually apologized to his father and asked for forgiveness. Even then, Brailsford's family provided him financial support only rarely and always begrudgingly. In 1726 Brailsford's father gave him £200 and released his inheritance from an aunt, but only after Edmund promised to refrain from making further demands on the family. Brailsford and his father's relationship further disintegrated after Edmund Sr. demanded custody of his grandson, Edward. The last evidence of Brailsford's life indicates that he died an impoverished man. Because of his estrangement from his family and their subsequent reluctance, even refusal, to aid him in Carolina, Brailsford could not hope for the success afforded someone immersed in a supportive kin network.[49]

Elizabeth Massingberd and Edward Hyrne faced the same problems when they moved to Carolina without the help of their kindred. In addition to marrying against the wishes of the Massingberd family, Edward was at least twenty-five years older than his seventeen-year-old bride. The Massingberds hated Edward because, among other things, as port collector he "misapplied" almost £1,400. When he married Elizabeth, Edward was deeply in debt and facing criminal charges, so he wisely decided it best "to remove himself from the proximity of his creditors." Much to her family's dismay, Elizabeth followed her new husband to Carolina. Alone, forced to work hard, often sick, and poor, she begged her family to send her supplies and money. The Hyrnes did everything they could to curry favor with Elizabeth's family in England. They alternately pleaded and insisted that her brother Burrell Massingberd, the executor of Elizabeth's father's estate, relinquish Elizabeth's inheritance. The Hyrnes even named their first child after Burrell, hoping he might feel a special affinity for his nephew and namesake, Burrell Hyrne, and send money for his education.[50]

The Hyrnes, however, found themselves continually disappointed. Neither their pleas for money nor their covert attempts to forge a relationship between their children and Elizabeth's family (and their purses) met with much success. Elizabeth wrote at length of the travails that they encountered. Their first few years in South Carolina were filled with heartache. Two of their children died, and their house burned. In the fire they lost most of their food and household possessions. This setback intensified their appeals to the Massingberds, who remained resolute.[51] The Massingberds' refusal to support the Hyrnes condemned them to failure.

Unable to gain the necessary support of her family, Elizabeth and Edward turned their attention to developing local kin ties. They bought land from a prominent planter, Thomas Smith, and tried to forge personal connections to him. After Smith's first wife died, he married Edward Hyrne's oldest child, Mary. Several years later Mary's brother Edward married one of Smith's daughters from his first marriage. But this recently acquired, tenuous kin network could not help the Hyrnes stave off economic disaster. Alone in Carolina without supportive relatives, the Hyrnes slowly realized the necessity of kin: "But blessed be God we have mett with some kind friends in this place or elce we had not bin for you ever to have heard more of us."[52]

Colonial South Carolina did not treat individuals kindly. The precariousness of early colonial South Carolina—death, disease, economic ruin—meant that it was no place for the unconnected. Immigrants who came to Carolina without a supporting web of kin and friends found colonization a perilous, if not impossible, ordeal.

Occasionally, of course, family problems did arise. One man accused his

Carolina cousin of "liveing like a prince, & here am I poor." Robert Colleton was shocked to find that his brother, instead of supervising Robert's estate in Carolina, had actually sold some of the land.[53] These subtle, passing complaints about disreputable kin sometimes gave way to more virulent fights. Some family problems, like those Edward and Elizabeth Hyrne faced, did produce open, noxious feuds. The Hyrnes, along with a few other colonists, endured especially intense conflicts with their relatives. Accusations of debauchery and threats of lawsuits tore some families (including the Hyrnes) apart. These rare but vehement fights demonstrate that, while cooperation and trust governed most of these relationships, suspicions and heartache could lie just beneath the surface.

But by and large these sorts of references to familial disagreements remained quite rare in the correspondence of colonists. Indeed, the scarcity of family conflicts in the historical record seems a bit too good to be true. The quest to build international family empires must have created competition and resentment among relatives on either side of the Atlantic. It would also seem that the logistics of creating these businesses (for example, assuming the debts of a faraway partner) would similarly complicate kinship relations. And the precariousness of life in the lowcountry, while it increased colonists' reliance on kin, must have made Britons skeptical about the entire enterprise and reluctant to blindly entrust their family resources to Carolina kindred. Little of this plausible speculation, however, can be substantiated by the sources that Carolinians left behind.

Whenever possible Carolinians avoided talking about kin troubles. No doubt many hoped that conciliatory language and wishful thinking might alleviate family squabbles. Kin held the keys to financial success and social inclusion in the lowcountry, so colonists who criticized their relatives risked far more than merely disrupting personal relationships. Given the importance of kin connections to economic success it is easy to assume that discretion frequently got the better part of valor. Moreover, it was simply not the practice of the day to talk about such issues. The first generation of colonists showed greater concern in their private writings for practical matters — when goods were being shipped, how to best produce rice, who was afflicted with what ailment. Complaining about relatives ran afoul of both their natural tendencies and their ambitions. Finally, it must also be added that the literary evidence favors those colonists who enjoyed harmonious kin ties. Estranged relatives do not, by definition, communicate with one another.

The relative silence of the sources on the question of family discord and the suspicions this silence raise do not, however, invalidate the words and actions of all the Carolinians who openly expressed deep regard for their kindred and lived their lives happily surrounded by family members. That some colonists apparently downplayed family disagreements can, in fact, be interpreted as further evidence of the importance of these bonds: kin ties simply mattered too much to sever them unless over the gravest of conflicts. From all indications, most Carolinians viewed reliable, interdependent kin ties in business ventures and personal relationships as both their expectation and their general experience. Strife, while real, remained the exception rather than the rule.

For the most part, the problems that the first generations of South Carolinians faced stemmed not from family tensions but from the absence of family support. In the early 1720s, Margaret Brett Kennett and her new husband determined to move from Kent to South Carolina. Margaret's father, Thomas Brett, worried that his daughter was irresponsible and unprepared for life in Carolina. As for his son-in-law, Thomas said only, "I cannot charge him with any Visciousness but only Imprudence and Misconduct." Although Thomas Brett arranged and financed the initial voyage of his daughter and son-in-law to Carolina, he did so in large part to teach them a lesson: "I hope a little biting on the bridle (which is our country proverb for suffering Hardships) may do them both good. And when they are in a place, where they have little money and no Friends or Acquaintancs I don't know but they may bite hard." As Thomas Brett predicted, Margaret could not make it in South Carolina without relatives or friends nearby. Only a few years after they settled in Charleston, Margaret's husband died and Margaret returned to her family in England.[54] Throughout her brief stay in Carolina, Margaret Kennett longed for family and friends. She eagerly awaited letters from her parents, brother, and several cousins and requested even more. Lonely in her new home, she "wish[ed] that half a Dozen familys of my acquaintance would come over and settle here." In particular, Margaret wished for "some friend from England, for there is no trusting a Carolinian." Margaret's brief stay and grievous experiences in South Carolina testified to the necessity of family connections. And her impressions of Carolinians no doubt reflected her exclusion from the increasingly closed society.[55]

THE COLONIZATION of early Carolina, not unlike that of much of British North America, rested on family ties. While hardly unique in the Atlantic world in this regard, Carolinians did encounter a number of factors that intensified their sibling and kin connections. The heavy reliance on kin abroad during initial colonization and early migrants' commitment to transatlantic trading meant that kinship played an especially important role in the colony. The demographic realities in the lowcountry accentuated this reliance on kin at the same time that it altered the shape of families. Succeeding, even surviving, in the lowcountry required both the protection of family relations abroad and the expansion of family networks in Carolina. The physical and fiscal reality of life in the lowcountry thus deepened Carolinians attachment to and their identification with siblings and intragenerational kin.[56]

The familial foundations laid by the first generations shaped South Carolina for years to come. The original intentions that drove migration into the lowcountry, coupled with the reality of life in the colony, produced an increasingly interrelated, closed elite that maintained connections abroad and secured them at home. By the 1730s, Charleston's interrelated gentry had turned a necessary adaptation of family life into a lucrative and powerful virtue.

The internal, emotional lives of elite Charlestonians followed a parallel path. The familial adaptations that enabled them to create their "earthly paradise" in the tumultuous, often deadly lowcountry also transformed their private lives. And their emotional and social attachments provided interrelated elites new avenues for pursuing power and new reasons to defend the power they acquired.

CHAPTER TWO

"A First, & Dear Connection"
Sibling Bonds and Kinship Networks across the Life Course

The earliest white immigrants to Charleston, South Carolina, no less than any other transplanted Europeans, wanted to recreate the world they had left behind.[1] They built their homes, fashioned their clothing, educated their children, and took their political and cultural cues from the English model. But the swamps and marshlands of the lowcountry proved an insuperable opponent in their struggle to replicate family life. Demographic and sociological factors conspired against the development of patriarchal, nuclear families in early South Carolina. In New England, long life expectancies, low mortality rates, a healthy climate, cultural hegemony, and religious ideology promoted stability and patriarchy; but in South Carolina, migration, disease, and death cut short the intergenerational connections between parents and children and the bonds between husbands and wives.[2]

All Charlestonians knew firsthand how frequently death, disease, and parental absence undermined relationships between parents and children. Constant reminders that parents suddenly and frequently perished surrounded young people. Most children could expect to lose one of their parents before reaching majority. Many lost both. Even those who did not personally experience the early death of a parent understood the likelihood that it might occur. Those lucky few children who were not orphaned lived in homes that opened their doors and hearts to less fortunate relatives.

In this society pervaded with parental death, lowcountry elites created a culture heavily dependent on siblings and intragenerational kin. Early Carolinians welcomed half and step-siblings, cousins, in-laws, and extended kin into their homes and hearts, and relied on these relatives as they constructed their emotional world. Family became more fluid, more broadly defined, more heavily intragenerational. For South Carolinians, relatives, especially siblings, formed the most consistently dependable part of the familial world. These relationships therefore provided a critical sense of psychological comfort and belonging.

Devotion, cooperation, and exclusivity formed the core of lowcountry elites' family values. Throughout the life course siblings and other close relations depended on one another for a wide array of emotional and practical needs. When apart, they wrote and visited regularly and lamented their separations. Family members cooperated with one another in myriad ways to promote their own agendas and undermine their adversaries. In these ways, interestingly, the behavior of eighteenth-century Charlestonians is remarkably similar to the theories and findings of contemporary social scientists who analyze siblings. In their path-breaking work on sibling relationships, Stephen Bank and Michael Kahn have discovered that children who lose parents intensify their reliance on and loyalty to their siblings. Orphaned siblings actively seek out each other and are distressed when separated. They are highly cooperative and sympathetic toward one another. They quickly and amiably resolve conflicts. And they adamantly defend each other against outside threats—precisely as eighteenth-century Carolinians did.[3]

Although encouraged by demographic instability in the early colonial period, dependence on sibling and kin was not determined solely by mortality rates. Siblings and kin mattered in the lives of individuals throughout early America. The demographic disasters plaguing early South Carolina increased, but did not create, the importance of these intragenerational relationships in that region. Certainly in the late seventeenth and early eighteenth centuries demographic factors blurred family boundaries and heightened the emotional attention paid to intragenerational kin. The first generations of white South Carolinians simply moved too frequently, sickened too easily, and died too early to inhabit stable patriarchal households. But even after the colony became safer, residents held fast to their siblings and extended kin. Quite apart from death rates and migration patterns, siblings represented an essential part of family life—both in and outside the Carolina lowcountry. By the 1740s Charleston's elites had learned not only that their siblings and kin could serve as a safety net in the absence of parents, but also that these ties formed a critical part of each other's emotional and social lives.

South Carolina experienced an exaggerated version of family patterns pervasive throughout early America. Parents were never the only, and often not even the most important, influence in their children's emotional world. Few colonists lived in households untouched by outside influences: visitors, apprentices, servants, kin, and orphans entered private households in every region of early America. And, when other adults resided in the household, they limited the power parents exercised over children.[4]

Further, in even the most isolated households, siblings contested parental power by building connections with and exerting influence over one another, independent of parental desires. For a long time, developmental psychologists emphasized a parent-child dyad—that is, individual child development was attributed primarily to relationships between parent (mother) and child. But recently researchers have moved beyond this paradigm, which considers siblings largely inconsequential. Researchers are slowly accepting that siblings have a "major impact on one another's behavior and development through mutual socialization . . . and companionship." Cultural anthropologists echo these findings, arguing that sibling bonds are "sorely underestimated."[5] While classical theories about child development excluded siblings as key socializing agents, more recent scholarship demonstrates that siblings provide a fundamental part of the construction of identity and the model for later intimate relationships. As one psychologist explained, siblings are our first peers, our "first real partners in life." From them we learn powerful lessons about social behavior as well as self-identity.[6] Certainly this held true in the eighteenth century, when siblings and kin formed a critical part of the psychological base on which individuals constructed their emotional lives.[7]

Although attention paid siblings and kin persisted, South Carolinians witnessed important changes in the tone of their familial world.[8] Within the kinship groups of Charleston's elites, affective ties increased over the course of the eighteenth century as relationships governed by necessity diminished. Kin in the late eighteenth century fulfilled markedly different roles than did their early-eighteenth-century counterparts. Whereas earlier generations depended on kinship networks primarily for physical and financial support, late-eighteenth-century Charlestonians also turned to their siblings, kin, and friends to help raise children, educate and socialize younger relatives, aid and advise in marital choices, and provide emotional support throughout their lives.

As their interdependence grew, members of the kin group blurred the lines of private households, which consequently challenged patriarchal prerogative. Literally from cradle to grave the intragenerational family was interwoven with the patriarchal. And it laid the foundation for an elite culture that blended egalitarianism and exclusivity and allowed Charleston to be simultaneously the most accepting and the most closed society in British North America.

Witness at the Creation

Involvement in an extended kin network began at birth. Women in eighteenth-century America faced a perpetual cycle of pregnancy and childbirth. White women in the southern colonies married young, and, if they survived, bore children for twenty or more years.[9] A sample of elite families from eighteenth-century Carolina reveals that married women typically delivered nearly seven children, and the time between births averaged just over eighteen months. So during their childbearing years, lowcountry women enjoyed less than ten months between delivering one child and conceiving another. Mothers also lost many of the children they delivered: in the first three decades of the eighteenth century, 26 percent of children within this sample died before reaching age five. The last generation of eighteenth-century Carolinians fared only marginally better. Between 1770 and 1800, parents buried 22 percent of their children in early childhood. Thus, motherhood represented a continual, and often a mournful, part of women's lives.[10]

Women's journals and daybooks recounted the almost unceasing rounds of childbirth within the lowcountry, and the illnesses that so frequently accompanied it. Elizabeth Wragg Manigault endured a typical eighteenth-century childbearing experience. During her first pregnancy in 1758, she was so sick she could not see company for almost a month, endured over twelve hours of labor, and needed her breasts lanced six weeks after the delivery. Elizabeth went on to deliver six more children before her early death in 1773. Of the seven children she bore in eleven years, three died within the first year of life.[11]

Such difficulties pervaded childbearing experiences, and women spoke often about it. Cousins Mary Pinckney and Margaret Manigault discussed a friend who had had a particularly trying pregnancy: bedfast for three weeks, she "was in such misery from a large swelling (near the child) that she was obliged to send . . . for a surgeon to have it opened," before the child could be delivered.[12] But the young woman's troubles were hardly over. When she could not nurse the child, her doctor "order'd that she should go to bed, & be cover'd with blankets till a perspiration was brought on, that she should live entirely on gruel & barley water. Notwithstanding the violent pain she underwent from having her breasts distended with the milk, this unfeeling man would not permit her to have them drawn, & at length the milk was to be felt like cakes in her breasts."

The young woman eventually grew so ill that her family could not recognize her. As an aside, Mary added that her friend "is again with child, & very unwell and pale."[13]

Although sickness and death often accompanied childbearing, sisters and kinswomen helped lessen the pain and sorrow. In eighteenth-century South Carolina, pregnancy was a family affair. Members of female kin networks faithfully provided each other with physical and psychological support during labor, and they often remained long after the delivery to aid new mothers in caring for their infants. Women like Anne Ashby Manigault wrote regularly in their journals of attendance to female kin who were "lying in." Not surprisingly, women became deeply troubled whenever circumstances kept them from their familial obligation. Sarah Read's sister Mrs. Harleston always traveled from her home in Virginia to stay with Sarah when she gave birth. The sisters expressed deep concern after Harleston missed the birth of Read's daughter in late 1795. The sisters had made plans to visit in early January, but the baby arrived before Harleston came to Charleston.[14]

Childbirth represented the first of many instances where siblings and kin intersected and ultimately transcended the private household. As pregnant women turned to their female kin during their "travail," they shut out their husbands. Indeed, at the very moment the patriarchal household was being formed, the intragenerational family intervened. While members of the female kin group ministered to pregnant wives, fathers remained outside the emotional process. Their physical removal from the household during labor symbolized this exclusion from a female kin experience. Painfully aware of the dangers of childbirth, but superseded by female kin, a father could do little more than worry about his wife and offer the occasional prayer. Everything else, fathers left to the women. William Read expressed concern about his wife's health during her second pregnancy, but he worried more that her relatives might not be able to attend her. Their absence, as the birth neared, weighed heavy on his mind.[15] Read's anxiety lay partially in his knowledge that his wife and child needed kinswomen to perform family functions that he never could.

The fact that children physically entered the world of lowcountry Carolina surrounded by these relatives provided a fitting start for a lifetime shared with siblings and kin. Single children were a rarity in South Carolina. The typical adolescent sibset within lowcountry elite society (accounting for early childhood deaths) included five children, spaced two to three years apart. Households of eight to ten children were not uncommon.[16] While most children grew up with several siblings close in age, death rates could subvert this pattern. For example, Henry and Mary Middleton produced twelve children between 1742 and 1760. But five of their first six children died early: one lived to age six, the others died in the first year or two of life. As a result, their eldest son, Arthur, was more than eight years older than his next surviving sibling, Henrietta. After Henrietta, Mary Middleton delivered five more children over the next ten years, all of whom survived to adulthood. By the time the youngest of his siblings was born (eighteen years his junior), Arthur was living in England with his uncle and attending Cambridge.[17] Undoubtedly he shared a very different relationship with his younger siblings than they shared with one another.

In extreme cases like Arthur Middleton's, birth order and difference in age dramatically altered sibling relationships. Since women bore children for so many years, even when deaths did not intercede, the eldest and youngest siblings could be separated by as much as twenty years. In those cases, as in Arthur Middleton's, elder siblings would no doubt seem more like parents than peers. Significant age differences gave elder siblings more authority over and respect from their youngest brothers and sisters, and thus complicate the picture of egalitarian sibling ties. A similar situation arose when fathers remarried and started second families with younger wives. Not only did blended families tend to increase tension and competition within the sibling and step-sibling set, but they also produced half siblings that were much younger. Second families, blended households, wide age discrepancies, and deaths all disrupted sibling relationships. They introduced new people and variables into the sibling world and produced ambiguous, contentious relationships in which siblings became more aware of rank and status.

Age and life experience could and did influence sibling relationships, especially if those differences were profound; however, there is little evidence that South Carolinians paid attention to birth order or sibling rankings in most cases. Siblings did not, for example, fill the roles and develop the character traits that recent birth order analyses theorize that they should.[18] Further, Carolinians indicated in both word and deed that birth order mattered little to them in practical matters. Elites made no concerted attempts to insure that older siblings married before younger siblings. Property was not divided according to age or rank except in cases where one or more heir was still a young child. And the letters siblings wrote rarely mentioned or even intimated the relative ages of the correspondents.

Although siblings sometimes faced complicated, difficult relationships with one another, the complexity did not originate in any inherent, biologically driven rivalry between first-born and later-born siblings.[19] Rather, it derived from the individual circumstances and personalities within the sibset. And despite all the struggles that could arise between sisters and brothers, siblings (and kin) continued to play a critical, formative role in one another's lives.

By and large, relationships within the sibling and kin group seemed to have been, either by choice or necessity, positive. The business interests and class identity of lowcountry elites hung on family connections. Most elites benefited from inclusion in a broad family network and saw little reason to complain. And if conflict did arise, most tacitly agreed to keep it quiet. Moreover, Charleston's elites expressed genuine, abiding affection for their siblings and kin.

From their entry into the world, children enjoyed the affection and attention of a wide array of kindred who invested themselves in their younger relatives' futures. When Margaret Manigault delivered her first child, her brother-in-law Joseph Manigault fawned over his new niece and insisted he could hardly wait to tell the rest of the family about her antics.[20] Most Carolinians, like Joseph Manigault, expressed great joy and love for new members of their families. They also prided themselves on making their presence felt in more practical ways as well. Siblings and other kin freely and frequently shared parenting advice with new mothers and fathers. Shortly after his nephew was born, William Read extended warm congratulations to his sister-in-law and brother but added that he hoped "she has too much good sense to spoil her lovely Boy." Parents actively sought the aid of relatives in the care of young children. Peter Manigault and his wife brought their first son to Peter's mother's home to be weaned. Henry Laurens's wife, Eleanor, similarly took responsibility for her brother's sick children. Some women even nursed orphaned kin.[21]

To repay the debt owed relatives and symbolize the importance of the kinship network, parents honored their most valued living kin by naming children after them. In the lowcountry, unlike other regions, parents did not primarily name children after themselves or their own parents.[22] Instead they selected the names of siblings and close kin. Jonathan Bryan named a child for each of his siblings, and they each did the same. William Blake named his son after his brother Daniel, who left part of his estate to his namesake upon his death. Henry and Eleanor Laurens named their oldest daughter after Henry's sister Martha. The three brothers, William, Henry, and Thomas Middleton, passed the names of their siblings on to their sons. William Middleton named his first three sons William Jr., Thomas, and Henry. Henry named his son Thomas. The elder Thomas named his only son William and his two eldest daughters Sara and Mary, after his brothers' wives.[23] These families were hardly unique in their naming patterns. Among the planter elite in the late eighteenth century there were almost no name innovations. Rather, parents chose to name their children after their brothers and sisters, parents, cousins, or other kin.[24]

Some scholars have interpreted the practice of naming children after family members or after deceased siblings as an indication that children were not valued as individuals. However, others argue that necronymic naming practices, far from indicating disinterest in children, represented the importance of kin as a means of "transcending death through progeny, of extending and enlarging each family's past through a link to the living present."[25] The naming of children after deceased siblings reflected a strong sense of family and a desire, in the face of high mortality and low life-expectancy rates, to memorialize the deceased. The evidence from Carolina complicates both these interpretations.

In the first place, South Carolinians typically named children after living relatives rather than deceased family members. The reason was twofold. In eighteenth-century South Carolina the best way to care for a child was to ensure she was connected to an array of kin. Naming practices among lowcountry elites reflected this desire to secure the child in the broader family network. Second, naming a child after a specially selected relative expressed the expectation, or at least the hope, that the elder relative would take a specific interest in his or her namesake. In the latter part of the eighteenth century, the growing predominance of naming children after kin paralleled an increasing desire to perpetuate the interconnections of the kin group and the growing affective nature of these ties. These naming patterns connected children to a wide web of kin and reminded relatives of their responsibility to the child. They also illustrated the intragenerational focus of South Carolina elites. For them, honoring the past was less important than securing the present—which depended on extensive kin networks. Like the birthing process, child-naming thus symbolized the practical and emotional importance of siblings and kin. But childbirth and naming was only the beginning. Connections to kinship networks had far more practical, tangible applications that transcended the life course.

The Lessons of Youth

Lowcountry culture required siblings and kin to play a significant part in the upbringing of children. Indeed, one of the most important tasks that intragenerational relatives faced was the socialization and education of the next generation. Children learned from their siblings and kin who they were and how to live in the world. Kin provided children with a sense of belonging, both to the family and to the Carolina lowcountry.[26] Social scientists have long understood that younger siblings learn key development skills and a greater understanding of the world from older siblings and other relatives.[27] They also insist that the lessons learned from siblings differ sharply from those passed from parents to children.

Parent-child relationships in early Carolina (and today) depended on inequity and hierarchy. No matter how much love and devotion existed, parents and children could never be equals. In early America, the rules were quite clear. Parents, particularly fathers, maintained authority. Parents instructed; children obeyed. If a child failed to accede to parental authority, her parents punished her. Although regional, religious, and class variations certainly existed, the rules remained fairly consistent—and perhaps not inappropriately.[28] Ranking and deference influenced many public relationships, so the household served as an important model for certain facets of society. Further, as any parent then or now would attest, escaping the power imbalance is both undesirable and impossible. All of this is not to suggest that parent-child relations were exploitive or bereft of affection. Parents, of course, taught children myriad life lessons. But at the heart of parent-child relations lay an imbalance of power and a commitment to authority and subordination.

Siblings, on the other hand, act like peers. They generally treat each other with equality and learn from one another how to build other egalitarian relationships. As one clinical psychologist observed, siblings teach one another "cooperativeness, sharing, caring, involvement in one another's lives, and placing the group above the individual."[29] Siblings and other intragenerational kin, who construct their relationships based on cooperation and mutuality, are thus powerful and unique sources of socialization. Siblings also usually represent the longest-lasting of all familial relationships. They consequently exert a tremendous influence over an individual's self-definition from early childhood throughout the life course.

In lowcountry South Carolina, parental absence and cultural patterns intensified the importance of sibling socialization. Siblings played an even greater role in one another's self-fashioning and attitudes toward the world. At the same time, the sibling model of cooperation and mutuality began to exert a profound effect on elite culture.

Among other things, this pattern of cooperation and mutuality guided elites' efforts to educate young people. Siblings and kin worked together to advance the education and careers of their relatives. Family members introduced younger male kin to established members of their intended profession and supervised and financed their formal education. Siblings and kin also served young men as personal tutors, moral guides, and surrogate parents. Wealthy young women similarly learned from elder sisters, aunts, and other kinswomen the lessons for their lives—how to read and write, speak French, and play music—and more often, how to cook and preserve, spin and sew, rear children and bear husbands. While less constant than caring for one's own children, educating cousins, siblings, nephews, and nieces represented an important, unavoidable family responsibility. That responsibility deepened when parents died. If a father's death predated his son's majority, male family members often assumed responsibility for the orphaned boy. When a mother died, female children frequently moved into the home of a sister, sister-in-law, or aunt so they could receive proper female guidance.

Of course, no formal system of public education existed in early America, certainly not in South Carolina.[30] Because the best formal training required a lot of money, travel abroad, and connections to schoolmasters, education belonged only to the wealthy. The elite young men of Charleston secured their educations through the cooperation of family and friends and under the careful supervision of relatives. Whether they traveled abroad or to schools in the north, whether they read law with an established barrister or served as apprentices in local counting houses, young men turned to their kin for support.

Established men in Charleston looked out for their younger relatives: they paid for tuition and expenses, arranged apprenticeships, supervised young men traveling away from home, and introduced them into society. This system benefited the young men, who acquired an education and forged invaluable professional connections. It also protected the interests of the larger family network by securing the future of the next generation and limiting the ability of outsiders (those without the right pedigree) to rise in lowcountry society. Kin networks provided the guiding force behind the education and careers of young men who later became business partners and political allies.

Men such as Charles Cotesworth Pinckney, Henry Laurens, and Ralph Izard used their connections in Charleston and throughout the British Empire to aid their younger kin. When young Daniel Blake, the son of William and Anne Izard Blake, traveled to New York in the spring of 1795, Ralph Izard wrote letters on Daniel's behalf to his New York family and friends. Izard had married into the prominent DeLancey family of New York, so his connection to them as well as his political positions and business interests earned him many friends in New York. Izard graciously introduced Daniel and informed his New York connections that he would be "obliged to you for any civilities you may be pleased to shew [Daniel]." This kind of introduction, and the doors it opened for Blake, was typical of the lowcountry. Although traveling to a strange city, Daniel Blake still remained protected by his supportive circle of Carolina kin—Ralph Izard assured as much. The "civilities" Izard sought included not simply invitations to balls, parties, and dinners, but also a place of residence, a watchful eye, and temporary loans whenever necessary. The connections between Blake and Izard were also representative of the lowcountry, if somewhat confusing. Daniel Blake was the nephew of Ralph Izard's sister, Margaret Izard Blake. He was also the son of Anne Izard, another relative of Ralph and Margaret. In other words, both Daniel's uncle and his father married Izard women—one the sister, the other the distant cousin of Ralph Izard. To further complicate matters, Daniel's Aunt Rebecca Blake married another Ralph Izard who was the uncle of Daniel's mother. Because of the elaborate connections between the Blakes and Izards, Ralph Izard wanted and was expected to advance Daniel Blake's career.[31]

Supervising younger members of the kin group kept established men like Ralph Izard busy. Several years before he wrote on behalf of Blake, Izard became involved in the education of another young kinsman, Henry Rutledge. Ralph Izard and Edward Rutledge, Henry's father, were distant kin and close friends. As Edward began planning Henry's education, Izard suggested that Rutledge send the boy to New York to live with him. Izard was in New York for political business, and he promised Rutledge that "if you determine to send him to this place, you may be assured that I shall pay the same attention to him, as to my own Son." Rutledge soon sent Henry off to New York, where he remained under the guardianship of Ralph Izard for two years. The offer to supervise Henry was not unusual—and not without strings attached. Sponsoring children was normally a reciprocal activity. Ralph Izard had three young sons of his own who would soon require mentoring, and Edward Rutledge controlled one of Charleston's most prestigious law firms. So a few years later, Izard sent his son Henry to Charleston to study law under Edward Rutledge. Izard had served Henry Rutledge well, so Rutledge owed Izard an important educational debt. Izard therefore had every reason to believe that Edward Rutledge would be as attentive to Henry Izard as Ralph Izard had been to Henry Rutledge. But Izard's old friend let him down. When Rutledge left Charleston to serve in the state legislature, Ralph Izard complained, "Your absence from Town has prevented my Son from availing himself, as much as I wished, of your friendly instruction." While he admitted that Henry would still "be able to acquire some knowledge of the Attorney's practice in your Office," clearly the connections Henry might develop to Rutledge were more important than any legal lessons.[32]

Although Ralph Izard's complaints were carefully couched, his concerns for his son's future were legitimate. In Charleston, what a young man knew mattered far less than whom he knew. Reading law only provided knowledge; knowledge without connections was virtually useless. When Rutledge left his Charleston office all his books remained. But he carried with him his connections and influence—the most important tools in Henry Izard's education. Rutledge represents a failure in Carolina educational networking. Indebted to his friend, he nonetheless ignored his responsibility to Henry Izard in order to pursue his own desires. This kind of rejection of kinship obligations, while rare, threatened the future of young people who depended on kin to acquire connections and status within lowcountry society.

Aware of the indispensability of extensive family connections, most Charlestonians, unlike Edward Rutledge, eagerly fulfilled their educational obligations to their kin.[33] George Izard chaperoned his nephew Harry Manigault, the son of Gabriel and Margaret Izard Manigault, when he enrolled in Princeton. George assured his brother-in-law Gabriel that Harry would do well in school and ultimately become a respected member of the gentry. Once in New Jersey, George and Harry noticed that some of Harry's classmates controlled their own spending money. George wrote his brother-in-law and sister: "Your son was desirous to have the same confidence placed in Him, & I judged it was proper to gratify him in this to a certain extent." While Edward Rutledge's son Henry traveled to Europe to serve as secretary to his uncle Charles Cotesworth Pinckney, Edward Rutledge used his influence with officials at Cambridge to introduce and protect Pinckney's son. After Stephen Moore took over the education of his nephew, he assured his sister Frances Moore Bayard that her son would soon "be put in a situation that would advance him [and] . . . he has not been without constant opportunities." During the 1780s and 1790s Charles Cotesworth Pinckney and Thomas Pinckney frequently involved themselves in the education of their nephew, Daniel Horry. They regularly corresponded with him, used their influence to advance his education, and helped his mother, Harriott Pinckney Horry, raise him.[34]

Women were not merely passive beneficiaries of this system. In fact, women actively cooperated with their male kin in these educational networks. Together with his mother-in-law, Alice Izard, William Loughton Smith arranged the careers of his son Thomas and his brother-in law George Izard. Throughout the late 1790s, Smith corresponded with his mother-in-law about launching George's career: "I have spoken with the Secretary of War [James McHenry] about George & he assures me that he will make some arrangements which will place George in a very eligible situation in the line of his profession." Smith assured Alice Izard that after he returned from Europe they would turn their attention to arranging Thomas's education.[35] Sisters and kinswomen also freely offered advice to young men. Eliza Lucas, for instance, counseled her brother about honor and morality in his profession as a soldier. "Remember then, My dear Brother," she cautioned, "that fortitude, a Virtue so Necessary in all stations of life and to all people, seems more particularly so to a Soldier." Later she urged him to "consider then to how many dangers you are exposed" and reminded him that "the greatest conquest is a Victory over your own irregular passions."[36]

Women also coordinated the education, such as it was, of younger female kin. While Eliza Lucas counseled her brother, she also taught her younger sister, Polly, how to play music and speak French. Young women learned more "appropriate" skills from female kin as well: how to be cooks, wives, housekeepers, mothers, and nurses. Unlike their brothers, who attended formal academies or worked in local businesses, young women acquired their education through extended stays in the households of sisters, aunts, and cousins, and through elaborate women's networks of trade and correspondence. Instead of Latin, law, or literature, women learned to quilt, slaughter animals, nurse bloody flux, preserve vegetables, and deliver children. Despite the differences in subject matter, girls depended just as much on their relatives as did their brothers. And both boys and girls learned to believe in the indispensability of kin.

Adults knew that immersion in kin networks held the key to young people's success and their inclusion in lowcountry society, so they admonished children to cherish their relatives and build strong connections to them. Time and again, parents urged their progeny: "Be good children, mind your learning, and love one another." Edward Rutledge insisted that while his young son lived with a relative, "he must take an interest in the Prosperity of your Family, & look forward to intimacy with your children." He later instructed his daughter to "consider yourself, as more than commonly fortunate, in being placed under the care of those who have taken charge of you."[37] When her two sons studied abroad, Eliza Pinckney wrote regularly to the elder brother, Charles Cotesworth, and charged him with the care of Thomas. She even arranged Charles's education accordingly. Eliza removed Charles and Thomas from one school because "the air of Camberwell does not agree with his dear little brother." When Charles contemplated moving to another, better school, away from Thomas, his mother refused because "the distance you must then be from your dear brother will be too great." And always parents instructed children to avoid conflict: "Family differences are the most bitter—avoid them, therefore, oh my Children."[38]

While instructing children to develop abiding attachments to their kindred, Charlestonians also taught two other critical lessons about family. First, family responsibilities were both economic and emotional. Carolinians raised their children to respect both the affective and the financial obligations to the larger kin group. Second, family needs should supersede individual desires. Children learned early and often that they must honor the needs of the family in order to contribute to its success. Eliza Pinckney articulated the interweaving of these two convictions in a letter to her sons as they studied abroad. Admonishing her children to remain ever mindful of their responsibilities to family, Pinckney explained that youth offered no excuse for wayward behavior that might imperil the boys' relatives: "Though you are very young, you must know the welfare of a whole family depends in a great measure on the progress you make." Twenty years later Eliza gave her grandson Daniel Horry essentially the same advice as she prompted him to always remember his family debts and duties. Harriott Pinckney Horry echoed her mother's advice to Daniel as she too directed her son to faithfully honor his responsibilities to her "as well as your other near connections."[39]

In their effort to encourage children to honor family obligations, lowcountry elites taught by example: they cooperated in these educational networks and willingly aided their kin when called. Their motives were not, however, strictly altruistic. Self-interest played a role as well. Certainly, most Charlestonians loved their younger siblings and wanted to see them succeed. At the same time, they recognized the shared benefits that came from promoting younger relatives. With the right educational and social foundations, young men and women grew prosperous and powerful, and their success benefited the kin network. While a few elites, like Edward Rutledge, failed to honor their commitments to younger kin, most welcomed the responsibility to help their relatives and, by extension, themselves.

Although the interdependence and affection prevailing in sibling and kin ties worked to the advantage of the larger family, it limited the power that elders could or would exercise over younger relatives. Their cooperative attitudes prevented them from mirroring parental demands for obedience and deference. Elder brothers and kin simply could not command the same authority as fathers. Many times they did not even want to try. A case in point was Richard Hutson and his nephew. While Isaac Hayne's father (also Isaac Hayne) traveled about during the Revolutionary era, Isaac and his sister Nancy stayed with their uncle Richard Hutson. Hutson assured their father that the children were healthy, happy, and well taken care of. Hutson secured a tutor for his nephew and carefully monitored his educational progress. Then, a problem emerged: the boy would not learn his catechism. Hutson, being a devoted uncle, "endeavored to remidy it by teaching him at home but that I found a fruitless attempt, for I [could not] . . . engage him to it by persuasion and I did not chose to exert my authority." Apparently, forcing the boy was not in the offing. Hutson's only solution, besides writing Isaac's father, was to encourage the tutor to try harder.[40] Male kin frequently avoided exercising patriarchal authority over younger kinsmen—that they left to the father.

Henry Laurens reflected this tendency toward cooperation rather than authoritarianism as he helped his sister arrange and finance the London education of her son John Bremar. When John refused to return to South Carolina, Laurens threatened to stop paying John's bills. He even went so far as to write his London contacts, the firm of Ross & Mill, and instruct them to cut off John's money supply. As Henry explained, John "resolves without consulting one friend here to stay an Extra Year in London & none of us approve of his project." The story illustrates the group effort behind education in Carolina. Apparently several Charlestonians had weighed in on the situation and disapproved. When John ignored the wishes of the people sponsoring him, his uncle was forced to step in. Here the story grows more interesting—and more telling. Henry Laurens wanted to be tough and rein in his nephew. He castigated John and threatened to cut him off financially. Perhaps if Henry had been John's father, he would have followed through with the threat. But Henry Laurens found himself torn between the need to control his nephew and the desire to protect him. The latter ultimately held sway. Even as he wrote his London contacts to "pay no more Money to my Nephew," Henry Laurens expressed second thoughts. In the same letter he relented. "Nevertheless as I love him & consider his Youth," explained Laurens, "if he shall be much pinched please to lend him 50 Guineas."[41]

The leniency of kin stood in stark contrast to parental control.[42] Young people studying under elder kin often found themselves torn between authoritarian parents and permissive kin. It was a difficult struggle for parents to win. In fact, siblings or other kin who lived in close proximity to children often challenged and even overrode the educational desires of parents. After John Drayton sent his sons abroad in the 1760s to live and study with their maternal uncle, James Glen, he fought a losing battle for influence over the boys. Drayton charged his sons with taking advantage of him and complained that "Charles little knows the many hot Summers I have been out in the field broiling my Head, while he is spending with care & pleasure what I've hard fatigued for." James Glen's perspective differed radically. Devoted to his nephew and closer physically and emotionally than Drayton, Glen insisted that Charles was an accomplished, forthright young man. As for Drayton's expenses, Glen maintained that "never was money better laid out."[43] While Drayton and Glen continued to squabble over Charles and his brothers, the boys, not surprisingly, sided with their lenient uncle rather than their distant, complaining father. Charles eventually grew so estranged that he refused even to write his father for over two years.

James Glen, like Henry Laurens and Richard Hutson, was a surrogate father in name only. Although solely in charge of his nephews, he would not exercise patriarchal power over them. Bound by affection and cooperation, and lacking the authority or the expectations of a father, surrogate parents treated their charges more like a sibling than a child. Kin-based education operated more as collaboration between equals than anything else, and fostered more independent-minded sons. Not surprisingly, young people living away from demanding parents and supervised by cooperative kin identified with those relatives and begrudged parental interference.

Close friendships also helped extend horizontal ties within the elite circle and could similarly be used to thwart parental authority over young people. When Peter Manigault studied abroad, he developed very close attachments to William Drayton and Andrew Rutledge. Peter characterized his relationship with Andrew as "a most intimate friendship," and William felt so deeply about Peter that, after Peter married, William claimed "a Brother's Part" of the bride's affections.[44] While all three filled their letters to each other with open displays of affection, they also found time to complain about and conspire against their fathers. As William's father made numerous attempts to get his son to behave more responsibly, William coyly informed Peter that he would never "accord my Father in his Desires of . . . getting more dutiful Children." When Peter voiced criticisms of his father, Gabriel Manigault (1704-1781), Andrew encouraged Peter to follow the path of least resistance: study hard and write often to his parents. This, Andrew assured his friend, would ensure professional success (Peter was training as a lawyer) and protect his share of the family estate. Andrew also confided that he secretly used his power as Gabriel Manigault's lawyer to protect Peter's future. When approached by Gabriel about changing his will, Andrew "dissuaded him from what I thought might abridge your power & lessen your consequence in the world."⁴⁵ Deep friendships like the one Andrew, William, and Peter shared thus had both emotional and practical consequences for parent-child relationships. Friends, like kin, offered young people another emotional focus in their lives and provided a means to challenge parental authority.

The behaviors of siblings and kin in eighteenth-century South Carolina share some striking similarities with contemporary analyses of sibling ties. In the past fifteen years a host of social scientists have begun to argue that sibling relationships are characterized by "relative egalitarianism." Some scholars further theorize that this equality, combined with the powerful socializing effect of siblings and kin, alters parental attitudes and transforms parenting efforts. There is, in essence, a give and take within family dynamics. Parents cannot exercise total authority over child rearing because siblings and other relatives exert not just *another* influence on children, but oftentimes a *contradictory* influence based on equality.⁴⁶ Lowcountry parents acted as if this were exactly the situation they faced.

Aware of the loss of power that accompanied placing sons with relatives and friends abroad, but equally aware of the necessity of those connections, lowcountry parents saw few options. Securing connections to members of the extended family remained essential to the success of young people. Parents needed to help children make those connections even when they undermined authority within the patriarchal household. Further, although local schools were reportedly "much improved" by the late eighteenth century, most lowcountry elites still continued to favor a European education.⁴⁷ Since parents could not uproot their lives to traipse about Europe following school-age boys, they continued to rely on kin abroad to supervise their children.

Lowcountry parents sometimes faced the choice of denying their children the benefits of extended kin connections or abdicating authority over them. Willful children, competing interests, and the communication problems that accompanied travel abroad complicated parent's abilities to guide their children and necessitated the intervention of relatives. For example, Alice and Ralph Izard found coordinating the educations of their sons Henry and George terribly difficult. George Izard refused to return to Charleston despite his parent's demands. George insisted that he needed more time to pursue his studies; consequently he ignored his parent's letters and even feigned illnesses to avoid leaving Europe. Unable to control George, Ralph Izard turned to George's brothers-in-law Gabriel Manigault (1758-1809) and William Loughton Smith and his kinsmen Edward Rutledge and Charles Cotesworth Pinckney. The responsibilities of these surrogate parents became so thoroughgoing that Ralph Izard admitted to Charles Cotesworth Pinckney that, since he was at his wit's end with George, he thought Pinckney should make any future decisions concerning the boy's education. Eventually he confessed complete ignorance about George's life: "Where he is I know not. . . . I am ignorant of what plan respecting him has been executed." John Drayton eventually relinquished control of his son Charles to James Glen because Drayton, like Ralph Izard, saw little choice. Charles Drayton neither wrote to his father nor responded to his father's letters. John complained that "as for my son Charles I hardly know I have such a Son. Not a scrap have I rec'd from him for these two years or more."[48] Drayton's emotional and geographic distance from his father and his growing attachment to his indulgent uncle intensified his sense of independence.

Taken to extremes, this independence could become insolence. Timothy Ford found the tradition of sending sons abroad to study self-defeating: "They generally return but little more improved & much more dissipated than they went -& after this much expense has been lavished upon them."[49] Ford's suspicions made sense. After all, these young men moved away from controlling parents to be supervised by siblings and kin. These surrogate parents typically saw themselves as equals rather than superiors, and only rarely and reluctantly exercised authority over their charges.

As parents and kin struggled to mold the hearts and minds of children, conflicts sometimes erupted. The struggle over the custody of young Edward Brailsford in the early eighteenth century illustrates the importance of both parent-child and kin relations and the resulting problems when the two clashed. Edward Brailsford traveled to South Carolina with his father and stepmother in the 1720s. Edward's father, Edmund, became estranged from his English family after he married his second wife without their approval. Despite this estrangement, when Edmund Brailsford's English aunt died in 1726, she left a large portion of her estate to her great-nephew Edward. According to Edward's grandfather, there was just one catch: the boy must move to England. The English Brailsfords insisted they had the right and the responsibility to bring Edward to England to live with them. Edward's English kin believed he was "losing his time" in Charleston, and disapproved of him "going on his fathers Errands & waiting on his Brothers, that he was made a perfect lackey, & sent from one end of the Town to the other." Edmund responded in an understandably hostile manner: "I may I think send my son on my Errands without being said why to by any one." Edmund, insulted by his family's charges, initially resisted their appeals for custody. He argued, "I do not think that any Bequest can convey a Title to any person to Supersede that propriety & Jurisdiction the Nature of the relation gives a parent in & over his child." Despite his conviction about the primacy of the parent-child relationship, Edmund eventually capitulated and sent Edward to England.[50] In part, financial considerations determined his decision. But Edmund also understood the necessity of extended family connections. Honoring his family's request might return Edmund to their good graces. It would certainly secure his son's future.

So strong was the pull of these intragenerational bonds that they could overwhelm the desires of parents. When Henry and George Izard studied abroad under the care of relatives, they disappointed their parents at every turn. Both chose careers against their parents' wishes, left schools without permission, spent too much money, became involved with disreputable people, and refused to return to Charleston. Not surprisingly, Alice and Ralph Izard expressed serious misgivings about entrusting the care and education of their youngest son, Ralph Jr., to others. Alice wanted desperately to be with her son, but, aware of the power of kin networks, she reluctantly let him go: "My reason is satisfied that he is better where he is."[51] Since both she and her husband knew the importance of being connected to a world of kin and friends, they simply saw no acceptable alternative. Keeping Ralph Jr. in Charleston not only denied him the best education but also undercut his ability to develop familial connections that, later in his life, would become essential to acquiring wealth and power. They wrung their hands, but they turned him over.

While parents like the Izards only reluctantly let go of their children, siblings and kin generally welcomed their younger relatives with open arms. As he supervised his nephew Isaac's education, Richard Hutson assured Isaac's father that "any assistance I can give him . . . will be cheerfully rendered." When his orphaned grandchildren came to live with him in 1773, Gabriel Manigault embraced his newfound responsibilities. Just before his grandson departed for school in England, Manigault discussed his commitment to the boy: "Nothing Shall ever be wanting in me to make everything Agreeable to you in this World, to the utmost of my power." And Ralph Izard assured Edward Rutledge that mentoring Rutledge's son was a joy: "If I can contribute to the accomplishment of your wishes, my friendship for you will make me do it with pleasure."[52]

When elite parents sent their children away for extended periods to study and work with relatives, the children secured both training in a particular field and ties to kin that lasted a lifetime. The broader their connections, the brighter their future. As children connected with siblings and kin, they deepened an essential psychological bond that provided a sense of comfort and belonging and enabled young people to thrive. Maintaining emotional and practical ties to these relatives represented a vital part of growing up, and growing away from parents.

Although parents struggled internally over letting their children go, no real choice existed. The power of kinship connections overwhelmed parents' desires for autonomy and isolation. Just as surely as female kin entered the private household and pushed out the patriarch to prepare for the delivery of a child, siblings and kin intervened in and sometimes overrode parental educational plans. Their justification and the reason for parental capitulation were the same: kinship networks provided an irreplaceable service. Its value to young people and the broader family network eclipsed any problems it created within the patriarchal household.

Parenting the Parentless

In part, the enhanced emotional intensity of and reliance on siblings can be attributed to the disease-riddled environment in the lowcountry. Parents throughout early America expected children to care for one another, but in eighteenth-century South Carolina demography and culture made this expectation a necessity. Historians have long assumed that high mortality rates threatened the stability of colonial societies because they weakened marital and parent-child relations. The turbulent Chesapeake has received far more scholarly attention than the lowcountry, but in both regions historians argue that demographic instability and short life expectancy, by undermining the patriarchal family, destabilized society. The end result: a society of supposedly unattached individuals.[53] But historians have generally ignored the ability of siblings and other intragenerational kin to step into the breach. The early death of parents certainly undermined patriarchal families, but it also intensified bonds between siblings.[54]

In early Carolina when parents died, siblings did not simply drift apart. Rather they grew ever closer, developing intense emotional connections that lasted the remainder of their lives. The Manigault brothers forged a particularly strong bond in part because they lost both their parents at a young age. Peter and Elizabeth Manigault died in 1773, leaving the fifteen- and ten-year-old brothers, Gabriel and Joseph, with only a young sister and aging grandparents. The Drayton brothers watched their mother die and their father, at age fifty-nine, remarry seventeen-year-old Rebecca Perry. As their father started a new family, Thomas and Glenn Drayton must have thought that, save for their uncle James Glen, they were alone in the world. Their experience in this regard was similar to that of Thomas and Charles Cotesworth Pinckney. Taken abroad as children, they resided in Europe when their mother wrote that their father had died. Heartbroken, Eliza Pinckney did not bring her sons home. Nor did she go to them. She simply informed them that their father loved them, and instructed the elder brother, Charles, to take care of young Thomas. The boys were eight and twelve.[55] Not surprisingly, siblings like the Pinckney, Manigault, and Drayton brothers who lost one or both parents clung all the more tenaciously to one another. In many cases, these attachments became the exclusive focus of emotional life. Young people turned to their siblings as well as their deceased parent's siblings, knowing that they would, as one young woman explained to her aunt, "Come—and supply the place of my long lost Mother."[56]

Throughout the eighteenth century, orphaned children remained a constant presence in South Carolina.[57] When parents died, sibling and kin stepped in to raise the children who were left behind. After their mother died, William, Isaac, and Sarah Hayne lived for a time with their uncle Richard Hutson and then with their aunt Mary Hutson Peronneau. Although their father, Isaac Hayne, survived his wife, politics monopolized his time and attention. When British troops captured and incarcerated Hayne during the occupation of Charleston, Mary Peronneau accompanied the children to jail to visit their father. After the British sentenced Hayne to death for treasonous acts against their government, Mary took the children to the house of British officer Nisbet Balfour. William remembered "going with my brother Isaac & Sister Sarah in Company with my Aunt Peronneau to Lieutenant Balfour's . . . and there on our knees presenting a petition to him in favor of my father but without effect." After Hayne's execution, Mary Peronneau took her nephews and niece home and assumed the role of their mother.[58]

In a few instances, grandparents became surrogate parents, but short life expectancy made grandparents a rarity in the lowcountry. Unlike their neighbors to the north, few Charlestonians even knew their grandparents. Certainly no one expected grandparents to care for orphaned children—to have done so would have been illogical. When grandparents did survive to know their children's children, affectionate relationships usually developed. But emotional ties across three generations remained anomalous throughout the eighteenth century.

When Gabriel Manigault's mother died in early 1773, he, his siblings, and their father, Peter, moved in with Gabriel's paternal grandparents, Gabriel and Anne Ashby Manigault. Peter was an only child—he had no sibling to whom he could turn. He stayed at Silkhope, the family's plantation home, for only a brief period before traveling to Europe in hopes of improving his own failing health. After Peter died abroad, his parents raised his young children.[59] Living with their grandparents, the Manigault siblings developed even deeper connections to one another. Joseph in particular forged an attachment to his elder brother that he retained for the rest of his life. When Gabriel went to Europe to study, Joseph wrote faithfully and begged Gabriel to write as often as possible. Joseph's grandmother worried about the boy after Gabriel left. "We are all very Dull," Anne Manigault lamented, "especially Joe." Years later, when Gabriel returned to Charleston and Joseph studied abroad, the letters continued. From London this time, Joseph again begged Gabriel to "write to me as often as you can, for you must know how much Pleasure it gives me to hear from you."[60] Even as grown men, married with children, established planters and politicians, the Manigault brothers continued to write and visit religiously. Their bond grew, rather than diminishing over time.

Although they lived many years with their grandparents and loved them very much, the Manigault siblings recognized that each was ultimately responsible for the other. Consequently, when Gabriel Manigault returned from studying abroad, he assumed responsibility for his younger brother's education and moved his younger sister from their grandparents' home into his own. After his father died, Arthur Bryan similarly brought his younger brother Jonathan to Charleston where they lived and worked together. Arthur launched Jonathan's career, taught him the mercantile trade, and provided valuable social and business connections. As Jonathan explained to his mother: "I cannot say too much of his goodness to me. . . . He really is a Father to me."[61]

A child did not have to be orphaned to live with relatives. When her cousin Eliza Lucas and the Lucas family migrated to South Carolina, Frances Fayweather came with them. She lived with her cousin outside Charleston and then moved to Boston to another relative's home. During the Revolution William Drayton sent his son John to live with John's maternal uncle Isaac Motte. When Motte could no longer care for John Drayton, he sent the boy to live with his paternal uncle Stephen Drayton in Virginia. Motte informed John's father after the fact, promising that "your Brother is very fond of him and has taken him under his protection."[62]

Influential political leaders often became so involved in their public careers that they could not ably parent their children. Further, most eighteenth-century men thought a maternal presence essential to successfully raising children, especially girls. Upon their wives' death, many fathers sought surrogate mothers, particularly for their daughters. Unsure what to do with young children and distracted by politics, many men sent their children to live permanently with female kin. After Sally Rutledge's mother died in early 1792, her father, Edward Rutledge, regretfully apprised her of the sad news. He then informed her that she was going to live with her step-aunt, Mary Stead Pinckney: "Mrs. Pinckney & the Major have taken you as their Child. They will treat you as such." When he traveled abroad, widower Henry Laurens left his daughters, Martha and Mary Eleanor, with his sister-in-law and brother in Charleston. Oliver Hart reported that his daughter Polly "lives with her Sister Severen, who is a mother to her." And shortly after his first wife died, Charles Cotesworth Pinckney sent his young daughters to live temporarily with his sister, Harriott Pinckney Horry. Widowed mothers similarly worried about their young sons having a proper male role model, and sometimes turned sons over to kinsmen. For example, several years after Harriott Pinckney Horry took in her widowed brother's daughters, she informed her son, Daniel, that his uncles would "have the management of you and your affairs."[63]

Although Harriott Pinckney Horry and her brothers did, in essence, swap children, she expressed grave doubts about assuming responsibility for her three nieces. When Harriott initially learned of her brother's return to Charleston with his motherless children, she and her friend Alice Izard commiserated about the situation. Izard later reported that Horry "looks melancholy, & no wonder. I dare say, she will spend the remainder of her life with him, in taking care of his Children."[64]

Horry's situation illustrates both the power of kin responsibilities and the limits of generosity between siblings. Horry dreaded the burden of raising her brother's children and complained about it. Clearly, all was not bliss and harmony within the sibling set. Yet while both Horry and Izard lamented the responsibility, neither thought for a moment Horry could refuse her brother. If parents died prematurely, siblings stepped—or were pushed—into the breach. Horry's brother needed her, and family duty required she honor those needs. It is also revealing that Izard voiced dejection about the situation but Horry remained silent. Indeed it is only because of the writings of her confidante that we know anything of Horry's reluctance. Horry's attitude, revealed only by her friend, demonstrates that responsibilities to siblings sometimes could not be avoided, regardless of personal desires. She also showcases the complex feelings that surrounded surrogate parenting. It is implausible to believe that no one else in the lowcountry shared Horry's fears. But literary sources, aside from the Horry case, reveal little on the subject. Most likely, other reluctant surrogate parents kept silent out of concern for the children they parented and the kin they needed to please, and let their sense of duty supersede their personal desires.

Today, turning children over to someone else to raise seems callous, if not cruel. But eighteenth-century Carolinians were simply doing the best they knew how. They acted out of a perceived necessity: daughters needed a maternal presence widowers simply could never provide. Clearly they made these decisions within the framework of social acceptability; no one looked askance at these fathers. Leaving children, sometimes permanently, with siblings or other relatives was simply a fact of life. After all, siblings had been taught all their lives to love each other and be responsible for one another.

The lessons of childhood persisted over time, and the attachments and devotion to kin so carefully fashioned in youth generally deepened in later life. Children brought up in a wide, strong circle of kin carefully maintained those networks into adulthood and immersed themselves in a series of kin-based responsibilities and rituals throughout their lives.[65] Sibling ties remained important throughout the life course in part because they lasted a lifetime. In this way, the eighteenth century is not so different from our own world. As one psychologist explained, "Our brothers and sisters are there with us from the dawn of our personal stories to the inevitable dusk." Sibling relations, in fact, represent the most enduring of any familial bond—lasting longer than relationships between husbands and wives, and between parents and children.[66] Further, they number among the most powerful. Siblings continue, long after childhood, to exercise a profound influence over the construction of identity and fulfill important psychological needs.[67]

This pattern of deeply felt, psychologically important sibling ties, while clearly the norm in eighteenth-century Carolina, was not universal. Although most sibling relationships promoted solidarity and felicity, others were fraught with tension. But because Carolinians remained essentially quiet about the subject of family feuds, evidence of conflict can be gleaned only from the occasional will that excluded close kin from the list of beneficiaries, or letter containing veiled references to wayward relatives. Very rarely does one encounter clear complaints about family obligations or fights.[68] Carolinians' reticence perhaps testifies as much to the need to appear cooperative as to the universality of harmonious sibling ties.

Still, it does seem clear that most lowcountry elites desired and experienced close relationships with their siblings. Moreover, the close horizontal ties between sibling and other intragenerational kin allowed them to transcend the authoritarianism of the patriarchal family. They constructed far more equal bonds than any other family relationships, and shared a strong sense of generational solidarity.[69] Siblings prized cooperation, interdependence, and loyalty. They worked together to make certain that individual life decisions protected the interest of the larger family network and bound family members ever closer.

Marital Matters

Because of their powerful emotional presence and their commitment to generational solidarity, siblings and kin exercised a great deal of influence over the major life decisions adults made. And no decision mattered more than marriage. Siblings, cousins, and other kin participated in courtship, advised one another on marital decisions, aided in coordinating weddings, and helped newlyweds expand their connections within the kin group. When they chose marriage partners, lowcountry elites were driven not only by personal passions but also by the desires and hopes of the family. Carolinians wanted love and personal happiness in their marriages, but they also welcomed the financial and political advances marriages brought. While families almost never arranged marriages, they carefully constructed an environment that fostered marriages within and between kin groups. In their marital patterns lowcountry elites showcased their duel conception of family—that it was at once emotional and economic.

Young people welcomed the assistance of siblings in matters of the heart (and wallet). Absent from Charleston during the American Revolution, Thomas Pinckney told his sister, Harriott Pinckney Horry: "If Chance should throw my Charmer in your way I charge you to make strong Love for me." Before William Gibbes began courting Nancy Manigault, he wrote her brother to request his blessing and ask whether he should worry about any competition. When Thomas Pinckney, Jr., courted Elizabeth Izard, he frequently wrote his cousin Harriott Pinckney (the niece and namesake of Harriott Pinckney Horry) to seek her advice. Frances Bayard encouraged her brother's courtship, insisting that "the Woman that makes My Brother happy must ever share my tender affection."[70] When parents and children disagreed over marital choices, kin interceded and tried to promote family harmony. Upon learning that the parents of Joseph Blake strongly disapproved of his bride, his aunt warned the family: "The sooner however, they are reconciled to it the better."[71]

Family historians traditionally have focused on the nature of authority—especially patriarchal authority—within families, and the transition over time from authority to autonomy. One often-studied component in this model is increased independence in marital choices. In the marriage practices of lowcountry elites, however, this paradigm breaks down. Parents were not the sole (and often not even the most important) actors in facilitating marriages. Instead, young people relied on their siblings and kin to help them choose a spouse. At the same time, marriage was far too important to leave simply to the whims of the young. Members of the kin group made certain that youthful passions did not derail family ambitions. So young men and women of the gentry class neither married according to the dictates of their parents nor acted independent of familial concerns. Rather, with the help of their siblings and kin, they cooperated on marital decisions and negotiated a compromise between family financial considerations and personal desires.[72]

Lowcountry elites routinely married their kin, and each new generation of newlyweds repeated the interweaving of families that had gone on before. Courting one's relatives was not merely acceptable; it was preferable. Not surprisingly, the family trees of the wealthiest planter-merchant families were, by the late eighteenth century, so interconnected that it is difficult to determine where one ends and the other begins.

Across cultures and over time, incest has had a variety of meanings.[73] Some cultures tolerated marriage between siblings, while others forbade unions between sixth cousins. Lowcountry Carolinians interpreted incest extremely narrowly. Eighteenth-century South Carolinians proscribed marriage between members of the conjugal family (fathers and daughters, mothers and sons, sisters and brothers) and between certain consanguineous or blood-related kin (uncles and nieces, nephews and aunts). But they embraced first cousin marriages and unions between most affinal kin (those related through marriage). Uncles, for instance, could and did marry their affinal nieces. Carolinians honored the incest taboo in its strictest sense, but they danced all around the edges.

Lowcountry elites demonstrated a particularly keen enthusiasm for cousin and exchange marriages.[74] Cousin marriage and exchange marriages (in which siblings of one family marry siblings of another) occurred for both emotional and financial reasons. Elite families traveled together, attended schools and social functions together, visited frequently, and generally shared a friendly yet exclusive social world. Members of the interrelated kin groups of Charleston selected as marriage partners those within their social circle, largely comprised of relatives. Cousin and exchange marriages thus pervaded the genealogical charts of eighteenth-century South Carolinians. The sisters Elizabeth, Susannah, and Mary Reid married the brothers John Julius and Robert Pringle and their stepbrother, William Bull. Charlotte Georgina Izard married Joseph

Allen Smith, the brother of William Loughton Smith, the husband of the deceased sister after whom she was named. Jonathan Bryan married Mary Williamson, the daughter by a prior marriage of his brother's wife. Thus Jonathan's mother-in-law was also his sister-in-law, and the women were not only mother and daughter but sisters-in-law as well.[75] The examples go on and on. These kin-based marriages occurred in part because of daily interactions, but they were not simply matters of convenience. Marrying family members helped prevent the fragmentation of family estates while it bolstered the financial and political power of particular families. These marriage strategies formed the cornerstone of elite wealth and class identity.

Close kin marriages, especially between cousins, also allowed members of the kin group to exert influence over conjugal households.[76] Like childbirth and education of the young, lowcountry marriage patterns reflected the interweaving of the intragenerational and patriarchal families. Young people did not simply create new, private households. They also expanded the emotional and economic connections within the kin network. These marriage patterns increased the bonds within families and fostered a greater sense of cooperation while they simultaneously advanced the exclusivity of the lowcountry. Through careful marriage choices, Charleston elites either reinforced existing family connections or created intergroup alliances. Both came to the same end: they deepened the tight-knit, exclusive nature of lowcountry society.[77]

Preserving the Connections: Visiting and Writing

These connections between Charleston's ever-growing concentric circles of kin continued throughout the life cycle. As they married and formed individual households, lowcountry men and women remained immersed in their other, kin-based families. The elaborate visiting rituals practiced by lowcountry elites offers one gauge of the importance of these attachments.[78] Visiting fostered a sense of belonging and provided entertainment, comfort, companionship, and safety. It physically expressed the emotional and social importance of kinship. Most importantly, it symbolized the constant interweaving of siblings and kin with the patriarchal household.

In the eighteenth century, visiting represented a daily part of the lives of elite men and women. Kin gathered together and shared special occasions such as births, weddings, and holidays, welcomed one another for frequent and extended visits, and mourned their separation when apart. Visiting served more practical functions as well. When residents fled Charleston to escape diseases that seasonally swept through the town, they sought solace at the homes of kin or elicited their aid in travel arrangements. As Anne Hart grew ill she asked her brother to take her to his home. Halfway through the trip she changed her mind and went instead to stay with her sister. When Judith Ball's Charleston doctor insisted that she move to a better climate in 1770, Henry Laurens, the widower of Judith's late husband's sister, wrote letters for her facilitating her travel north. He made sure his friends in Rhode Island befriended Ball, provided her a place to stay, and secured the best doctor in the colony. Furthermore, Henry made it clear he would provide any money Ball needed by informing local merchants that he assumed responsibility for any expenses she incurred.[79]

Life's trials seemed somehow more bearable with relatives nearby. Whenever people got sick or lost loved ones, they traveled to the homes of family members. Alice and Ralph Izard's daughter-in-law remained sick after the birth of her first child, so she traveled with her sister and husband to Alice Izard's family's home in New York. After her beloved husband died, Eliza Pinckney took refuge with family and friends. Grief-stricken "beyond the power of words to utter," she could not return to her home for several weeks. Anne Hart recuperated from an illness at her sister's home for nearly seven weeks.[80]

Siblings also provided a natural, genial environment for young people. Some young women, like their brothers being educated abroad, preferred living with siblings to their own parents' homes. Given the powerful emotional role siblings played in one another's lives, parents could only resign themselves to living without their children. Alice Izard reluctantly accepted her daughter Anne's frequent and lengthy visits with relatives because "she is so happily situated there with her Cousins that I am, on that account, reconciled to lieving without her."[81]

Visiting expressed the deep emotional connections that kinfolk shared. The fact that women and men visited a wide array of kin attests to their broad definition of family. That they visited often demonstrates the powerful role relatives played in their lives.[82] Eighteenth-century elites seemed to be constantly on the go, visiting from house to house. Explaining her social activities to her husband, Alice Izard noted that when she visited the Kinloch plantation, she found Mrs. Kinloch away, visiting her sister. Alice then visited Mrs. Horry, who was also away making visits, but Alice stayed the night anyway. After leaving the Horry plantation, she "unexpectedly met Mrs. Motte & Mrs. J. Middleton . . . & I dined, slept, & breakfasted with them." On the same trip she also visited Ralph's mother, an aunt of her nephew, and her daughter's mother-in-law. None of this seemed particularly unusual to Alice.[83] Her schedule was similar to Anne Izard Deas, who wrote her brother: "Mrs. Deas and Nancy are now with us, Your Sister, Mr. Manigault, & their family are coming this day, & I expect your Brother, & his family the end of this week."[84]

Both Alice and Anne recounted their activities as just that—daily activities, not unique experiences. And they were not alone. Other prominent lowcountry women kept similar accounts of their lives, which literally flowed from household to household. Far from isolated within the patriarchal household, lowcountry women also lived in the homes of sisters, kin, and friends. Visiting was so commonplace that women would even "carry our work abroad with us so that having company . . . is no great interruption to that affair."[85] As they traveled from home to home, women blurred the lines of the private household and publicly demonstrated the power of intragenerational kinship ties.

While women often became the primary "kin guardians" of southern families after the mid-eighteenth century, the desire to remain connected to a broader kin network was not gender specific.[86] Both women and men actively maintained frequent physical and emotional contact with their siblings and kin. For example, the brothers Joseph and Gabriel Manigault routinely visited one another and missed each other when apart. On one occasion Joseph returned to his Charleston home after a visit with Gabriel and immediately sent his horse back to Gabriel so he could visit a few days later. When Gabriel traveled to New York with his father-in-law in 1789, only limited funds prevented Joseph from going along. The following year, as Gabriel traveled to Columbia for a legislative session, Joseph implored his brother to stay only briefly in the capital. Gabriel and Joseph Manigault, like many other Carolinians, made up for their separation with frequent, loving letters. During the 1789 trip to New York, Joseph and Gabriel wrote each other every few weeks and discussed a host of subjects including family finances, the political climate, and Charleston's social scene. With his brother away, Joseph complained of his boredom in Charleston, insisting he found nothing to do "but Tea drinking Parties, to which I am compliant enough to attend Mrs. Manigault when ever she goes." Joseph admitted at the heart of his discontent lay a "wish to be with you." Like Gabriel and Joseph Manigault, Charles Cotesworth and Thomas Pinckney clung throughout their lives to the emotional connections forged in youth. The boys studied at Oxford and lived in England for almost sixteen years. Separated from their mother and grieving the loss of their father, Charles Cotesworth and Thomas Pinckney shared an emotional connection and a sense of reliance on one another that surpassed any other familial connection in their lives. Even more devoted, the brothers John, Benjamin, and Peter Waring lived together throughout their lives. None of the three ever married; they chose instead to remain at their Pine Hill plantation where, according to one visitor, they lived in great harmony.[87]

Between visits, siblings communicated through the written word. Their letters offered them a means of visiting across space and testify to the emotional significance of their bonds. Even if we could not read their words, the volume and frequency of letters between siblings showcase their deep attachments. For example, after Andrew Pringle complained that his brother Robert did not write often enough, Robert reminded Andrew that between early October 1739 and late May 1740 he wrote twenty-five letters. (Andrew remained in England, while Robert resided in Charleston.) Twenty-five letters in thirty-two weeks still did not satisfy Andrew, who requested even more frequent communication. Not even warfare and the occupation of Charleston interrupted the correspondence of the Pinckney siblings. During the Revolutionary War, Charles Cotesworth and Thomas Pinckney wrote each other and their sister almost daily.[88]

In order to remain part of one another's lives when separated, siblings and kin wrote elaborate descriptions of their daily lives. No detail seemed too small. Correspondents described clothing, meals, and the minutia of their daily routines—all in hopes of maintaining intimacy. And they voiced unfailing, sometimes pseudo-erotic devotion to one another. Writing his elder sister Margaret Izard Manigault, Henry Izard typified the intimate nature of sibling relations in eighteenth-century elite families. Playfully chastising his sister for her failure to correspond, he wondered, "What is the reason my dear Sister of your inveterate silence? . . . Does the gentle string of fraternal love no longer vibrate in your heart?" These were not the sentiments of a young boy but of a twenty-seven-year-old married man trained in the military. Still, he courted his thirty-three-year-old sister's attention. For years, Stephen Moore and his sister Frances Moore Bayard carried on a similarly affectionate correspondence. Frances worried a great deal about Stephen when he traveled abroad and wrote that her "Hearty Prayer is that at this time My Dear Brother is safe arriv'd in London." When Stephen married, he hoped Frances found his new wife "worthy of the esteem of the few like my dear Sister." Thomas Pinckney, Jr., also carried on a loving correspondence with his first cousin Harriott Pinckney. When she failed to respond to one of his letters, he wondered: "Oh Harriott! how could you let such an opportunity escape. Not a single line or even a message." Thomas urged Harriott to write often and insisted, "Every thing you can tell me will be interesting. I shall even receive pleasure in being informed how the sands blow."[89]

On one level, correspondents like the ones above genuinely doted on one another. They showed considerable interest in each other's lives and overtly expressed their feelings. Indeed, in some exchanges, like that of Margaret Izard Manigault and Henry Izard and Thomas Pinckney, Jr., and Harriott Pinckney, the language seems more romantic than platonic. The flirtatious tone of their letters, however, points out another dimension to sibling exchanges: all is not exactly as it seems.

Letters offer the greatest evidence of sibling attachments, but they must be read with a bit of skepticism. In the first place, letter writing was an important symbol of gentility in eighteenth-century America. While elites primarily used their correspondence to perpetuate family and friendship ties, letters were, secondarily, consciously constructed representations of gentility. Literate men and women manipulated their language in letters to reflect their self-image as refined gentlemen and ladies. Indeed, early American correspondents thought of every letter as a literary performance, and each correspondent tried to fit the prescribed ideals of society. This was particularly common at the end of the eighteenth century, as a new wave of advice literature encouraged young people to carefully manicure their public image. Writers like Lord Chesterfield instructed men and women on the fine art of self-fashioning for public consumption, and correspondence, like dress and demeanor, bore the imprint of this new wave of advice.[90] Writers always kept the expectations and the status of their recipient in mind. And they knew that letters rarely remained private exchanges between two people. Instead they were often shared with other family members and kept for posterity.[91]

In some ways, then, letters portrayed the carefully constructed self, influenced by societal ideals and fashioned for outward consumption, as much as they chronicled real experiences. The letters of lowcountry elites must therefore be read as both displays of idealized sibling relationships (brothers and sisters who appeared dutiful and affectionate) and credible evidence of honest experiences and emotions between sisters and brothers (siblings who acted dutifully and felt affectionate toward one another). The fact that letters between siblings wove together reality and ideal poses one set of problems for the historian. The scarcity of conflict in those letters brings up another.

To begin with, there is the question of siblings who did not write to one another. While Gabriel and Joseph Manigault corresponded with one another regularly throughout their lives, few letters exist between the brothers and their sister Anne. Why? Were the brothers estranged from Anne or indifferent to her? Do the absence of letters indicate some divisive gendered sibling experience? Or did Anne live so close and see her brothers so regularly that writing more often proved unnecessary? Were letters written, but destroyed? Did descendants decide that only male letters merited conservation and donation to archives? Furthermore, what should be made of the paucity of conflict in sibling and kin correspondence? Was the pervasive pleasantness in these letters sincere? Did it grow out of Carolinians' hopes of building some affectionate attachments? Or did fear of retribution keep feuding relatives quiet?

Collectively, their relative silence about conflict, the absence of certain collections of correspondence, and the power of idealizations and self-fashioning that are present in others make it inappropriate to always accept the words of Carolinians at face value. But neither is it fair to completely discount their words. True, lowcountry elites employed rhetoric in their letters to their kindred. And they used those letters to help construct an idealized version of themselves and their world, particularly family relationships. But their words were not hollow. They did not convey sporadic professions of devotion—they wrote regular, sometimes weekly, accounts of their lives and their responsibilities to one another. In short, Carolinians spent their time and money caring for one another throughout the life course. Their letters sincerely represent—not simply reify—their close attachments to siblings and kin.

In addition to expressing their deep attachments to one another and showcasing their genteel idealizations of self, siblings' letters also highlighted their near-obsession with sickness. Their graphic descriptions of ailments take some of the wind out of the argument that letters were really idealized versions of life. Rarely did letters pass between kindred without detailing a litany of family illnesses. Flux, fevers, coughs, cancers, rashes, swellings, boils, abscesses, headaches, gout, sore eyes, sore throats—the list of maladies went on and on. One woman interwove her health obsession and her sororal attachment when she insisted that "I wrote a few lines to my sister . . . with a hand which trembled so much from the sickness I had endured that I could hardly hold a pen."[92] The pervasiveness of sickness in the lowcountry no doubt fueled Carolinians' health fixation. Being surrounded by disease and death made people think early and often about their mortality. Even as a young woman, Eliza Lucas recognized the uncertainty of life and discussed her concerns with her brother: "But old age, you will say, is a long way off from you and me. True, and perhaps we shall never reach it. 'Tis then an additional reason why we should make use of the present and remember no time is ours but the present."[93]

Whenever one sibling reported an illness, the others felt great anxiety and turned to one another for solace.[94] Mary Pinckney grew frantic after she learned of her cousin's illness, which the women suspected might be cancer. Eliza Lucas expressed similar emotions when she learned that one of her brothers had been "given over by the Phisicans."[95] When the inevitable death of a beloved relative occurred, family members left behind professed great sorrow and affliction. The loss of his brother-in-law John Coming Ball was, according to Henry Laurens, "a great stroke to mine & will detach me very much." Alice Izard found her sister's death "a subject that afflicts me so greatly." When William Smith died, his former sister-in-law Margaret Manigault wrote her daughter: "You can suppose that we had the sensations of pain and surprize that Mr. Smith had so suddenly left this world." The interesting thing about Margaret's reaction is that Smith's marital connection to her family would seem to have been severed twenty years before, when Charlotte Smith (Margaret Manigault's sister) died. But Smith's inclusion in the Izard family transcended his marriage to Charlotte. He was still a brother-in-law, an uncle, a friend. Since Smith remained emotionally connected to the Izards and Manigaults, his death represented a great blow. While some lamented their losses, others found themselves welcoming death as a respite from pain and suffering. One woman attended her brother-in-law on his deathbed, hoping to forestall the inevitable. In the end, however, she admitted that "when I saw his Sufferings, and thought it [death] wou'd be a happy release for him I cou'd with a degree of composure resign him."[96]

For most elite Carolinians, only death could sever the ties to siblings and close kindred. And since siblings and kin played so many roles and held such emotional sway in each other's lives, death could devastate those left behind. Individuals spent a lifetime cultivating sibling and kin ties. Literally from the moment a child entered the world she was surrounded by these relatives. As she grew, her family grew with her, and her dependence on them increased. Sibling and kin provided a fundamental part of self-identity and an important source of emotional and practical support. When a brother or sister died, their siblings lost that source of support and identity. They also lost a friend, a life partner, and an irreplaceable link to family. As one lowcountry woman explained simply: "It is hard to be severed from a first, & dear connection."[97]

While death brought most kindred together, it tore some apart. Margaret Glen Drayton's death helped destroy the bond between her brother, James Glen, and her husband, John Drayton. Distraught over his sister's death, James Glen blamed John Drayton for failing to "make necessary provision" for Margaret when she first fell ill. Glen never got over the loss of his sister, and he never forgave Drayton for his role in her passing. A few years after Margaret's death, and after the brothers-in-law disagreed vehemently over the education of John's sons, they cut all ties with one another. Glen explained to his nephew that his father's "cruel and unjust treatment has put a final period to all future correspondence between him and me."[98]

Making the Rough Places Smooth

On occasion, because of the interweaving of the kin group and the private household, family feuds could erupt. The evidence undoubtedly belies the full extent of family conflicts. But the ways relatives handled even rare fights reveal a great deal about elite Carolinians' values. In most cases when conflict occurred, relatives recognized the greater importance of the kin network and interceded to reconcile quarreling family members. When James Penman, for example, argued with his brother Hugh, a family friend urged him to "not be too angry with him. Consider he is a Young Man & really seems to desire to ... please tho he may sometimes mistake the means." Because of the tremendous importance of family connections, when conflicts arose kin generally believed "the Relations of the Family should interest themselves in promoting a reconciliation."[99] If individuals deliberately visited trouble upon their relatives, the family viewed them with disdain and even scorn. After the adult daughters of William Wragg sued his second wife, Henrietta Wragg, in 1778, her niece Margaret Manigault complained to her husband about the women's abominable behavior.[100] Siblings and kin did all they could to foster harmony and prevent strife. Their connections were simply too important to allow two or three individuals to undermine them.

In their relationships with siblings and kin, lowcountry elites prized mutual cooperation and balanced reciprocity. They expected their relatives to work together and help one another no matter what. When one sibling failed to live up to his part of the bargain, the others expressed surprise and pain. Jonathan and Arthur Bryan openly worried when their connections with their brothers, Francis and Samuel, weakened. Jonathan found himself "very uneasy about the familys situation" and longed "to hear of the settlement of Sam'l." The relationship between Jonathan and Arthur and their brother Francis weighed even heavier on their minds: "Frank appears to have secluded himself from Society altogether & will not even write us & further than that not answer our letters." Jonathan and Arthur recognized the emotional benefits derived from close brotherly bonds, and their brothers' disinterest in developing and preserving such ties puzzled them. Thomas Reaston seemed equally perplexed over his brother-in-law Nathaniel Broughton's failure to write: "I am not conscious of haveing given any just cause for being deprived Corresponding with one I so much esteem so I am at a loss how to account or atone properly for it."[101]

South Carolinians intensely disapproved of individuals who did not fulfill their familial obligations. Joseph Manigault scornfully reported to his brother that one of Joseph's school friends suffered because of a brother's neglect: "His Brother seems to be insensible both to the Feelings arising from so near a Relationship, and to those of Humanity." The man's insensitivity toward his brother stymied Joseph. It simply did not make sense to Joseph that a brother could abdicate his family responsibilities because siblings in his world did not abandon one another.[102]

There were, needless to say, extreme cases of sibling rivalry and contempt. Ironically, one of the most bitter sibling relationships existed between Joseph Manigault's nephews. Unlike their father and uncle, who shared a deeply committed relationship, Charles and Harry Manigault despised one another. Harry wrote that his brother was "a Wild, incontrollable Youth, giving his family much trouble." Charles, insisted Harry, "had little, or *no Sincerity*, for on any important subject *You could not believe a word he said.*"[103]

The callousness of Manigault's remarks were surpassed only by their peculiarity. Whenever most Carolina elites talked about their kin they expressed devotion and affection. Catherine Read loved her niece "so much as to be interested in every thing she says and does." Joseph Manigault seldom ended a letter to his brother Gabriel without expressions of filial love and well-wishes to his relatives. Concerning his Aunt Wragg, Joseph wrote: "I should consider it as a great [pleasure] to love the good Opinions she entertains of me." Edward Rutledge told his nephew Charles Rutledge: "There is scarcely a Misfortune to which Humanity is subject that, I would not endeavour to lighten, by dividing it with you; or a pleasure which you could enjoy that, I would not endeavour to multiply."[104] Their words were not mere hyperbole. While the sentiment reflected genteel patterns of language usage, it also demonstrated the sincere desire of elite Carolinians to truly matter in the lives of their kindred.

THROUGHOUT THE LIFE COURSE, lowcountry elites made siblings and kin a vital part of their emotional worlds: in childbirth, education, marriage, and the internal lives of individuals. These intragenerational ties were not, however, their only family experiences. Eighteenth-century Charlestonians also inhabited patriarchal, conjugal families, and a great deal of interplay occurred between the two. Siblings and kin often transgressed the bounds of the conjugal home and overrode the desires of patriarchal heads of households.

They physically entered the patriarchal household to deliver children, educate young people, and conduct visits. Their emotional presence was even greater: as young people made important life decisions and fashioned their emotional lives, they turned to their kin. There were conflicts, to be sure. Not everyone subscribed to this vision of siblings and kin. Some relations were ambiguous, others estranged. To further complicate matters, Carolinians adopted a style of letter writing that downplayed conflict and magnified harmony. Despite the ambiguity and the rhetoric, a pattern of affective interdependence is clearly discernible in the words and deeds of lowcountry kin groups.

The values that these intragenerational relatives embraced ran counter to those of the patriarchal family.[105] Hierarchy and deference governed relationships within the patriarchal household; conversely, sibling bonds fostered equality and cooperation. In lowcountry Carolina, the mutuality and cooperation of the sibling set balanced the authoritarianism and hierarchy of the patriarchal family.

Finally, in addition to exerting a powerful emotional influence in individual's lives and providing a counter to the authoritarian, patriarchal household, the kin group also served as the model for elite culture. It fostered, throughout Charleston's elite ranks, a strong collective identity and a deep commitment to interdependence that shaped both their affective ties and their public behavior. Interestingly enough, this mutuality among siblings and throughout elite society was not limited to men. In fact, the egalitarianism of sibling and kin relations, along with the constant interplay between the intragenerational and patriarchal families, held powerful, surprising implications for the definition of gender in lowcountry Carolina.

CHAPTER THREE

Sibling Ties and Gender Values

Throughout the 1780s, Eliza Wilkinson carried on a lively correspondence with her close friend "Miss Mary P." Eliza wrote Mary about the British occupation of Charleston and the behavior of the troops, mutual friends and family members, the comings and goings of her active social schedule, and the problems facing young unmarried women in the lowcountry. In particular, Eliza and Mary puzzled over "why the two Sexes shou'd act as if they were in continual open war with each other; and to commence a friendship with, or behave socially to a Gent. should put us under the dread & fear of some sad Catastrophe." Eliza concluded that "such notions are a bane to Society, they keep us under a constant reserve & constraint, and we fear to open our mouths, lest the enemy should find some advantage over us." While she encountered possible marriage partners with "reserve & constraint," Eliza interacted with her brother on dramatically different terms. In the midst of complaining about courtship woes, she happily reported that she had received a letter from her brother, who promised to visit her soon. Although relations with potential mates left her "under the dread & fear," Eliza rejoiced at the prospect of seeing her beloved brother. Their relationship bore none of the apprehension and stiffness that undermined amiability in courtship. Indeed Eliza insisted, "I really long to see him; he's among those I highly value."[1]

Eliza Wilkinson's letters reflected three pervasive trends in the family lives of eighteenth-century women. As numerous early American historians have argued, men and women in the eighteenth century seemed to inhabit distinctly different and frequently segregated worlds.[2] In theory men occupied the public world of politics and economics, while women held responsibility for the private world of family and household—although even this was controlled by the family patriarch.[3] Parents raised children to accept and perpetuate this highly gendered worldview. The divergent socialization of boys and girls frequently yielded courtship and marital relationships bereft of openness and ease.[4] Eliza's fears about courtship demonstrated this distance, which pervaded much male-female romantic interaction in the eighteenth century and presaged women's concerns about living in households under the unchecked governance of family patriarchs. Eliza's choice of a correspondent and the candor with which she wrote are similarly revealing. Enduring what one historian called "lives distorted by patriarchal power," young women like Eliza and Mary immersed themselves in a female world. Women spent their emotional energy and time visiting, corresponding, and building intimate connections with other women. Thus they simultaneously created a unique female culture that centered on kinship and friendship and embraced cooperation and affection.[5] Eliza Wilkinson typified both the "constant reserve and constraint" women experienced in courtship and marriage and the emotional importance women placed on female kin and friends.

Her letters also demonstrate a third, powerful component of early American family life: the ease and mutuality of sibling relations. While Eliza confided in her friend about her courtship worries, she also expressed longing and genuine affection for her brother. Sister-brother relationships, like that shared by the Wilkinson siblings, provide a new way of understanding the nature of male-female interaction and the status of women within families. They also force us to reevaluate what we think we know about the separate worlds of men and women, the sharp divide between public and private life, and the meaning of women's culture in the eighteenth century.

Eighteenth-century women and men inhabited a variety of families during the course of their lives. Within those varied families, individuals fulfilled a number of roles and responsibilities. Looking at women only within the patriarchal household (that is, in marital and parent-child relations controlled by fathers) obscures the reality of women's lives by overestimating their subordination within families and exaggerating gender lines.[6] Broadening the definition of family and taking a closer look at gender relations between siblings and intragenerational kin reveals another, contradictory, dimension to women's familial experiences. In short, interaction between the sexes encompassed far more than male prerogative and female subjugation, although that was clearly a part of certain relationships.

Although women typically deferred, in both word and deed, to their fathers and husbands, these unequal relationships by no means reflected the totality of women's experiences. Societal norms required the subordination of women to their fathers and husbands, but such values did not govern relationships between sisters and brothers. Not confined by the laws and customs governing parental and marital bonds, siblings and other kin constructed relationships that rarely conformed to rigid gender norms. Among siblings, age and stage of life mattered as much as gender in determining the locus of power within relationships.[7] Women's letters to and from brothers and male kin reflected an ease and equality that differed dramatically from correspondence with husbands and fathers. Younger brothers sought and followed the advice of their elder, more established sisters in a wide array of matters. Men treated their sisters with greater equality than they ever thought of treating their wives and daughters. For their part, women often acted as the equals of their brothers and male kin, challenging and castigating them in a manner unthinkable of a wife to her husband.

Just as their relationships with brothers allowed women to transcend their inferior status within the patriarchal family, so too did the connections women maintained with their female kin. Women built important, equitable relationships with one another that provided a source of joy and belonging and offset the subordination that accompanied married life. The most important and longest-lasting female connections existed between sisters, who enjoyed remarkably close relationships that were often the most reliable and honest of all family connections. Further, sororal bonds altered both the shape and tone of conjugal families. The connections between sisters along with other female kin bound together families and blurred the lines of patriarchal households. Like their connections to their brothers, these ties also provided women an emotional refuge from the subordination and distance they faced in their marriages.

The bonds between women and their sisters and brothers offer a more complete understanding of the diverse roles of women within families and an alternate way of conceiving of gender not only in the lowcountry, but throughout eighteenth-century society. Elite Carolinians paid careful attention to marital and parent-child relationships and set rigid, highly gendered guidelines for appropriate behavior within the patriarchal family. Brothers and sisters, however, escaped this and remained free to construct relationships as they saw fit. Among the lowcountry gentry, the primary requirements for sibling interaction were reciprocity and equity. Siblings were supposed to be dependable and loyal and treat one another as equals, often regardless of gender. Thus, women demonstrated a greater degree of authority and independence with their siblings and kin than was conceivable in marriage. These egalitarian relationships within the kin network, particularly between siblings, stood in sharp contrast to the subjugation women experienced within the patriarchal household.

Gender Relations in the Patriarchal Household

Most family historians, adhering to a patriarchal paradigm, have found that eighteenth-century wives and daughters occupied subordinate positions within their families.[8] Part of this argument is accurate. In white families throughout the colonies, relations between fathers and daughters and husbands and wives remained starkly unequal and frequently exploitive. Social custom, religious institutions, political ideology, and legal systems all reinforced the superiority of fathers over daughters and husbands over wives. Ideally, elite wives and daughters were quiet, ornamental, and deferential.

Girls learned from the earliest stages of life that the head of the household must be obeyed. The lessons of patriarchy were hammered home in stories and by law codes. Most important, mothers taught their daughters, through example, the appropriate way to treat the head of the household. As daughters grew into women, they retained the lessons of childhood, approaching fathers in a deferential manner. Even Eliza Lucas, South Carolina's famous indigo planter, knew she must follow this rule, though she ignored many others. A manager of three lowcountry plantations at age sixteen, a woman who at one point insisted that "a single life is my only Choice," and an avid reader of Locke and Virgil, Eliza broke all the rules for eighteenth-century women, save one: despite her achievements and her strong will, she always deferred to her father. Eliza regularly made assurances to her father such as, "I shall always endeavour to deserve your favour by the strictest filial duty and obedience."[9] In spite of Carolina's temperamental climate and tumultuous economy, Eliza became a very successful planter, and she recorded her achievements in frequent, meticulous letters to George Lucas. But the tone of those letters remained solicitous even as she grew older and more experienced. Eliza always kept in mind the deference she owed her father and prayed that she would never disappoint him.[10]

Their continued commitment to hierarchy and deference within patriarchal family relationships put Carolinians somewhat outside the mainstream of parenting practices in the late eighteenth century. Elite households in other areas of the south grew increasingly child-centered in the decades following the American Revolution.[11] Parents became more openly affectionate toward their offspring and encouraged children's autonomy. In the Carolina lowcountry, however, the incredible affluence of the planter-merchant class and their nearly single-minded drive to expand their wealth and power curbed some of the affectionate tendencies of parents and limited parental enthusiasm for autonomy of children. Advancing relatives remained the top priority of most lowcountry elites who embraced the new ideals of family life as long as they did not conflict with the financial aims of the larger family network.

That is not to say that affection and parental devotion were absent from the households of lowcountry South Carolina. Some fathers openly doted on their children. William Read thought his young daughter Elizabeth "very handsome, quite a lively prattler, and in fact is the delight of my Eyes." When Elizabeth's sister Sarah was born, William bragged to his brother that the infant "takes notice of objects around her, coos, & laughs with us" and never has "given us a moments uneasiness since her birth." The way that William Read and his brother Jacob wrote about their children is quite telling about the values and involvement of fathers, at least within the Read family. The brothers cherished their children—and they were hardly alone in their affection and devotion.[12] Edward Rutledge referred to his daughter Sarah as "my dear little Angel." Whenever Gabriel Manigault traveled away from home, he urged his wife to take particular care of the children and give them hugs from him. After their father died, Eliza Pinckney informed her sons, Charles Cotesworth and Thomas, that "his affection for you was as great as ever was upon Earth! . . . He blessed and thanked God for you." And Henry Laurens so enjoyed the presence of his three small children that he maintained "their noise which would disturb anyone else serves to lighten my labors."[13]

Other fathers, like Ralph Izard, appeared more detached from their offspring and concerned themselves primarily with their children's health and improvement. Izard rarely expressed emotion regarding his children. Instead he focused on arranging a proper education for his sons and advantageous marriages for his daughters. Ralph, whose active political life separated him from his wife and children for long stretches of time, instructed his wife to exercise strict vigilance over the children and insist upon their constant self-improvement.[14] While he occasionally wrote letters that voiced concern about the children's illnesses, he exhibited virtually no affective reaction to them. Izard's concerns for his sons were of a political nature: "There are two objects very near my Heart, which if I live to see accomplished, will be an ample compensation for every thing that I have suffered. I wish to see a good solid federal Government established, & my Sons so educated as to afford me a prospect of their being Men of abilities, & honour, & their becoming useful, valuable Citizens of their Country."[15] As for his teenage daughters, he concerned himself almost exclusively with grooming them for successful marriages. For example, Izard encouraged his eldest daughter, Margaret, to learn to play the harpsichord, an appropriate hobby for a prospective wife. He also warned her mother to make certain Margaret did not fall in love with a European. Margaret's job was to become a desirable commodity on the Charleston marriage market. Her father therefore made her pursue interests he felt would make her more attractive and avoid relationships he deemed unacceptable.[16]

Children garnered even less attention from some fathers. Samuel Wragg voiced more concern over his plantations than the birth of his child. In the fall of 1756 he sent Peter Manigault a lengthy letter about their shared holdings, but could not find time to write his mother about the recent birth of his daughter. Instead, Wragg asked Manigault to convey the news for him.[17]

Henry Laurens perhaps represents the middle ground between the emotional effusions of William Read and the detached indifference of Samuel Wragg. Regarding his children, Henry wrote: "One of the highest delights I have in life is that which accompanies a constant attendance to the manners & morals of these little People & I am never happier than when they are round me in health & good humor."[18] Still, as much as he loved them, Laurens confessed that "I am not so much attached to them or to home as not to interfere at all in the concerns of my Country." Henry Laurens thought that, more than unconditional love, he should give his children the tools to improve themselves and the desire to serve their family and society. Laurens therefore believed his most important parental responsibility was "to attend them, to inspect their Education, to cultivate their Manners, and to train them in the manner they should go."[19]

Most lowcountry fathers, irrespective of their level of emotionalism, shared Laurens's deep commitment to improving their children through education and social guidance and encouraging proper friendships and marriages. Women could give voice to the same attitudes about children. One grandmother wrote her twelve-year-old grandson that her heart "overflows with tenderness and a longing . . . to take you in my Arms and tell you how truely, how fondly I love you." But, she went on, "these emotions . . . must have bounds": her feeling would not override her demands for his service to family and country.[20]

This commitment to personal and, more important, familial aggrandizement often made parents, particularly fathers, temper their affection toward their children. Furthermore, men sometimes criticized their wives for failing to similarly distance themselves from their children. Fathers complained that mothers spoiled children (particularly sons) by being overly devoted or lenient. When young Thomas Drayton grew lazy and insolent, his father, John, blamed Thomas's behavior on the boy's mother, who, he charged, gave in to the boy's wishes too often. John Drayton, never one to avoid passing the buck, insisted: "I am certain his mother does him a good deal of Injury in spareing the rod."[21]

Regardless of distinctions in levels of affection, fathers in early South Carolina demanded certain behavior in exchange for their good favor. Children had to earn their father's love through paternal respect, self-improvement, and family devotion. Edward Rutledge's affection toward his daughter Sarah, for example, was superseded by his desire to see her behave properly and live up to his expectations. As Sarah traveled abroad in 1792, her father informed her that he expected her to "return to me, with good Sense, good Manner, and good Temper." He went on to demand that she focus her full attention on improving herself. *If* Sarah fulfilled her responsibilities to herself and her father, Edward promised, "I will receive you, my dearest Girl, with all the affections of the fondest Father."[22]

Children's responsibilities to the head of the patriarchal household were clearly defined and highly gendered. Gentry fathers expected sons to fulfill their familial duties by following their fathers into public life, becoming successful, virtuous citizens. Henry Laurens's highest hope for his son was that he might become a productive, useful member of society. Other lowcountry fathers agreed. William Read bragged that his young son seemed poised to advance the family name by serving his community. Edward Rutledge's son similarly enjoyed his father's esteem because he was a "Credit to himself and his Country."[23]

A daughter, on the other hand, brought advancement or shame to the family through her marriage. A father's highest expectation for a daughter was to marry well. Failure to do so could be the source of his greatest displeasure. A daughter who refused to fulfill this duty incurred not just her father's disappointment but sometimes complete rejection. Eleanor Austin provides a compelling example of this attitude. In January 1762, Eleanor married John Moultrie against the wishes of her father, George Austin. She naively believed her father would come to accept her marriage. When he did not, Eleanor fell into a deep depression. By the following May her uncle feared she would not survive the summer if George Austin refused to forgive her. John Laurens similarly rejected his daughter Mary when she married Nathaniel Gittens against his wishes, going so far as to expel her from his house. Only years later, after John Laurens's death, did the family make overtures of reconciliation.[24] The trouble in both these cases was not that Nathaniel Gittens and John Moultrie were especially objectionable men. Rather, both couples abrogated paternal power and failed to financially enrich the larger family network. Marriage in eighteenth-century South Carolina provided a critical opportunity to expand family connections. Mary and Eleanor not only squandered that opportunity for familial advancement, they also blatantly repudiated their fathers' influence over a monumental life decision. Both women paid a high price for their independent-mindedness. Each lost her conjugal family of origin.

The message for Mary and Eleanor and other women like them was clear: the head of the household could not be challenged and the obligation to the larger family unit could not be ignored. Throughout their youth, girls like Mary and Eleanor were instructed to defer to their fathers, bending to their will without question. Those who failed to follow the rules could no longer be considered part of the family: ostracization was the price women paid for their refusal to accede to patriarchal authority. Sons, while also expected to defer to fathers, were simultaneously training to become heads of their own households. Parents encouraged greater independence in sons and their transgressions against patriarchal authority seemed easier to accept. If sons erred too much, they lost access to extended family connections, which, in Charleston, represented financial and political devastation. While fathers demanded submission from both sons and daughters, sons had a longer tether—a privilege within the patriarchal family that could never be extended to daughters.

The lessons about parental, especially paternal, devotion and duty numbered among the experiences boys and girls shared as they grew up. As many scholars have argued, boys and girls underwent widely divergent patterns of socialization. Their different experiences frequently complicated courtship and marriage. Indeed, romantic relations between men and women were often awkward, even unpleasant. Platonic relations, however, particularly those between siblings, differed sharply from this pattern. As one visitor to South Carolina observed, "The maxims of the country have taught them [women] & custom has forced them to almost consider a sociability on their part with gentlemen as an unbecoming forwardness—& they are by this means circumscribed within such narrow bounds as exclude the frankness & care which are necessary to put people on the most agreeable footing."[25] Consequently, women often felt emotionally estranged from their suitors and husbands—what Eliza Wilkinson called "the dread & fear." As young people started to court, they stumbled over words and agonized over actions. Many found themselves utterly nonplussed by romantic matters.

Typical of the strained interaction between young men and women is a story recounted by young Joseph Manigault, one of Charleston's most eligible bachelors. Joseph visited with a group of women in the winter of 1786, and the afternoon was filled with a series of social blunders. In the midst of the chaos, one young woman told a story about a cow, but "unfortunately she mistook the Gender and told that *he* ... gave most excellent Milk." The afternoon went downhill from there; any composure the young women possessed quickly disappeared. The afternoon ended when two sisters present "had a great dispute [over] which had committed the greatest Blunder."[26] The story highlights a common problem: divergent socialization patterns often left young women and men grossly ill-prepared to relate to one another in a romantic manner.

Unfortunately, this problem did not diminish as young people reached adulthood. Indeed, the inequality and distance governing relationships between fathers and daughters, which were also quite prevalent during courtship, persisted after marriage. Husbands assumed control of their wives from their new fathers-in-law and exercised similar authority over them. Women rarely retained an independent legal status after marriage, and their property typically came under the dominion of their husbands. While the mid-eighteenth-century rise of romantic love and increased individual autonomy in marriage choices eased some of the abject power men exercised over their wives, marriages in early America never operated as egalitarian partnerships. Instead, most marriages continued to be inequitable alliances in which women deferred to husbands.[27] As one lowcountry woman explained, her greatest responsibility was "to make a good wife to my dear Husband ... to make all my actions Corrispond with that sincere love and duty I bear him ... and next to my God, to make it my Study to please him."[28]

Throughout British North America, marriages were unequal by design, and many men wanted a worker and/or benefactress rather than a partner.[29] In South Carolina, lowcountry elites clung longer and more tenaciously to older traditions because for them, marriage continued to be heavily influenced, if not governed, by the financial and political aims of relatives. Within lowcountry elite culture, marriage provided the most reliable means to secure and preserve family wealth and power. Not surprisingly then, South Carolinians cared less about personal fulfillment and mutual affection than about improving their own and their family's lot. Upon marrying, one man explained to a friend that he knew he would be pleased with his new wife since "I am sure I want one to look after my House and Negroes as much as any Body in the world."[30] More subtle Charlestonians expressed similar notions about married life. George Lucas welcomed his daughter's marriage to Charles Pinckney since he believed Charles would treat Eliza properly, and particularly because "of the Blessing Providence has bestowed on me in your Alliance."[31]

The prevalence of financially motivated, inequitable marriages did not necessarily negate the possibility of happiness. In fact, despite the inequity that accompanied married life, many found marriage a source of pleasure.[32] According to one prominent Charlestonian, "I enter'd into a Matrimonial partnership & in this state have alternately enjoyed the blessings & felt the Afflictive hand of divine providence. But . . . the former does greatly predominate & demands my incessant thanks."[33] In their letters, husbands and wives often expressed great devotion to one another. Oliver Hart wrote his wife that "the moment I had the Happiness of calling you my own, I thought my self one of the happiest of Men, and truly you have rendered me so." Anne Hart responded: "I strive to bear this long and painfull separation. . . . In imagination I see you, converse with you, I endeavor to call back some of the happy hours we have past, over again." When temporarily separated, couples like the Harts often wrote such passionate letters to one another. Margaret Izard Manigault assured her husband, Gabriel, that during their separations in the early years of their marriage, "I count the days now that you are absent." Her loneliness was palpable: "There are moments when melancholy reflections take possession of my mind . . . [and] I am anxious, uneasy, restless beyond description." She longed for his company because "your presence & conversation used never to fail in dispelling my dismal recollections." He responded in kind, assuring her "the only agreeable moments I have passed today, have been those employed in writing you." Not just young couples like the Manigaults shared such sentiments. Catherine Read admitted, "I am at present a forlorn widow my Spouse being absent on his fall Circuit. Tho' so old a married Woman I always feel pain at his departure & now the brightest ideas I entertain is to look forward at the pleasure of his return."[34] Many eighteenth-century Carolinians would no doubt agree with Charles Pinckney, who insisted that "the wedded life [is] the only happy life in this world."[35]

South Carolinians viewed mutual happiness and devotion as a positive, even desirable, consequence of marriage, but not the basis for marriage. Marriage was simply too important a tool in building wealth and power to be squandered on personal passion.

Regardless of the level of devotion between wives and husbands, women remained subservient to their husbands, and everyone knew it. Legally, socially, religiously, economically, and politically, women were subordinated to their fathers and later their husbands. Men oversaw the activities of their wives in much the same way as they did their daughters. Husbands controlled most family finances, second-guessed their wives' child rearing, and even tried to control their wives' movements. When, for example, James Glen invited his ailing sister to move to England in hope of improving her health, her husband, John Drayton, interceded. Drayton assumed the decision was his to make. And while he found the offer generous, he remained unwilling to accept it.[36]

Most husbands excluded their wives from decisions about economic and political matters. Even those men who did choose to discuss such issues with their wives adopted a commanding tone in their correspondence, leaving little room for doubt as to who wielded authority. Ralph Izard frequently wrote his wife, Alice, about the political turmoil of the Revolutionary era and sought her advice about handling their planting affairs, but he always addressed her as a subordinate, not as an equal. Ralph also carefully supervised Alice's parenting. Although she remained the primary—and because of his active political life, frequently the only—parent to their children, Ralph scrutinized everything from her handling of courtship and education to the treatment of minor illnesses. Through their letters he also closely monitored her behavior and chastised Alice whenever she failed to maintain their frequent correspondence.[37] When the Revolutionary War held up the mails, he complained that Alice did not write often enough and failed to include duplicates of previous letters in each new mailing. Ralph's frustration with his wife's infrequent letters was not from emotional longing but from a loss of control over Alice that he could not abide. Although they were separated by his own volition, Izard refused to abdicate his authority over Alice.

Women in the eighteenth-century South, like their more frequently studied daughters in the nineteenth century, also endured the sexual power the patriarchs maintained over them. Laws and custom seldom limited the patriarch's sexual access to his wife and female slaves. By and large, white men found that, within their households and particularly in the slave quarters, their sexuality was confined only by their own desires. Both black and white women were compelled to accept this prerogative.[38]

The sexual, legal, and social control that husbands exercised over their wives, coupled with the divergent socialization of women and men, ensured that, in marital relations, women would remain subordinate to the family patriarch.

Eighteenth-century historians often tell this story of deferential wives and controlling husbands. One consequence was that women, while intimately connected to their fathers and husbands, nonetheless remained excluded from their world and subject to their desires. A further result, many historians argue, was that eighteenth-century men and women simply lived separate lives and created separate cultures. Men inhabited the public world of politics and finance and shared a competitive culture centered on the ever-increasing acquisition of money, land, and power. Even male leisure activities took on this competitive air: cockfights, horse races, and gambling were all public displays of male competition. Women, conversely, constructed a female culture of cooperation and mutuality and they inhabited the "private" sphere of home and kin.[39]

Within the patriarchal family some of this was true. Women often found themselves psychologically and physically removed from the day-to-day lives of their husbands. Daughters approached their fathers with veneration, even trepidation. Lowcountry culture directed wives and daughters to defer to husbands and fathers, and therefore essentially precluded mutuality within the patriarchal household. In their letters and in their demeanor, most women acquiesced to this subordination, and they accepted that gender circumscribed their lives within the household.

But the divisions between male and female seldom remained as sharp as patriarchal family ideals held they should. Men and women crossed and blurred these lines, and shared lives where male and female cultures blended. Moreover, the household did not represent the totality of women's experiences within their families and communities.

"My Brother Is a Friend Indeed"

Contrary to the subordination of wives to their husbands, brothers and sisters enjoyed gregarious, equitable relationships. Indeed, affection and mutuality mattered far more than power. Sisters and brothers cooperated in a multitude of family matters, wrote and visited regularly, and depended on one another. Many echoed the feelings of Anne Hart, who insisted that "my brother is a friend indeed." When Eliza Wilkinson talked about her brother, she expressed "sisterly wishes for his wellfare and happiness." Eliza Lucas spoke often of her "much loved brother." Brothers expressed similar sentiments, writing often to "beloved" or "dear" sisters, insisting they were "a Brother who tenderly loves you."[40]

In archival collections of family papers, the difference between siblings' letters and those of husbands and wives or of fathers and daughters is immediately obvious. Correspondents actually tell a great deal about their relationships in the first line of their letters. Women and men addressed their fathers as "Honoured Sir" or "honoured Father." But when writing siblings, they called each other "Beloved Brother," "Dear Sister," or "Affectionate Friend." Individuals closed their letters in equally telling ways, giving "duty" and "honour" and "esteem" to parents, while offering "love" and "devotion" to siblings. Thomas Dale expressly instructed his friend to "give my duty to [my father] & love to sisters, and service to all friends." Other relations between kin of disparate ages followed this pattern. As a young man, Henry Laurens signed his letters to his stepmother, "Your oblig'd and Dutifull Son." Illustrating the status of women within patriarchal families, fathers rarely referred to their married daughters by their first names. For example, when Oliver Hart discussed his family, he wrote about his daughter and future grandchild as extensions of his son-in-law: "My Son-in-law, Mr. Severen is but poorly . . . his Family well, and his Wife in a hopeful way of bringing him another child."[41] Other fathers stopped writing to their daughters altogether and corresponded instead with their sons-in-law.[42] Siblings, however, remained "dear Brother" or "beloved Sister," regardless of marital status and corresponded directly with one another throughout the life course.

The differences in sibling and paternal relations, while obvious at first glance in family correspondence, ran far deeper than greetings in letters. Relationships with brothers and sisters numbered among the longest-lasting and most important familial ties. Throughout their lives sisters and brothers depended on one another for practical and financial aid, personal and professional advice, and psychological comfort. Sisters and other female friends acted not only as surrogate mothers for younger brothers and the children of their brothers, but also served as agents, mentors, and partners in family matters. Brothers reciprocally advised and comforted their sisters. Across gender lines, siblings built relationships based on mutual respect and abiding affection, which served to controvert the inequality of romantic relationships. Brothers and sisters felt comfortable with one another, confided in each other, and cooperated in family decisions.

In these ways, interestingly enough, sibling relations and kin ties seemed to mirror the values and behaviors traditionally associated with the cooperative "female world" of the eighteenth century. This, in turn, complicates the image of female powerlessness within families and women's consequent identification with a strictly female culture. In fact, the evidence from South Carolina indicates that the values often attributed to women's culture actually crossed gender lines within the sibling and kin group. Brothers shared deep emotional bonds with their sisters and acted in a cooperative manner toward them. Moreover, sibling ties challenge perceptions about the gendered nature of competition and cooperation. In Carolina, competitiveness occurred between family insiders and outsiders rather than informing a predominantly male culture. And cooperation governed sibling connections across gender lines. Thus, the competition-cooperation dichotomy better describes relationships between members of the sibling/kin network and unrelated outsiders than male and female behaviors.

Careful attention to sustaining close sibling ties lay behind much of this cooperation. Because maintaining sibling connections represented such a crucial family responsibility, sisters and brothers engaged in extensive correspondence with one another. Women, however, played the greatest role in this supervision of family connections. They took charge of coordinating elaborate letter-writing networks and chastising those who ignored their sibling duties. The cousins Mary Pinckney and Margaret Izard Manigault, for example, presided over a complex, multigenerational letter-writing group that included their sisters and brothers, their in-laws, and a host of other kindred. Even before their daughters were old enough to write, Mary and Margaret sent messages back and forth between the girls. By including childhood conversations in their adult letters, the women introduced the girls to their elder relatives and taught the youngest members of the kin group the importance of correspondence. It required a vast amount of time and energy to coordinate this kind of writing network. Mary and Margaret gathered information from their expansive kin group and then passed news on to other correspondents. Their letters typically recounted stories about health, travel, and family finances, and sometimes included admonishments to "have patience" when the letters were slow to arrive.[43]

Women took their duty of protecting kin correspondence very seriously. After she married, Eliza Lucas Pinckney vowed to be not only a good wife but also a good sister to her and her husband's siblings. She even took her husband's first wife's kin as her correspondents. Eliza accepted that she might fall short of the first Mrs. Pinckney on many fronts, but swore "I shall equal her in preserving a due regard to her relations and a readiness to do every thing in my power to serve them."[44] Like many other women in the lowcountry, Eliza eventually stood at the center of an extensive kin network. And by shaping the information that flowed between these relatives, she was able to exercise significant power over her circle of kin.

Women overtly expressed that power when relatives neglected their letter-writing obligations. Although thrilled to receive a visit from her brother, Eliza

Wilkinson also took him to task because, during their separation, he failed to write her often enough. Elizabeth Hasell similarly complained that her cousin Joseph Manigault "is very Delinquent in setting down every thing the least Intertaining in order to send a Pleasing Letter."[45] When John Lloyd apologized to her sister for letting their correspondence lapse, he urged her to "not attribute my silence to any want of affection for you." Women not only castigated siblings who failed to write directly to them: they interceded in controversies between other relatives as well. When, for instance, Richard Moore failed to correspond regularly with his brother Stephen, their sister Rebecca Moore intervened and wrote to Richard "to chide him for not answering your letters wrote long ago."[46]

In contrast, women did not chide their husbands. When they wrote letters to their brothers, however, women could disregard most deferential language. They teased, advised, and chastised younger brothers, addressing them alternately with devotion, condescension, affection, and concern. Brothers accepted this attitude and acceded to their sister's authority in family matters.

The mutuality of sibling connections did not stop there. Women not only advised brothers about the maintenance of family connections, but commented freely on more "public" aspects of lowcountry life as well. Even military service, the most masculine part of eighteenth-century life, was not off limits. When her brother Ralph Izard, Jr., entered the navy, Anne Izard Deas told him she expected "to hear you spoken of as an exemplary character, & that courage will be ranked as only one among many excellent qualities." She expressed her devotion to her brother and hoped he would find happiness and honor in the navy. Anne further counseled her brother: "A knowledge of every branch of your profession, & of every thing that can tend to the health, & happiness of Seamen must be your study, & I trust you will attain it." Similarly, when Eliza Lucas's brother joined the army in 1741, she urged him to avoid self-serving actions and "make proper distinctions between Courage and rashness, Justice and revenge." Eliza also admonished him "to be particularly careful of his duty to his Creator, for nothing but an early piety and steady Virtue can make him happy."[47]

If expectations went unmet, sisters leveled criticism. Sisters openly expressed disapproval of their brothers in ways they never would display toward fathers or husbands. Margaret Izard Manigault's brother-in-law Joseph Manigault frequently served as a messenger when financial and political obligations separated Margaret and her husband, Gabriel. When Joseph failed to comply with her instructions and delayed a trip to see Gabriel, Margaret complained that "his loitering vexes me," and insisted she "was very good this morning not to abuse him." After Thomas Pinckney erred in one of his errands, he quickly apologized to his sister, Harriott Pinckney Horry, hoping to avoid a stern lecture. Harriott sarcastically wrote a friend abroad about her other brother's failure to maintain contact: "If you should see a youth call'd Chas. Pinckney, let him know that he has a mother and Sister in this part of the World to whome he is very dear, that would be glad to hear from him often." Margaret Izard Manigault similarly complained about her wayward brother, whom she referred to as "that good-for-nothing boy George."[48]

The language that Margaret, Harriott, and other women used regarding their brothers showcased their power and their interest in sibling relationships. It may also indicate their brothers' growing detachment from the sibling set. Women felt confident they could lecture and reproach their brothers when they failed to meet familial expectations. But fraternal disregard for these familial obligations forced women to exercise this authority. Thus, the letters between kin-guardian sisters and wayward brothers must be read as both a manifestation of female influence over their relatives and as symbols of male inattention to their sibling duties.

Still, the judgmental, confrontational language employed by women writing their brothers could never be used in letters to husbands and fathers. While Alice Izard could criticize her former son-in-law, William Loughton Smith, for frequent, protracted absences from his children, she dared not question her husband when he behaved the same way. Although Alice and Ralph spent year after year of their marriage apart because of his political activities, she couched all her frustrations in deferential language. Infrequently she might confess she missed him or felt anxious about her children. While she remained silent about any contempt she felt about her husband's extended absences from their home, she proved far less reticent about criticizing William Smith. Alice wrote Ralph that she believed Smith should return home after his term in Congress expired. Six years, she insisted, seemed far too long for a man to be away from his family and community.[49] For Ralph, who spent much of his married life pursuing a political career that took him away from his family, the implication must have been clear. But social mores prevented Alice from directly confronting her husband. On the other hand, Alice openly reproached Smith for choosing politics over family. Voicing disapprobation toward William also allowed Alice indirectly to vent some of her frustrations about her husband's protracted absences.

Women did not simply speak differently to their brothers than their fathers and husbands; they behaved differently toward them as well. Within the patriarchal family, men exhibited a protective, authoritarian demeanor toward female family members and assumed control over their financial lives. For example, when seventeen-year-old Elizabeth Ball married Henry Smith in 1764 just two months after the death of her wealthy father, Elizabeth's uncle Henry Laurens stepped in as her surrogate father to protect her interests. Henry Laurens quickly entered into a lengthy conflict with Elizabeth's new husband about the settlement of John Ball's estate. Smith insisted Laurens owed his wife more land. Laurens, assuming Smith married his niece to advance his wealth, adamantly opposed Smith's plan for the distribution of the land. As a young wife and heiress, Elizabeth doubtless felt caught between the demands of her new husband and the desires of her prominent uncle. We do not know her opinion about this, however, because while the two Henrys squabbled over her inheritance, neither discussed the matter with Elizabeth. The equal of neither her uncle nor her husband, Elizabeth found herself excluded from the affair.[50]

Siblings and intragenerational kin, however, did not operate this way, and women dealing with brothers and certain other male relatives escaped this sort of treatment. When, for instance, Anne Edgar thought her brother-in-law Jacob Read tried to cheat her out of part of her inheritance, she quickly confronted him. Jacob's sister-in-law's accusations left him chastened. Read profusely apologized to Edgar for his behavior and promised that she would never lose any money owing to his actions.[51]

The conduct of Elizabeth Ball and Anne Edgar was not merely a manifestation of differing personalities. Rather, their actions reflected general patterns of behavior in lowcountry society. Women in Elizabeth Ball's situation rarely overtly challenged the authority of their fathers (biological or surrogate) and husbands. On the other hand, women like Anne Edgar felt confident asserting their power within the sibling and kin group. The behavior of the men in these families is equally telling. Just as Anne Edgar wrote things to her brother-in-law that she never would have written her father, Jacob Read responded to her in a manner radically different than the manner in which he would have reacted to his wife. In fact, Jacob Read's wife was actually the direct heir to the contested estate, but Jacob controlled her share. While he negotiated with and capitulated to his widowed sister-in-law, Read's wife and her interests remained solidly under his authority.

Such different patterns of interaction often occurred within individual families. When, in 1733, Mary Laurens married Nathaniel Gittens against her father's wishes, he forbade his daughter ever to return to his house. John Laurens's wife and children acceded to his demands, and throughout his life Mary remained estranged from her parents and siblings. No one within the conjugal family dared challenge John's authority over his daughter. For fourteen years they did nothing. But after John Laurens died in 1747, Mary's brother Henry Laurens attempted a family reconciliation. While Mary's father could never forgive her disobedience, her brother encouraged her to return to Charleston and offered to help her financially. In fact, he promised to supply anything she needed. Henry also suggested his sister accept her responsibility in the family split. After begging Mary to "pardon my severity," Henry expressed his belief that she appeared partly to blame for the family trouble. In Henry's opinion, Mary's fault lay in her failure to "act the part of a dutiful Child." Since she owned her brother no such obligation, he could forgive her behavior. Her father needed to bend her will, but Henry simply wanted to alleviate Mary's financial crisis. Then he hoped to bring together the remaining members of his family. "Our Family," he wrote, "is now reduced to three Vitz. Sister Bremar, Brother Jemmy, & my self. If you can come over here & add to the Number, you may be assur'd . . . of a sincere welcome & all the assistance in our power."[52]

Henry's expectations of his sister, and therefore his attitude toward her marriage, differed sharply from his father's. Deference governed father-daughter relationships. Siblings, conversely, based their relationships on mutuality, affection, and cooperation. Whereas John Laurens found it impossible to forgive a daughter's abrogation of his authority, Henry Laurens could not help reaching out to a sister in need. This story illustrates both the divergent patterns of interaction between siblings and parents and children, as well as the limits of those differences. Although Henry Laurens felt differently about his sister's behavior than did their father, he could not express his attitudes until after his father had died. Indeed, he and his other siblings kept silent for many years. So while sibling interaction provided a different experience within the family, it did not always override the power of patriarchy within lowcountry society. It does, however, clearly demonstrate that patriarchal authority was not the only force influencing family interaction.

Brothers and sisters and other intragenerational kin rarely expressed the authoritarianism and subservience that characterized other male-female familial relations. Instead, they interacted with one another in more open, equal ways. When his brother George died, David Hunter quickly wrote his sisters to inform them of George's death and discuss the disbursement of his estate. Hunter treated Elizabeth Dunlap and Margaret McDermitt as equals in the matter and assured them he would gladly help his sisters in any way they saw fit. Together Elizabeth, David, and Mary made their brother's burial arrangements and coordinated the settlement of his estate.[53] Siblings Thomas Pinckney, Charles

Cotesworth Pinckney, and Harriott Pinckney bound themselves together and ignored the gendered norms of the patriarchal family throughout their lives. At the close of the eighteenth century, Harriott oversaw Charles's holdings in Carolina and retained power of attorney over his estate. She paid his and Thomas's bills while they traveled abroad. Well into the nineteenth century, Thomas and Harriott cooperated on planting ventures, eventually expanding into cotton production. And all three siblings corresponded regularly with one another throughout their lives.[54]

Of course all sibling relationships did not operate so smoothly, and conflicts did occasionally erupt. If brothers failed to treat sisters in a suitable manner, the women called them on the carpet. After Elizabeth Massingberd's brother Burrell refused to release her inheritance because he did not trust her husband, Edward Hyrne, Elizabeth wrote a fiery letter in which she lambasted Burrell for telling her friends she "*married a broken Merchant* and one that was a fool not fitt to be trustd with money." Elizabeth angrily insisted that her brother release her part of the family holdings, but Burrell held out until he was convinced that the money would be used solely for his sister and her children. Ironically, his capitulation to his sister's demands came too late: by that time Edward Hyrne had been thrown into debtor's prison.[55] The exchange between Elizabeth and Burrell was both typical and unique—typical in that Elizabeth felt comfortable confronting her brother, unique in the discordant tone of the confrontation. While disagreements sometimes occurred, few brothers and sisters resorted to such hostile language in their correspondence.

Far from contentious, most siblings filled their exchanges with expressions of devotion and love. The letters between Thomas Pinckney and his sister Harriott Pinckney Horry typified the correspondence between Charleston's elite siblings. In his frequent letters to his sister, Thomas poured out his most intimate feelings and explained his daily routines. He wrote his sister, "I have nothing in the world to say. . . . As however I know you are fond of receiving Letters, even more than writing them, I have just sat down to make my Mark upon this Paper by way of giving you a momentary relief from the Ennui of a Sick Chamber." Harriott and Thomas obviously loved and respected one another a great deal. He closed one letter, "Adieu my Dear Girl, . . . believe me to be your loving Brother." When separated, adult siblings like the Pinckneys longed for one another. Henry Izard wrote his sister Margaret Izard Manigault: "I ought to tire you to death with an account of all the instances in which my thoughts have been with you, of the wishes that I have of enticing you into the Country

& of all the airy visions which . . . you make a principle figure." When Margaret failed to write as often as Henry, he implored her to pay more attention to their relationship: "Have you entirely forgotten that there exists a Brother who tenderly loves you & who secluded in the solitude of the Elms stands in need of a little notice from you?"[56]

Men like Henry Izard sought the attention and approval of their sisters in ways quite unheard of in the patriarchal family. Younger brothers and kinsmen often confided in and deferred to elder female relatives, and they relied on female kin as close confidantes and respected advisors. For example, first cousins Harriott Pinckney (the namesake and niece of Harriott Pinckney Horry) and Thomas Pinckney, Jr., shared a strong bond they expressed in frequent, devoted letters.[57] Thomas chronicled his courtship efforts, sought Harriott's advice in social matters, and shared information about family and friends. Thomas and Harriott even worked out the details of his clandestine engagement to Elizabeth Izard. Through it all, Thomas assured Harriott he would follow her advice religiously. Far from expecting subservience from Harriott, Thomas deferred to his elder cousin. Once when Harriott failed to write as often as Thomas wished, he upbraided her. Upon receiving a letter that had crossed his, he profusely apologized: "I am truly contrite for my impetuosity, and for supposing, even for one moment, that you would withhold from me. . . . Forgive me! I will sin no more."[58] Romantic sentiment clearly underlay some of this language, but the letters between these cousins did not evidence a love affair. While seeking his cousin's affections and advice, Thomas was not courting her as a potential mate. Instead, he was using his close relationship with Harriott to plan his courtship strategy and try out his romantic rhetoric. She acted as his partner in coordinating the affair.

Parents contributed to this pattern of interdependent partnerships between siblings and kin by holding up female kin as examples to male relatives. Anne Broughton numbered among the many mothers who urged their sons to follow the moral example of older sisters: "I have often desired you to look over your catechism . . . which it is now high time for you to think of renewing at the lord's table as your sister has done."[59] Instead of resenting this, brothers actively sought the approval of sisters, particularly when they planned to marry. One man promised his sister that his new fiancée was "the most amiable of women," and hoped she would therefore gain his sister's approval. Another man similarly assured his sister that his new wife would exceed her expectations: "Each following day proves her more worthy the esteem of the few like my dear Sister."[60]

Exceptions to Egalitarianism

Despite the general pattern of equitable relationships between brothers and sisters, there were limits to how far even the most egalitarian sibling ties could go. Although siblings and other intragenerational kin generally approached one another with equality and affection, age or stage of life could alter these relationships. Letters between siblings of widely disparate ages lacked the ease and mutuality of correspondence between brothers and sisters closer in age. Younger siblings, particularly girls, tended to be more respectful when they wrote their elder brothers. When Eliza Lucas, a prolific writer and unregenerate counselor, told her elder brother, Tommy, how to be a good soldier, she began with an apology "for a girl of my early time in life presuming to advise."[61] The respect shown an older, established sibling never equaled children's deference to parents, and it applied to older sisters as well as older brothers. Eliza Lucas may have apologized to her elder brother, but when she offered similar suggestions to her younger brother, she felt no need to justify her behavior. She simply explained, "I am a littler older than you and [advise] on that account."[62] This was not simply a gendered phenomenon. The same kind of age ranking also influenced relationships between female kindred such as aunts and nieces. Because of birthing patterns, a woman could have an aunt close to her own age, or she could be separated from an aunt by thirty years or more. Age discrepancy determined whether the aunt and niece saw one another more in the sibling or in the parental model, which, in turn, shaped the dynamic of their relationship.

If siblings underwent significantly different life experiences, similar patterns prevailed. A brother or sister who was educated, married, traveled extensively, or attained a significant measure of power within the community acquired the respect of less-established siblings. Elder sisters and brothers offered advice based on their greater experience, and younger siblings followed it. Consequently, their relationships sometimes took on a tone more akin to parent-child patterns than the sibling model. At the same time, siblings at different stages in their lives sometimes lacked the comfort and ease of sisters and brothers who had more in common. When younger sisters wrote to older, more established brothers, they tended to adopt a tone more similar to that used to address fathers: their letters bore a sense of detachment and deference. After failing to write her elder brother Gabriel, sixteen-year-old Anne Manigault worried he would "think me a very indolent Girl" and beseeched him to not be angry.

Gabriel, while only four years older than Anne, no doubt seemed a lifetime away from her in experiences. Studying abroad, Gabriel had little in common with Anne, who still lived on her grandparents' plantation and had only recently been allowed to see suitors. When she finally did write, Anne confessed she hardly knew what to say and worried that Gabriel would find her letters "very Nonsensical & short."[63] Try as she might, Anne simply did not know what to say to her brother. She knew little of his world, while hers, she suspected, seemed irrelevant to him. In cases like Anne and Gabriel, age and stage of life altered the emotional connections between siblings and moderated the equality of their relationships. Still, the differences between their worlds, not their gender, tempered their connections.

Just as age discrepancies sometimes altered the mutuality of sibling bonds, so too did the patriarchal values of lowcountry society. After all, the general equality of sibling bonds still existed within a patriarchal framework.[64] Although sibling bonds could and did influence relationships within the household, the reverse was also true. After George Austin flew into a rage about his daughter's unapproved marriage, his sister, Eleanor Laurens, interceded. Although Eleanor's appeals on behalf of her niece kept George from "fall[ing] into such violent outrages as the mention of that subject used to produce in him," and restored some semblance of peace to the family, he remained intractable on the subject. As much as he respected his sister, even she could not persuade him to set aside his outrage over Eleanor's defiance. Everyone in the family suffered because of the rift. Henry Laurens particularly lamented his brother-in-law's attitude because he found it a troublesome impediment to "that mutual intercourse & happiness that would otherwise subsist."[65] Henry, like other members of the family, proved unwilling to challenge Austin, however, and accepted his authority over the situation.

As they negotiated their relationships, brothers and sisters respected the patriarchal norms of the conjugal family. For example, during the War for Independence, as Elizabeth Hayne's health deteriorated during a pregnancy, her brother Richard Hutson and sister Mary Hutson Peronneau decided it would be better for her to stay with them off the coast of Charleston than at her home in the country. But they needed the permission of her husband, Isaac Hayne. Throughout the summer of 1776, Richard and Mary tried to coax Isaac into letting their sister join them. They promised him they would provide the best of care. Then they warned him that Elizabeth should not remain alone in the countryside while pregnant. Finally, they informed Isaac that they had hired armed guards to protect their estate—surely Elizabeth would be safer with them. Hayne rejected all these offers, and in September Hutson wrote the Haynes to congratulate them on the birth of the child. Obviously annoyed by Isaac's obstinacy throughout the ordeal, Hutson slyly added, "The United States are not likely to want Subjects I think at this rate."[66] Although the Hutson siblings resented their brother-in-law's behavior and longed to be with their sister, they did not directly challenge his control over her. As important as sibling relations were, they could not override patriarchal authority.

Except in rare cases, custom and law precluded sisters from entering law firms or counting houses, forbade overt female political activism, and circumscribed women's ownership of land and involvement in various legal transactions. Women did step into running businesses and plantations whenever male relatives left for extended periods of time. And the work of women—running households, overseeing kinship ties, offering counsel—allowed men the time to pursue political office and travel extensively.[67] Still, women's involvement in business and politics tended to be temporary and compensatory. Embracing women's ongoing, independent participation in these activities simply lay beyond the scope of possibilities in the eighteenth century.

But the absence of what to lowcountry elites would have seemed like impossibly radical social behavior does not mean that the divergent patterns of cross-gender interaction exemplified by sibling relations were insignificant. Within the context of eighteenth-century sensibilities, the relationships between brothers and sisters pushed the envelope of acceptable male-female behavior and blurred the lines between men's and women's worlds. While sibling ties did not subvert patriarchy, brother-sister interaction represented another part of family life in which both women and men could put aside patriarchal attitudes and construct mutually supportive, egalitarian relationships. In fact, women's relationships with their brothers looked a lot like their relationships with sisters—affectionate, based on cooperation and interdependence, and a source of inclusion and mutual aid.

Women's Other World: The Sororal Bond

Although women created partnerships with their brothers and kinsmen that blurred the lines between public and private, they simultaneously sought out a uniquely female world. Female kin shared the milestones of their lives with one another. They comforted each other during pregnancies, illnesses, and family deaths, and together they celebrated weddings, baptisms, births, and holidays. Sisters and other kin wrote to one another faithfully and visited regularly. They empathized with one another's struggles, mourned their separations, and deeply grieved their deaths.

Historians have traditionally interpreted this female culture as an outgrowth of women's exclusion from public institutions and oppression within patriarchal society. According to received wisdom, the disparate roles of men and women within the patriarchal family and the subordination of women to their husbands produced disjunctive and adversarial male-female relationships. As a result, women immersed themselves in a distinctly female world.[68]

Viewing women's lives in the context of the sibling and kin group challenges this interpretation of the roots of women's culture. As the South Carolina example indicates, the female world arose from far more diverse and complicated origins. In the first place, the adversity and distance attributed to male-female interaction held true primarily of romantic relations. And these relationships, as we have seen, differed dramatically from attachments between siblings. Far from adversarial or estranged, brothers and sisters tended to forge harmonious, affectionate connections. Further, women in early America had much more in common than exclusion from the patriarchal power nexus. The rhythms of their lives and their own desires drew them together. Finally, women's culture did not exist in relative isolation from the rest of society. Instead, it infused other relationships and cultural practices in the lowcountry.[69]

Sisters represented the most important connection in this female culture. Ironically, despite the wealth of recent historical scholarship on women and family, women's social networks, and female friendships, surprisingly little has been written about this most fundamental bond.[70] Social scientists, who pay more attention to sororal ties, insist that relationships between sisters are the closest of all sibling bonds and rival other family connections. Some of these sibling scholars argue that in the late twentieth century ties between sisters still "run much deeper than those between husbands and wives." And, like all sibling ties, they last longer than relationships between parents and children. Besides their emotional value and longevity, sororal bonds provide a powerful source of self-definition. Women learn more about who they are from their sisters than anyone else. And, as one psychologist explained, women's relationships with their sisters serve as a training ground for all other relationships.[71]

In the lives of eighteenth-century lowcountry women, sisters provided all this and more. For most women, sisters were the most enduring of all family members. Sisters and other female kin provided one another with practical aid, moral guidance, social advice, and emotional support throughout their lives.[72] While parents, husbands, children, and friends all held profound meaning for women, each represented only a part of a woman's life. Parents died, children grew up and left home, friends moved away, and husbands were often physically and emotionally absent. The bonds between sisters, on the other hand, lasted a lifetime. In eighteenth-century South Carolina, sororal bonds also fulfilled an important psychological function. In a culture that favored sons over daughters, enforced a strict hierarchy between parents and children, and required the subordination of wives to husbands, sisters provided one another a refuge of mutuality and respect much like the relationships between brothers and sisters.

Women spent a good deal of time and emotional energy maintaining meaningful relationships with their sisters. One sister wrote about another: "She is very much the subject of my thoughts." Another explained that her sister "gives me the greatest comfort I can receive."[73] Sisters also served as the model for other kin relationships between women. Margaret Izard and her cousin Elizabeth Stead developed a close friendship as children. Years after her death, Margaret's son Charles Izard Manigault remembered that his mother and Elizabeth were "*two Bosom Friends*" who remained "*more Devoted to Each Other, than ever till Death alone severed them.*"[74]

Throughout the life course women demonstrated a strong resolve to protect their bonds with sisters and other female kin and a fierce resistance to separation. When Eliza Lucas's father planned to send her younger sister abroad to study, Eliza begged her father to allow her to teach her sister at home instead. Living abroad without her favorite cousin, Sophia Penn insisted, "Willingly I would exchange a Dozen of Public entertainments, for one evenings conversation with you, dear Charlotte." Mary Pinckney traveled to Europe in the late 1790s and she longed for her favorite cousin, Margaret Izard Manigault. "If anything could lighten the weight that sits so heavy on my mind," Mary wrote, "it would be to have your company."[75]

Sisters shared a lifetime of experiences and often became best friends. Margaret and Charlotte Izard typified this trend. Born in February 1768 and 1770, respectively, Margaret and Charlotte were not only close in age, but were also the two eldest Izard children to survive infancy. Following the births of six brothers, another female child did not join the household until Elizabeth was born in 1777; she died at age seven. Margaret and Charlotte's next closest sister, Anne, was ten years younger than Charlotte. Since Ralph and Alice Izard often sent their sons abroad for travel and education, there were long stretches of time when Charlotte and Margaret were, in effect, the only children in the household. As the sisters grew up in Charleston, traveled to London and Paris, and immersed themselves in an active social life, they grew closer and closer. In May 1785 Margaret married Gabriel Manigault, one of Charleston's wealthiest and most desirable bachelors. One year later Charlotte followed her down the aisle, marrying the equally respectable if slightly less prosperous William Loughton Smith.[76] While Margaret lived a long and happy life with Gabriel Manigault, her sister was not so lucky. She died in 1792, probably from complications suffered during pregnancy. The day Charlotte died, her mother, Alice Izard, wrote Gabriel Manigault about Charlotte's passing and urged him to prepare Margaret for the shocking news. "The trial," Alice warned, "will be a severe one." Just as her mother feared, the untimely death of her sister and close friend devastated Margaret. Months later Margaret reported she had "lost one of my great enjoyments as you well know, in being deprived of my Sister."[77]

Indeed, many lowcountry women echoed Margaret's sentiments: the death of a sister numbered among life's greatest losses. As a woman neared death, her sisters left their own families behind to care for her. When Hannah Moultrie's sister died, her husband wrote Hannah at her late sister's house to express his sympathies and tried to comfort his wife. At least, he said, Hannah had moved to her sister's home to nurse her and the sisters had been together at the end.[78] Both men and women recognized the great loss the death of a sister presented to a woman. When Alice Izard recounted the deaths of the Brewton family at sea, she worried most about Mrs. Brewton's sister. It was, according to Izard, "a most dreadful accident, & one that makes even an indifferent Person shudder; how must it affect an only Sister?"[79]

Women who lost sisters and other kinswomen through estrangement felt similarly pained by the experience. Catherine Read deplored her alienation from her sisters-in-law. She knew neither the root of their coldness toward her nor a means of remedying the situation. Her repeated attempts at reconciliation all failed, and she was left "extremely mortified" by the whole situation.[80]

Detachment from sisters created such a profound sense of loss because women frequently found, in their sisters, a closer thing to a soulmate than they enjoyed in their husbands. Within a world of loss and exclusion, sisters offered consistency and acceptance. Sororal connections held tremendous emotional meaning for women and gave them a source of power within the larger family. Being detached from those ties through death or disagreement could be devastating. Moreover, as they guided younger kin, supported one another, and oversaw family life, women gained a greater sense of self-worth and demonstrated the importance of this female world.

SINCE SIBLING AND KIN CONNECTIONS exercised so great a presence in women's lives, they held important implications for the patriarchal household. Intragenerational female ties bound together conjugal families and blurred the lines between private households. While women learned from their female kin the lessons of patriarchalism, they also learned how to transcend it. For the most part, women set the rules for their relationships without the direct influence of fathers and husbands.[81] Although women did not conspire to destroy patriarchy, women's relationships with sisters and other female kin provided an alternative experience within families: a pattern of interaction based on collaboration, affection, and mutual respect.

This world of cooperation and mutuality was not, of course, unique to women. It also governed their interaction with brothers and select male kin. Brothers and sisters shared emotionally salient, generally egalitarian relationships and moved beyond the rigid gender constructs embraced within patriarchal households. Women counseled their brothers on a wide array of issues, and they sometimes took control over family holdings when male relatives were absent. Their involvement in male activities, as both advisors and participants, complicated the distinctions between male and female and offered women greater latitude in participating in more diverse family matters.

Throughout the eighteenth century, women's lives remained intricately connected to their families. They retained primary responsibility for caring for young children, maintained the household, and supervised family rituals. Women were not, however, simply powerless pawns in the patriarchal family. Rather, they acted as partners in both the construction of their own female world and in their relationships with their brothers. Since women assumed responsibility for attending to family obligations and overseeing their relatives' behavior, they amassed significant power. Because they served as the primary kin guardians for their families, for example, women not only supervised the correspondence between their kindred but also controlled the flow of information within these letter-writing networks.

These letters also represented an important part of women's involvement in the construction of class identity. Letter writing, along with dress, leisure activities, and houses, served as symbols of refinement in the eighteenth century.[82] Women, by holding dominion over these vestiges of gentility, acted as the arbiters of class identity. The activities of elite women—maintaining homes and gardens, leading leisured lifestyles, attending plays and balls, writing—reified and publicly demonstrated the class of the family. And women's attention to kin ties made them the protector of family identity, which, in the lowcountry, was intimately linked to class.

Women's attention to family relationships, their maintenance of the symbols of class, and their involvement in the activities of their male kin collectively moved women beyond the confines of the household and the limited range of "female" activities. These factors simultaneously allowed men the time to pursue political careers and to travel away from home for extensive periods without fear of imperiling family holdings. Women and men's partnership in these practical and symbolic matters thus played a critical role in the construction of family wealth and class identity.

The mutuality and interdependence shared between siblings transcended the emotional lives of the lowcountry gentry and the personal interaction of men and women and provided a model for this interrelated elite's cultural style. Lowcountry elites carried these attitudes into Charleston's counting houses and plantations, where, as we shall see, they used their intragenerational family values and connections to make themselves a wealthy ruling class.

CHAPTER FOUR

Making Money, Making Class

In the late seventeenth century, Affra Harleston Coming and her husband migrated to South Carolina hoping to build a new life together and to profit from the small tract of land they had purchased. Unfortunately, her husband succumbed to the harsh Carolina environment, and her family in England failed to come to her aid. Writing her sister, Affra explained her predicament: "Having no relations to comfort me, nor friends to assist me.... By all that I can perceive at present, I appear as a sheep in the midst of wolves."[1] Coming was right. Kinship networks dominated businesses, trades, and credit in the lowcountry. Prosperity thus remained firmly linked to inclusion in these interconnected webs of kin. The absence of kinship connections to established Charlestonians derailed Affra Coming's financial plans and left her impoverished and demoralized.[2]

In Carolina, as in much of early America, economic power traveled through family blood lines. This interweaving of family and finances shaped both the economy and the culture of the lowcountry.[3] Through careful integration of their economic and familial activities, a small group of interrelated planter-merchant families increasingly controlled the land, slaves, businesses, and contacts necessary for fiscal success. Their quest for economic supremacy also led them to adapt family life to fit their financial agendas. They made strategic marriage choices and carefully distributed personal estates. As elites grew more powerful and more interrelated, they also cooperated to exclude those outside their familial world. Guarding their relatives' financial interests came to mean undermining any potential rivals. Elites in other regions made similar attempts to amass wealth by blending the familial and the financial, but lowcountry elites achieved the greatest mastery of this practice. By the mid-eighteenth century, South Carolina society was highly stratified, and the paths to economic prosperity were increasingly blocked to anyone unrelated to established lowcountry gentry families. Within Charleston's concentric circles of kin, wealthy planters and merchants inhabited a culture of mutual aid and cooperation. They bought land and slaves together, formed business partnerships, socialized, and intermarried. Carolinians outside the circle who, like Affra Coming, lacked the requisite kinship connections, found themselves surrounded by—but excluded from—the greatest wealth in mainland America.[4]

Family Businesses

South Carolina's first white settlers laid the foundation for this interplay between economy and family even before they arrived in the colony. The influence of family abroad and the ability to expand familial connections within the province determined the financial success or failure of Charleston's early residents. South Carolina's first planters and merchants drew on kin networks that spread from Charleston to the West Indies to Europe.[5] The Colletons, Bulls, and Middletons came from the West Indies, while the Rutledges, Pinckneys, and Manigaults left Europe to expand family empires on the coast of South Carolina. The plantations that spread along the Ashley and Cooper Rivers and the merchant firms that developed on Market Street operated as family enterprises.

In the initial decade of settlement, Stephen Bull helped establish South Carolina's first major export commodity when he consigned deerskins to his brother, a London merchant. Joseph Blake, nephew of Admiral Robert Blake, used his familial connections to expand the skin trade in the early decades of colonization. Also during the initial colonization, brothers John and Isaac Motte started a successful mercantile firm, as did Pierre Manigault and his brother Gabriel. Brothers Samuel and Joseph Wragg built the largest slave-trading business in Carolina in the early eighteenth century when their uncle, London merchant William Wragg, bankrolled them. The biggest ship-building interests before 1740 were controlled by the Wragg brothers, the Holmes family, and a partnership of kinsmen William Gibbon and Andrew Allen. Robert Gibbes settled in South Carolina in 1672 and traded through his West Indies family. Benjamin Godin was connected commercially to his kinsman Stephen Godin of London. Paul Jenys immigrated to South Carolina in the late seventeenth century while his brother Thomas remained in Bristol, so they could cooperate in a number of business ventures.⁶

Familial connections to Europe and the Caribbean brought access to markets and credit while simultaneously diminishing the risk of individual failure. Deeply immersed in international kin networks, these families eventually attained unrivaled wealth in Carolina. But despite substantial support from relatives, amassing a fortune in early Carolina proved an arduous task. Widespread disease, conflict with Indians, and unrealistic expectations forced a continued reliance on kin abroad and hindered success in the colony. As early Carolinians searched for a profitable commodity, they tried exporting naval stores, tobacco, sugar, fruits and vegetables, livestock, hemp, silk, flax, soap, and lumber. All produced disappointing profits. Only the deerskin trade provided a lucrative export product during the 1710s and 1720s. In the first fifteen years of the eighteenth century, over two hundred Carolina merchants exported an average of 54,000 skins annually. In 1707, the high point of trade in that period, South Carolinians shipped 121,335 deerskins to England. By that year, Indian traders traveled as far as one thousand miles to obtain skins from interior nations, including the Creeks and the Cherokee.⁷

In the early eighteenth century, deerskins were the colony's most valuable commodity and a source of income for a wide array of traders. As the trade expanded, however, merchants relied more and more on securing market contacts abroad and political favors at home. And a diminishing number of kin-based trading houses controlled both. As a result, the power of a few elite families increased dramatically at the expense of smaller traders. By the middle third of the eighteenth century, the deerskin trade was monopolized by a small circle of interrelated elites. Between 1735 and 1775, over 650 individuals or firms exported deerskins from Carolina. Most traded only briefly, however, and paid less than £100 duty. Ultimately twenty-three individuals or firms, just 13 percent of all exporters, controlled the lion's share of the deerskin trade. Even that number is inflated because membership in the large firms frequently shifted. For example, Benjamin Stead was the largest exporter for the entire period. He was also a partner in the firm of Stead and Evance, the third largest exporter. Brothers-in-law Henry Laurens and George Austin owned the fifth largest exporting firm, while Austin's individual trade in skins ranked twenty-first and Laurens's twenty-third. The deerskin trading firms that eclipsed smaller traders were overwhelmingly family-based. The five largest exporters included brothers Samuel and George Eveleigh, brothers-in-law George Austin and Henry Laurens (and later Austin's nephew George Appleby), and kinsmen

Benjamin Stead and Thomas Evance. By the 1730s large merchant families, exploiting the personal nature of eighteenth-century business, had supplanted the vast majority of smaller traders and gained control of South Carolina's deerskin exports.[8]

Despite the success of the deerskin trade in those early years, the South Carolina economy remained unstable. Neither the expansion of the trade nor the substantial aid of kin fully ameliorated the difficulties facing early colonists searching for profits. Economic life remained uncertain until the 1730s when Carolinians finally began to make steady profits from rice. The marshlands, rainfall, and long summers in Carolina combined to produce an excellent environment for rice cultivation, and rice soon supplanted deerskins as the colony's most valuable export commodity. Between 1699 and 1709, rice exports from Carolina increased tenfold. By the 1730s rice was clearly the most important and lucrative staple crop in the colony.[9]

Just as with deerskins, the wealthiest and best-connected planters and merchants benefited most from the expansion of the rice trade. They alone possessed the slaves (who knew how to grow rice), land, and connections abroad that rice production and marketing demanded. Because they already controlled the best lands and cooperated in international family partnerships, they stood ready to exploit Carolina's rice crop. Furthermore, most had a long-standing familial tradition of using slavery as a system of labor. African slaves had lived in Carolina as long as whites. Colonists brought slaves with them from the West Indies sugar plantations they left behind, and in the early colonial period whites made limited use of slaves on their farms and businesses. With the advent of rice, a highly labor-intensive crop, lowcountry elites, particularly transplanted Barbadians, possessed both the money and mentality to expand their slaveholdings and maximize their rice production.

The growth of rice production thus accelerated the emergence of an elite-controlled, slave-based economy. The availability of labor and land at home and capital and markets abroad facilitated the emergence of an economic elite that alone could produce enough rice to meet market demands. Their power and wealth increased with each successful crop. The rice boom fostered greater demands for slaves and financing, which in turn produced larger profits, increased monopolization of the trade, and enhanced economic power.

Rice monoculture also encouraged greater stratification of wealth. With the crop's increased profitability by the 1730s, the planter elites invested most of their energy and money in rice production. Rice exports skyrocketed from

10,849 barrels in 1717 to 48,238 in 1731. Rice planters left the less lucrative exports to the yeomen farmers. As the largest planters increasingly focused on rice cultivation, both the volume and profitability of other export products declined. In 1717, Carolinians exported 444 barrels of beef, but by 1731 beef export figures dropped to only 39 barrels. In the same period, tar exports fell from 29,594 barrels to 2,242. Flour exports similarly plummeted from 1,245 barrels in 1717 to 303 barrels in 1731. While South Carolina continued to export these products, rice and indigo constituted over 75 percent of the value of the export trade by the late colonial period. One resident who unsuccessfully urged greater crop diversification attributed his failure to "planters [who] are so much attached to following Rice being a commodity most contracted for paying merchants and factors for Negros &c."[10]

The South Carolina slave trade expanded in tandem with rice culture, and a shrinking number of merchant firms similarly controlled the slave trade. Between 1735 and 1775, the eighteen largest importers of slaves controlled 90 percent of all imports. When multiple listings of traders in the annual enumerations are taken into account, only eight different commercial houses controlled more than 90 percent of the slave trade for forty years. The number of powerful firms decreased over time, but their command of the market grew. In 1735 five importers of slaves paid 86 percent of all duty. By 1760 four slave-traders paid 88 percent of the total.[11]

Kinship lay at the center of these trading houses. Kinsmen formed partnerships with relatives abroad and in the colony and successfully monopolized the importation of slaves into South Carolina. The five largest slave-trading firms in the colonial period were Austin & Laurens, Powell, Hopton, & Company, Joseph Wragg & Company, Middleton & Brailsford, and Miles Brewton. Austin & Laurens was a partnership between brothers-in-law. Robert William Powell and his father-in-law, William Hopton, ran Powell, Hopton & Company; brothers controlled Wragg & Company; Samuel Brailsford and Thomas Middleton were distant kin. Only Miles Brewton operated as an individual trader, but he got his start working fifteen years with his stepbrother-in-law, Benjamin Smith, and step-nephew, Thomas Loughton Smith.[12]

Landownership followed the same pattern. In South Carolina, the line between planters and merchants was obscured beyond any significant meaning. Planters frequently pursued mercantile-business interests, and merchants and professionals, such as lawyers and doctors, often owned plantations. Furthermore, no discernible difference existed between their agendas. Planters and merchants married one another, assumed complementary roles in society, and crossed occupational lines so frequently that the planter-merchant dichotomy retained no real significance.[13]

The ownership of land and slaves thus paralleled trading patterns. While a great many slaveholders held fewer than ten slaves each, a small group of planters owned increasing percentages of the South Carolina slave population. In 1745 seven lowcountry men owned more than one hundred slaves. While they represented only 1.6 percent of the total number of slaveholders, they owned over 12 percent of all slaves in South Carolina. Over the course of the eighteenth century, the proportion of slaveholders owning more than twenty slaves increased, while the number of slaveholders owning fewer than ten slaves declined.[14] Not surprisingly, the men who owned a growing proportion of slaves in Carolina belonged to the same families that dominated Charleston's businesses and monopolized the lands used for rice cultivation. Wealthy planter-merchant families controlled the land best suited for rice production, and rarely considered parting with it. The result, according to one Carolinian, was that "the valuable land is chiefly engrossed by the wealthy."[15] Rice production, from planting through international marketing, was therefore concentrated in the hands of a few interrelated planters and merchants.

For these interrelated elites, then, monopolization of one part of the economy was not enough. They diversified their interests and involved themselves in all of South Carolina's lucrative trades. Merchants traded throughout the colonies and abroad in deerskins, rice, indigo, and slaves. For example, in 1735 William Wragg & Company was one of the top three traders in both deerskins and slaves and among the twelve largest dealers in rum. During the 1760s, Austin & Laurens imported more slaves than any other firm and were one of the five largest exporters of deerskins. These interrelated gentry families not only controlled the distribution of Carolina's most lucrative commodities; they dominated the production of the crops as well. As in their merchant firms, lowcountry elites collaborated on their planting interests, bought slaves and property together, shared the risks and rewards of planting, and eventually eclipsed smaller farmers. Merchants abroad exacerbated this growing stratification of wealth in South Carolina. British and Caribbean merchants maintained kin connections with South Carolinians and therefore exhibited far more interest in promoting their relatives' economic prosperity than that of strangers.

The two most successful merchants of the first half of the eighteenth century, Gabriel Manigault (1704–81) and Joseph Wragg (1695?–1751), typified the path to economic success in Charleston. Both Wragg and Manigault headed family businesses that they operated with their brothers. Each diversified his interests: Manigault traded in rum, rice, and English goods and owned a number of plantations, while Wragg, also a large landholder, sold slaves, rice, and deerskins. Both enjoyed the support of kin abroad and extended those contacts as their wealth grew. They marketed their goods in a variety of places including Barbados, London, Bristol, Philadelphia, New York, and Jamaica. The two families merged in 1755 when their children, Peter Manigault and Elizabeth Wragg, married.[16] Charleston's gentry repeated this pattern again and again. By mid-century, they had established control over not one, but all of the most profitable commercial and agricultural interests in the colony.

While they diversified their interests and monopolized control over lowcountry businesses and crops, these elites simultaneously became a self-conscious, interrelated ruling class, intent on acquiring ever more wealth and power while distancing themselves from those outside their ranks. The gulf between rich and poor widened as gentry merchant families extended their holdings at the expense of less established firms. Inside the family circles, however, something profoundly different transpired. While they sought to draw clearer and stronger distinctions between themselves and the unrelated "lesser sorts," within their own ranks elites constructed a sibling society of sorts, based on cooperation and mutuality.

The Culture of Cooperation

Rather than creating a culture of competition and engaging in rivalries between kin groups, lowcountry elites cooperated regularly with one another. The kinship connections between planter-merchant families, along with their desire to protect their economic preeminence in Carolina, fostered a sense of shared interests. (Family was, after all, both emotional and financial.) Their immersion in this family network placed their focus on cooperation and mutuality rather than individualism and competitiveness.

The largest merchants, whom one might suppose vigorously competed with one another, actually collaborated in business endeavors. When a friend of Henry Laurens set up his nephew in a new merchant firm, Laurens assured his friend that he would "do every thing in [his] power to promote them as Merchants," although this new firm would compete with Austin & Laurens.[17] Lowcountry merchants often brought the younger kin of their "competition" into their own establishments as apprentices. Owners of rival firms owned ships together, introduced one another to contacts abroad, and bought and sold slaves and goods together. Miles Brewton and Henry Laurens frequently corresponded with each other and owned a number of ships together. They, along with other large slave traders, promoted joint agendas and excluded challengers. Planters behaved in much the same way, by offering aid to one another and buying and selling property and slaves together. Far from fearing competition, many of Charleston's most prominent merchants welcomed new firms into their circle, provided they held the proper kin connections.

While a great many early Carolinians formed legal partnerships with brothers, cousins, and other kin, still others cooperated informally. The brothers Andrew and Robert Pringle illustrate this pattern. Andrew established himself as a merchant in London in the 1740s while Robert operated out of Charleston. The two brothers never entered into a formal partnership, but they frequently borrowed and loaned money, introduced one another to important business associates, and corresponded about a wide host of financial matters. In 1740 one of Andrew Pringle's debtors failed to pay an overdue account. Andrew urged Robert to ask the debtor's brother in Charleston for the money. Robert assured Andrew that he would do everything in his power to collect the debt, but he implied that neither of the brothers could be counted on to pay their debts. William Stead of London and his brother Benjamin of Charleston similarly operated merchant firms in their respective cities and worked together to protect investments and connections and increase profits.[18]

Charleston's elites also sought out relatives to aid them in the operation of their plantations. When one of Ralph Izard's slaves, Andrew, proved too difficult for Izard to control, he asked Peter Manigault to step in. Izard explained that sending Andrew to Manigault's rice plantation would both end Izard's troubles and save Andrew's life: "If he was to stay long in this country he would certainly be hanged." When George Lucas's daughter Eliza married Charles Pinckney, Lucas's new connections to the Pinckney family enabled him to expand his planting interests in Carolina. Like many lowcountry planters, brothers-in-law Isaac Hayne, Richard Hutson, and Arthur Peronneau owned plantations, horses, slaves, and supplies together.[19]

When men traveled away from Charleston, they depended on their relatives to oversee their interests in the colony. While in New York, Ralph Izard wrote Peter Manigault concerning a ship they owned together: "I trust you will manage my share of her to the best advantage." Manigault also looked after Izard's planting interests, and when Izard needed extra money in New York he acquired it from Manigault. After James Glen's return to England in 1760, his brother-in-law John Drayton maintained his plantations in South Carolina. Glen and

Drayton corresponded frequently about the rice crops, and Drayton assured Glen that "nothing in my Power shall be left undone to serve you as long as life." While studying abroad in the 1780s, Joseph Manigault acted as an informal agent for his elder brother, Gabriel. After Joseph returned to Carolina, he continued to oversee Gabriel's affairs from time to time: he made decisions about their shared investments and supervised Gabriel's overseers at his Silkhope and Goose Creek plantations.[20]

Powerful men embraced this cooperation within and between families because it advanced their interests and protected them against outside rivals. By sharing their resources and interweaving their families they created not only a powerful ruling class, but also a uniquely cooperative culture within that class.

Because economic interests were familial rather than simply male concerns, women joined in the efforts. Women ran plantations and businesses in the absence of their male kindred, and made it possible for their relatives to focus on politics and international trading. Eliza Pinckney and her daughter, Harriott Pinckney Horry, for instance, took control of their family estate when Harriott's brothers went off to war and then pursued political careers. Eliza was, of course, practiced at running plantations. She oversaw her father's lands in her youth and maintained her husband's holdings after he died. For women like Eliza and Harriott and for the men in their families, female involvement in financial matters made perfect sense: it protected the family's economic interests. Female involvement in family finances should not, however, be overinterpreted. In the first place, their roles were provisional and auxiliary. Women operated as surrogates for their absentee male kin, and they did not demand independent plantations or positions in trading firms in return. And second, women were not propelled into these positions by any pre-feminist ideology; rather it was family needs that led to their involvement. Still, women played essential parts in the successful development of family empires, both through their participation in businesses and in their commitment to financially influenced family strategies.[21]

"Pluming Themselves on Rank and Fortune"

While they worked together to secure control over lowcountry businesses, the planter-merchant elite also infused the most intimate parts of their personal lives with their economic agendas. Using their kin connections, they devised a number of tactics to advance their economic authority over the colony. Marriage provided elites their most important and most commonly used resource in this quest for wealth and influence. Through cousin, exchange, and intergroup marriages, wealthy Charlestonians protected the financial interests of their family while binding themselves to an increasingly closed and self-conscious elite class. Members of the planter-merchant class embraced the financial advantages that flowed from strategic marriages. And from it they gained a greater sense of cohesion and exclusivity.

Elite South Carolinians paralleled almost to the letter the theoretical models developed by anthropologists studying kinship and class. For example, anthropologists argue that within elite classes, wealth and privilege depends on the careful conservation and distribution of family resources. One of the best ways to assure this preservation of privilege is by making careful marriage choices. By marrying only within a closed, interrelated group, families avoid diluting their resources. Simultaneously, they intensify the attachment of members within the group and increase the advantage of group inclusion. This in turn limits competition within the group and potential threats from outsiders.[22]

This is exactly what happened in South Carolina. Those Carolinians intent on conserving their family's financial interests often entered into exchange marriages, which decreased the fragmentation of family estates. These kinds of marriages pervade South Carolina genealogies. The three daughters of James Reid, for example, married three brothers. Elizabeth, the eldest, married William Bull, the stepson of Robert Pringle. Susannah married John Pringle, Robert Pringle's son, and Mary married John's brother, Robert Pringle, Jr. Timothy Ford married Sarah DeSaussure, the sister of his sister's husband.[23]

Sometimes intermarriage could get even more complicated. John Rutledge married his brother's stepdaughter. Samuel and Joseph Wragg married two sisters who were also their first cousins. The marriages of the Blake siblings are both genealogically confusing and typical of lowcountry elites. Four of Joseph and Sarah Blake's children reached adulthood. One resided abroad while the other three remained in Charleston. All three Charlestonians married members of the Izard clan. Daniel Blake married Margaret Izard, and when she died in 1760 he married her second cousin, Elizabeth Izard. In the meantime Daniel's brother, William, had married Anne Izard, a first cousin to Elizabeth Izard. Rebecca Blake extended the familial and commercial connections between her siblings and the Izards when she married Ralph Izard, the uncle of both Elizabeth and Anne. Thus, Ralph Izard became the brother-in-law of his two nieces; Elizabeth and Anne Izard were both cousins and sisters-in-law; and Elizabeth and Anne's sister-in-law, Rebecca Blake Izard, became their aunt.[24]

The richest merchants also bound their fortunes together through carefully coordinated marriages. Mary Wragg, the daughter of merchant Joseph Wragg, married the wealthy merchant Benjamin Smith. Mary's sister, Henrietta, married her first cousin, William Wragg, the only son of Samuel Wragg and heir to his businesses. Henrietta and Mary's other sister, Elizabeth, married Peter Manigault, the only son of prominent merchant Gabriel Manigault.[25]

This pattern of intermarriage created a strong group identity and a growing exclusivity within the elite class. As planters and merchants married to protect or extend family wealth, they bound themselves ever closer into one interrelated elite class. Their cohesion allowed them to protect their interests at the same time that it provided even more opportunities for wealth and power, which in turn intensified their desires for exclusivity.

Carolinians outside this inner circle of kin and power realized that marriage offered them the one real chance for rising in the lowcountry. So colonists, especially men, who aspired to the planter-merchant class tried to court individuals who offered an entry into Charleston's elite. Robert Pringle, whose sons' exchange marriages conserved family resources, had first gained acceptance by Charleston's elite through his marriage to Jane Allen, the daughter of a wealthy merchant. When she died he married Judith Bull, the widow of the lieutenant governor's son. Through his marriages, the elder Robert Pringle connected himself to established merchants as well as key political leaders in the colony. Henry Laurens exhibited the same degree of skill in his selection of a marriage partner. Henry's wife, Eleanor Ball, belonged to one of the most important Carolina families, and his marriage to her provided a trading partnership with merchant George Austin, Eleanor's brother-in-law, and co-ownership of Wambaw plantation with Eleanor's brother, John Coming Ball. Women also married for inclusion in Charleston's elite class. Mary Mackenzie married Thomas Drayton when his wife, Elizabeth Bull Drayton, died. After Drayton died, Mackenzie married the widower of Elizabeth Bull Drayton's sister.[26] But outsiders faced an uphill battle in their quest to "marry up" because they needed to counter both the social insularity of elites and the tendency of relatives to warn against such unions. Not surprisingly, marrying up worked better in the early eighteenth century when class lines remained more permeable.

The financial motives for marriage took a toll on the emotional lives of young Carolinians. While visiting South Carolina in 1785, Timothy Ford declared financially driven marriages the norm, and marital turmoil a frequent consequence: "I hear of more family troubles & especially of the conjugal kind than in any other place. I every day hear of unhappy marriages both in time past and present. This however I fancy may be partly attributed to the share which sinister views are apt to take, among people who plume themselves on rank & fortune, in the making of matches."[27]

Many openly admitted as much. Thomas Dale's haste to marry so soon after the passing of his first wife grew out of the economic connections his second wife provided: "I have allied myself to a very numerous and wealthy family which enlarges my Interest more ways than one." Some were a bit more subtle than Dale. While Sarah Rhett served as surrogate mother for Sarah Amory, she arranged for the younger Sarah to marry Arthur Middleton. Writing Sarah's brother, Thomas Amory, about the wedding, Rhett assured him that Middleton was "a sober, ingenious man worth eight hundred to one thousand pounds.... I doubt not but she [Sarah] will be very happy." Whatever the degree of tact, almost all members of the Carolina elite endorsed the pursuit of wealth through marriage.[28]

While many families strengthened their interests through advantageous marriages, few so single-mindedly devoted themselves to the purposeful construction of a family dynasty as did the Bond sisters of Hobcaw Point. Through their marriages between 1745 and 1754 they unified and virtually monopolized the Carolina ship-building industry. Elizabeth, the oldest of seven sisters, married the master of a privateer in Charleston. Susannah married an English mariner. Mary married Job Milner, a Charleston merchant who dealt primarily in shipping stores. Rebecca married James Reid, the owner of the only ropewalk in Charleston. Sarah married a British naval officer turned shipbuilder. Hester married the owner of Carolina's biggest shipyard. Only the youngest sister, Catherine, married someone unconnected to the shipping business.[29]

Leading families in the lowcountry knew how critical the right marital decision could be to the success of the kin network. So they both encouraged economically advantageous unions and actively discouraged marriages that jeopardized family status. After John Lloyd learned that his nephew, Richard Campion, was about to make "a very imprudent matrimonial connexion," Lloyd urged Richard "to reflect on the fatal consequences which inevitably arise from a conduct that must incur my highest displeasure." Worried that the woman Richard proposed to marry would not bring sufficient status or money into the family, Lloyd then warned his nephew about the perils of "indulging a rash & thoughtless passion" that ignored familial needs. Never, insisted Lloyd, should Richard pursue a serious relationship without consulting his kin. When Richard ignored this advice, Lloyd then moved on to threats: "Unless you come to that resolution you must not expect any assistance from me whilst I live, or, to be remembered in my Will." Shortly after receiving that letter, Richard Campion broke his engagement.[30]

Relatives discouraged marital choices out of concern for what the marriage represented to the larger kin group rather than simply because of personal objections to the intended spouse. When Elias Ball married his second wife, his first wife's sister, Ann Bulkeley, criticized his apparent disregard for the financial security of his children. Elias's second wife was nearly the same age as Elias's oldest daughter. The implications for the children of the first marriage were devastating. This second wife would almost certainly outlive her husband and inherit a share of his property and holdings. Furthermore, she might bear children who would make claims on the estate and reduce the inheritance of his first wife's children. Realizing the threat to her nieces and nephews, Ann Bulkeley expressed outrage at her brother-in-law's behavior to her brother, John Harleston: "If he had done his best for them children, I should a loved him as if he had been my own brother; if he had stayed unmarried, or married for their advantage, as a good father would a done, but just please himself without any regard to their welfare, I shall never have a favorable thought of him."[31]

Coming of age in this kind of marital culture, young people sometimes found themselves torn between their familial obligations and their own hearts. As a cautionary tale, one Charlestonian recounted the story of a young man who placed his own passions above his relatives' needs. In the midst of youthful "revelling & carousing," he married a poor, disreputable girl without the consent or even the knowledge of his family. Upon learning of his inopportune marriage, his relatives urged him to move temporarily to the Caribbean and forget about his new wife. After he returned, they would arrange a better marriage for him. When he refused, they issued an ultimatum: Either abandon his wife or face disinheritance. Upon declaring that he could neither live without his wife nor bear to lose his family, the young man committed suicide.[32] Elite Charlestonians could not be moved on the question of marriage—it was simply too important to squander on personal passion. Instead they embraced marriages that protected the economic interests of the larger kin network, could serve as a basis for business partnerships, countered the fragmentation of family estates, and encouraged a greater sense of family identity.

Charleston's interrelated elites were, of course, hardly alone in embracing such marriage patterns. Colonists in other regions of early America often replicated their behavior. Merchant families in Massachusetts developed similar marriage practices that countered the division of family wealth, protected family firms, and heightened their class consciousness. Virginia's gentry married relatives at a very high rate, which advanced their planting and political interests and created a strong sense of class identity. In Connecticut, colonists lived in communities "composed mainly of interrelated and interdependent families." And free blacks in colonial Louisiana used kinship and intermarriage to carve out an autonomous place in society between free whites and enslaved Africans. As one scholar explained, Louisiana's free blacks, or Libres, "wove intricate family patterns and utilized complex kinship strategies to promote their own well-being and that of succeeding generations."[33]

South Carolinians were, however, consistently focused on and particularly successful at linking their marriages with their economic objectives. Philadelphia merchants engaged in some intermarriage, but social and cultural differences between the city's elites undermined the creation of one cohesive, intermarried class. Philadelphia elites were never successfully integrated; marriage patterns there as well as in New York fostered divisions rather than class cohesion. In Massachusetts, ephemeral alliances often yielded conflict rather than consensus. And in Virginia, where planters and their families lived great distances from one another and created an economic system and a culture aimed at self-sufficiency, the commitment to economically driven marriages waned over time, replaced by a new interest in individual choice and romantic love.[34]

The difference between lowcountry Carolinians and other early Americans, then, was one of degree and not kind. Carolinians faced few religious, cultural, or geographic obstacles to their acquisitiveness and insularity. They did not live on far-flung, independent plantations like wealthy Virginians, and they lacked the cultural plurality of elites in New York and Philadelphia. Charlestonians formed a strange hybrid: business people who lived in a homogeneous, irreligious city and who possessed one uncompromised goal—to acquire family power. To that end, intermarriage and interdependence pervaded all of the elite class. Like other eighteenth-century Americans, they used marriage to protect and enhance their wealth and to create a strong sense of class allegiance—but lowcountry elites were more persistent and more successful.[35]

At the same time that this high degree of economically influenced intermarriage helped produce a unified ruling elite, it also engendered a greater sense of cooperation within this gentry class. When Timothy Ford traveled to Charleston with his sister and new brother-in-law in 1785, one of the first things he noticed was the pervasive pattern of intermarriage and the accord it fostered. An adjunct member of the planter-merchant class by virtue of his connection to his brother-in-law Daniel DeSaussure, Ford marveled at these networks of kin: "The inhabitants are almost all connected by some family relation; which makes them sociable & friendly. A stranger taken notice of by one gains an early access to all."[36]

Planning for the Inevitable

Intricate and powerful in life, the kin relations of lowcountry elites were on display in death as well. As their wills demonstrate, the gentry inhabited larger family networks than either less wealthy Charlestonians or backcountry residents. Wills showed who really mattered in the deceased's emotional and financial world. They were, as one historian explained, "self-conducted surveys of the identification and relative importance of different relations."[37] In short, testators left property and personal effects to the most important people in their lives. In Carolina this invariably included siblings and close kin.

Members of powerful lowcountry families were far more likely than other Carolinians to name kin in their wills. John Crowley has conducted the most extensive work on eighteenth-century lowcountry wills, revealing much about the class and regional variations in estate dispersal. Crowley found kin-naming varied according to gender, age, and marital status. But the two greatest variables were wealth and region. Crowley ultimately concluded that kinship did not matter a great deal in early Carolina, in part because he found that only 56 percent of testators named kin in their wills, while 65 percent named non-kin.[38] Members of Charleston's elite families sharply diverged from this pattern. In the wills written by members of eleven of Charleston's richest and most powerful families between 1700 and 1800, 85 percent of testators named kin in their wills.[39]

Not only were members of Charleston's inner circle more likely to name kin in their wills, they also named a greater number of relatives than other Carolinians. For the poor and "middling sort" and for small farmers, extensive family connections could bring more problems than benefits since dispersing estates across a wide array of kin weakened the financial position of the conjugal family. Many shopkeepers and craftsmen simply did not own enough to leave bequests to anyone besides their spouse and children. Similarly, backcountry farmers could not afford to fragment their holdings. But lowcountry elites had a long tradition of involvement in extensive kin networks. Broad family networks helped their international businesses and contributed to their sense of class identity. Furthermore, they possessed enough land and money to care for all their children and many of their kin without a loss of status.[40] Crowley found that testators whose estates inventoried at more than £500 named more than twice as many kin (2.69 per will) as those with estates worth less than £500 (1.31 per will).[41] Again, the discrepancy appears all the more dramatic among Charleston's wealthiest families. On average, they named 3.87 relatives in their wills. That represents a 44 percent increase over the kin-naming patterns of all benefactors with estates over £500. It also means that members of Charleston's most powerful families included in their wills almost three times the number of kin named by poorer Carolinians.[42]

Lowcountry elites' wills reflected this inclusive, extensive conception of family. They named a wide array of consanguineous and affinal kin in addition to members of the conjugal family. John Izard's will named not only his wife but also his sister and brother-in-law. Miles Brewton made bequests to an array of kin including each of his sisters and brothers-in-law, a half brother and half sister, and a niece and nephew. Elizabeth Middleton named her sisters, several brothers-in-law, nieces, uncles, cousins, and even a goddaughter. Through their wills, prominent Charlestonians demonstrated a uniquely broad definition of family and a strong sense of interdependence and cooperation within the kin group.[43]

Siblings, of course, represented the most important part of the intragenerational family, and they were the most commonly recognized kin in wills. Brothers and sisters named one another beneficiaries, guardians for children, and executors. Among the eleven families surveyed only one person out of seventy-five discussed his sibling in a negative light. Joseph Wragg warned his children that he often bickered with his brother, London merchant Samuel Wragg, and he expected the fighting to continue after his death.[44] Only five testators, including Wragg, had a sibling at the time of their death and failed to name that sibling as either beneficiary or executor. In fact, among this group, fully 86 percent who had siblings named them as either beneficiaries or executors.[45]

Wills showcased both the advantages and the obligations that flowed from inclusion in Charleston's concentric circles of kin. Bequests of business partnerships, land, and houses enriched the holdings of recipients. The acquisition of money and real and personal property through estate dispersal also symbolized the value of the individual beneficiary to the larger family. Kin receiving bequests therefore enjoyed both the financial fruits of their relatives' labors and the status of being a valued member of the family. At the same time, testators entrusted their relatives with important familial duties and used their wills to remind both executors and beneficiaries of their responsibilities to the benefactor. All this played out when parents confronted the daunting task of naming a guardian for their children. Guardians oversaw the upbringing of orphaned children, so they played a key role in the fate of the family. They had to be a trusted ally. Not surprisingly, lowcountry elites often turned to their siblings to serve as surrogate parents for young children.

Choosing an executor also numbered among the most important decisions a testator made because executors faced the monumental task of protecting the family's interests. If executors acted honorably and thoughtfully, the family would be enriched. If they failed their duty, the family could be imperiled. Executors did everything from negotiating the complicated financial transactions of mercantile houses to preparing for young children's futures. Sometimes the responsibility lasted a lifetime. Elias Ball instructed his executors, brothers-in-laws George Austin and Henry Laurens, to oversee his son William Ball's share in his estate, since William was "subject to fits" and might not understand how to care for his inheritance. Elias trusted his executors to retain William's share and "lay it out" for him as they deemed proper.[46] As they chose executors, lowcountry elites again demonstrated their strong commitment to siblings and kin. In fact, 60 percent of the wealthiest and best-connected Charlestonians named kin as executors.[47]

Within Charleston's planter-merchant class, wills represented an important intersection between the patriarchal and intragenerational families. Testators, not surprisingly, took care of their spouses and children first. Members of the gentry wanted to protect the family estate and ensure the success of the next generation. At the same time, they knew they needed to perpetuate their kin connections. The only escape from this dilemma came when no conjugal family member survived. Eliza Blake's husband and daughter, as well as her only sister, died before her, so Eliza left her property to her nephews and cousins. Hannah Bull split her estate between her brother, cousins, nieces, and nephews. Others devised contingency plans to provide for children and kin. Joseph Blake, for example, left the bulk of his estate to his only daughter, Rebecca. But he also left clear instructions that if she died before reaching age twenty-one, the estate was to go to his cousin, William Day. William Wragg left his holdings to his wife and children. Upon their death, he instructed his executors to split his money between his sister (£5,000), two sisters-in-law (£2,000 each), his brother-in-law (£2,000), and other kin.[48]

But sibs and kin represented far more than merely potential replacements for the conjugal family. Most members of Charleston's elite class made careful arrangements for both conjugal family members and important kin. James Laurens typified this behavior. He left most of his estate to his wife, but also bequeathed money to his brother, two sisters-in-law, and several nieces and nephews. William Bull also left money and personal effects to kin and the "remainder of estate" to his wife.[49] In fact, 76 percent of individuals who could have named only their conjugal family as beneficiaries and executors named siblings and kindred also. Only five testators from the eleven prominent Charleston families surveyed ignored their siblings when they made out their wills, regardless of their conjugal family situation.[50]

Charleston's elites used their wills for a variety of purposes. They honored lifelong attachments to kin. They ensured the future success of their family. And they protected their descendants by reminding their relatives of their obligation to the next generation. Those who had both conjugal families and siblings sometimes faced a difficult struggle between dynastic concerns and intragenerational family obligations. Most took care of children first, but left property and responsibilities for select kin as well. In the end, Charleston's elites knew the best way to care for the next generation was not merely to bequeath them property and money, but also to ensure their attachment to kin. That, after all, was what counted in the land of the living.

A Safety Net for Kin, a Barrier against Rivals

Elite Charlestonians went to great lengths to safeguard members of these intragenerational kin networks from outside threats as well as their own failures. As one Carolinian explained, "We all know one another of any fashion or Consequence, and we have so many . . . family parties, that a person must take any disadvantageous Character with great allowance."[51] To protect their consanguineous and affinal kin, lowcountry families provided one another with a financial "safety net" that simultaneously protected individuals within the family and preserved the status and wealth of the larger kin group. Stephen Bull provides an example of this safety net in action. When Bull died in 1750, his estate appeared to lay in ruins. He had mortgaged half his slaves and sold 3,000 acres of his land. Surprisingly, this financial reversal only slightly altered his lifestyle. In the last years of his life, he remained on his plantation and continued to reap the profits from his planting interests. Why did Bull not face financial ruin and social disgrace? When forced to dispense with his land and slaves, Stephen Bull sold the land to his brother-in-law, John Drayton, and mortgaged his slaves to his brother, William Bull II. While he appeared financially devastated, his brother and brother-in-law ensured that his straitened circumstances did not diminish his position in the community or the status of the Bull-Drayton clan.[52]

If their less fortunate kin needed money, South Carolinians felt personally responsible and quickly came to their aid. When William Bampfield and his wife traveled to Rhode Island for her health, Henry Laurens wrote his contacts there informing them that the Bampfields were kin and should be welcomed into society. Laurens even instructed his business contacts to charge William's bills to Henry's account.[53]

Whenever Charlestonians needed help, they turned to their siblings or other relatives. In early 1734, for instance, brothers Charles and William Pinckney organized America's first fire insurance company. Although initially quite successful, they faced crippling losses in the fall of 1740 when a great fire swept through Charleston. After the fire, in order to "alleviate his brother's financial pressures," Charles took in his nephew, Charles Pinckney, and funded his education. Similarly, when Gabriel and Joseph Manigault faced financial problems in 1784, the brothers shared the losses and maintained much of their holdings. Although forced to sell part of their property to pay their debts, Joseph assured Gabriel that he implicitly trusted Gabriel's handling of the matter. Gabriel proved worthy of Joseph's confidence, and the brothers soon recouped their losses.[54] Meeting the financial and practical needs of relatives represented a critical component of family duties, and Carolinians assumed that their kindred would come to their aid if called. They did not think that asking for help was a sign of weakness. As one Carolinian put it, "Why should we have Friends, if we never make use of 'em."[55]

On the other hand, wealthy men could be expelled from Charleston's inner circle if they failed to fulfill their family obligations. Egerton Leigh, for example, lost his claim to the gentry class after alienating his relatives. In 1756, Leigh married Martha Bremar, the daughter of Francis and Martha Laurens Bremar. Henry Laurens was Martha's brother and Francis's business partner, and after Leigh married Henry Laurens's favored niece, Laurens allowed Leigh to handle most of his legal matters. Laurens urged his business associates in London to support Leigh and lend him "whatever sums he might need, up to the limits of [Laurens's] own credit." But Leigh squandered this opportunity when he impregnated his wife's underage sister. Once the scandal came to light, virtually all of Charleston shunned Leigh. The only friend he could find was Fenwick Bull, a social pariah who had been horsewhipped for trying to bribe a jockey to lose a horse race.[56]

Stephen Bull's son, another Stephen Bull, also incurred the wrath of his kinsmen after he betrayed an uncle. During the Revolutionary War, the younger Stephen Bull became a patriot, while his uncle, William Bull, remained a loyalist. Fearful of losing all his holdings in Carolina, William Bull transferred his estate to Stephen, his favorite nephew, with the understanding that when peace came Stephen would return the property. In the meantime, Stephen would pay allowances to his uncle. Stephen, however, reneged on the gentleman's agreement, and his uncle and aunt were forced to sue him. Stephen lost the case and was financially ruined. By 1790 he owed more than twice the value of all his assets. Most devastating of all, his relatives rejected him, and even his stepmother took him to court. He died "a ruined and broken old man, forgotten and unmourned."[57] Such egregious behavior was rare, however, because most prominent Charlestonians cautiously guarded their familial connections. They understood that their relatives held the key to their inclusion in Charleston's elite class.

A few Carolinians did voice opposition to this pattern of kin interdependence. Brothers John and Edward Rutledge had enjoyed a close, mutually beneficial relationship for most of their lives, but experienced a falling-out in old age. The evidence is sketchy, but it seems that John grew ill in late 1795, and he suffered from occasional mental lapses until his death four years later. Responsibility for his estate fell to Edward, who resented it: "I am very much engaged in the affairs of my Brother, and I wish to bring them to a close whist I am on this side of the Grave." Edward failed, however, to reach his goal. He died in January 1800, and his ailing brother lived six months longer. Although apparently mentally incapacitated, John Rutledge was lucid enough to understand the conflict and instruct his children to avoid similar problems in their own sibling relationships. In his last advice to his children, John Rutledge warned them that "dearly bought Experience" had taught him hard lessons about blending family and finances. "Money Transactions," he wrote, "betwixt near Relations, have not only disturbed, but Totally broken, the peace of Families, dissolved, as it were, the Ties of Blood, & converted Love into Hostility—of all Evils, Family differences are the most bitter."[58]

Most elites did not, however, express such concerns about or contempt for the interweaving of kin and commerce. They accepted, even welcomed, the duties and benefits of these family networks. And for those who honored their family obligations, the safety net provided by kindred ensured that economic difficulties would not mean loss of land and businesses or expulsion from the elite class. On the contrary, once family contacts ensured an individual's inclusion in Charleston's ruling class, loss of money alone could not force him out. But by the same token, wealth without the proper pedigree could not ensure acceptance. As long as a man honored his relatives, they worked hard to ensure his success and protect the interests of the larger kin group. In short, they took care of their own.

There was, of course, another side to this coin. While they cooperated to protect their kin, Charleston's interrelated elites also worked together to exclude those outside their ranks. Lowcountry elites consistently blocked potential rivals from the paths to economic power. In 1745 William Vernon traveled to South Carolina to expand his and his brother's Newport, Rhode Island, firm. Vernon quickly found out that interrelated merchants monopolized Charleston's business opportunities. He ultimately concluded that his trip to Charleston was "the unlucks affair I ever undertook" and returned to his business in Newport. Margaret Kennett, who immigrated to Carolina in the 1720s and built up a successful shop, found herself forced out of her place of business because "our Lanlord has taken the Business into his own hands and only put one of his Relations into the House." When asked to help place the son of James Habersham in a Charleston mercantile firm, Henry Laurens agreed to try but warned Habersham that it might be a futile effort because "most of the Houses in this Town are under engagements to take Sons, nephews or relatives." In his response to Laurens's pessimism, Habersham admitted, "I am very sensible of the Difficulty of getting him into a proper House in Charlestown, as I have now no interesting Connections there, which really puts me to a loss, how to dispose of him."[59] The web of kin that bound elites together formed a safety net to protect relatives at the same time it created a barrier to block unrelated rivals. Habersham was on the wrong side of the net.

"All of One Mind"

By the second half of the eighteenth century, an interrelated group of elite families had transformed the harsh lowcountry environment into the most opulent community in British North America. Slaveholders in Charleston owned more slaves than any group on the American mainland. Rice and indigo planters turned greater profits than almost any other colonists. Lowcountry planters and merchants poured hundreds of thousands of pounds into the British economy each year. White South Carolinians enjoyed the highest per capita income of any colonists.[60]

The city was nothing short of awe-inspiring. Traveling from Rhode Island in 1764, Moses Lopez reported to his brother that Charleston "is twice as big as when I was here in the year 1742. It has increased with sumptuous brick houses in very great number. One cannot go anywhere where one does not see new buildings." According to Lewis Thibou, "The port is never without ships and the country is becoming a great traffic centre." John Toblers agreed: "The commerce which is carried on there is quite considerable, is continually increasing and is very advantageous. It is hardly believable how quickly merchants with good business attain to great wealth." Travelers to Carolina seemed uniformly impressed with the beauty of Charleston. During his visit to the city, one Englishman found that Charleston "makes a most beautiful appearance . . . in grandeur, splendour of buildings, decorations, equipages, numbers, shipping, and indeed in almost everything, . . . all seems at present to be trade, riches, magnificence."[61]

Charleston's gentry wore their wealth like a badge of honor. They exhibited great sophistication and an unrivaled penchant for consumption. They dressed in the finest clothes, maintained majestic houses and gardens, threw lavish parties and balls. Their public presentation of self—the clothes, houses, and leisure activities—both supplied a powerful visual representation of elites' concerns over gentility and showcased the dramatic class divisions in the lowcountry. Visitors could not help but be impressed by the show the planter-merchants put on. After visiting Miles Brewton's home, Josiah Quincy of Boston bragged that he had dined in "the grandest hall I ever beheld." An Englishman visiting Charleston expressed surprise upon finding the houses of elite families "large and handsome, having all the conveniences one sees at home." Timothy Ford marveled that the prosperity of elites in Charleston "seems to be showered upon them."[62]

Women played critical roles in this elite self-construction for public consumption. Just as women served their families as the primary kin guardians in the late eighteenth century, they also became the paragons of gentility. By maintaining dominion over their opulent houses and gardens and by being the most conspicuous consumers of the material artifacts of gentility, elite women came to embody notions of refinement. The leisured lifestyles of elite white women also distinguished them from other classes and races of women. In all these ways, women thus reified elites' sense of gentility and their class identity.[63]

The expansion of elite wealth and class identity, so inextricably linked to kin networks, came at the expense of poorer colonists.[64] By mid-century, lowcountry elites were not only incredibly rich, they were also fervently protective of their status. The gulf between rich and poor grew ever wider. Charlestonians could honestly proclaim that "the Men and Women who have a right to the Class of Gentry... are more numerous here than in any other Colony in North America." But they also had to concede that the vast number of Charlestonians possessed only "a bare subsistance." Or, as Josiah Quincy found during his 1773 visit to the colony: "The inhabitants may well be divided into opulent and lordly planters, poor and spiritless peasants and vile slaves."[65]

The attitudes elites expressed toward those outside their class stood in sharp contrast to the treatment insiders received. As we have already seen, the commitment to egalitarian relations patterned after the sibling bond complicated eighteenth-century beliefs in rank and deference. Within their kin networks and their interrelated class, elite Carolinians by and large enjoyed amiable, mutually beneficial connections. This did not, however, carry over into relationships with people outside the gentry class. Indeed, elite Carolinians treated poor whites, slaves, and artisans ruthlessly. Elites imposed a rigid hierarchy on relationships outside their class. By the middle of the eighteenth century, unconnected whites faced virtually insurmountable obstacles to rising in lowcountry society. Established elites monopolized most businesses and the best lands. Marriages were carefully orchestrated in order to limit access to wealth. And powerful families cooperated in every conceivable way to promote their interests at the expense of others.

A thoroughgoing analysis of slavery is beyond the scope of this work, but slavery does offer a particularly compelling example of elite treatment of people outside their ranks. Philip Morgan's excellent *Slave Counterpoint* recently underscored the rigidity and morbidity of lowcountry slavery. Morgan primarily concerned himself with black experiences in the Chesapeake and lowcountry and the cultural consequences of slavery. But he simultaneously illuminated the violence and callousness of lowcountry slaveholders who went to unimaginable lengths to extract work from their slaves.[66] In the end, it seems that slavery in Carolina was perhaps more brutal and cruel than anywhere on the American mainland. And slavery played a more crucial role in the lives and culture of slaveholders in the lowcountry than in any other region of early America. Everything that elite Carolinians imagined that they were — rich, powerful, genteel — hung on slave labor. Living in a black majority and utterly dependent on slave labor, elite whites could not envision a world without slavery. Not surprisingly, then, Carolinians voiced the greatest outrage over the debate concerning slaveholding at the Constitutional Convention in 1787, and set themselves up as the primary defenders of the institution during the early national and antebellum eras. They also consistently demonstrated that no means of violence and cruelty seemed too great to maintain Carolina's rigid racial order. Slaves suffered the greatest burden, then, for the aspirations of elite families.

South Carolina paid a heavy price for the excesses of its interrelated gentry in other ways as well. Determined to protect themselves and their kin from any potential rivals, elites refused to spend money to advance the public good. They failed to finance educational systems, encourage an artisan community, promote broad diversification of crops, or develop manufactures. Even in the very late eighteenth century, Charlestonians, according to Pelatiah Webster, possessed "very few mechanic arts of any sort, & very great quantity of mechanic tools are imported from England & the North'd Colonies." Timothy Ford also noticed that "manufactures are neither patronized encouraged or pursued; and they seem to be perfectly content to supply themselves from foreign markets." Even visitors such as John Toblers, who otherwise praised the lowcountry, lamented the lack of schools and colleges.[67]

The tremendous affluence of certain families fostered among their members a combination of acquisitiveness and dissipation. Timothy Ford observed that most wealthy Carolinians did not even bother handling their own estates and businesses. According to Ford, they directed their attention elsewhere: "Pleasure becomes in a great measure their study." Almost everyone who traveled to the lowcountry agreed that the Charleston gentry loved wealth and all its manifestations. One observer found that "the generality of people here are more mindful of getting money and their worldly affairs than they are of books and learning." Another remarked that "the people of Charleston live rapidly, not willingly letting go untasted any of the pleasures of life." And a third wrote that they often whiled their lives away "in idleness and dissipation."[68]

Carolina's gentry were so notoriously greedy and irreligious that they stunned ministers who traveled to the lowcountry. One visiting clergyman lamented that Carolinians cared only about "eager pursuit of the things of this world" and seemed utterly indifferent to religion. Another appalled minister agreed: "Their whole Lives are one continual Race: in which everyone is endeavouring to distance all behind him; and to overtake or pass by all before him; everyone is flying from his inferiors in Pursuit of his Superiors."[69]

As they became wealthier, South Carolina elites also turned further and further inward. Their obsession with family led them to discount anyone unrelated to them. Henry Laurens, for example, denounced poorer Carolinians because "all that the bulk of them aim at is Victuals & clothing no matter how mean. Few of them seem to covet more." Eliza Lucas agreed, insisting that "the poorer sort are the most indolent people in the world or they could never be wretched in so plentiful a country as this." When Joseph Manigault stayed in Charleston during the Christmas season of 1786, he complained to his brother Gabriel that only working people, whom he found "vulgar," remained in the city. Unconnected Charlestonians knew elites viewed them with scorn and disdain. Outsiders found "the rich [are] haughty and insolent, and all of them are remarkably indolent" and insisted they were "all of one Mind . . . [and] very Cautious before whom they speak."[70]

Slaveholding also contributed to elites' sense of superiority and exacerbated the tendency toward "dissipation." As he traveled through South Carolina, Ebenezer Hazard wrote: "The *country gentlemen* are . . . accustomed to tyrannize from their infancy, [and] they carry with them a disposition to treat all mankind in the same manner they have been used to treat their Negroes." Timothy Ford concurred: "Accustomed to have every thing done for them they cannot or will not do anything for themselves." According to Ford, many of the largest planters "know little about the process & art of planting," and "all is committed to overseers and drivers."[71] The slave-based nature of the lowcountry economy certainly permitted members of the planter-merchant class a great deal of leisure time. Overseers and drivers did most of the supervisory work on plantations. Slaves performed the hard labor. After finishing college at Nassau (later Princeton), Richard Hutson returned to the Carolina lowcountry. Explaining the rigors of plantation ownership to his college friends, he wrote: "Since my arrival I have done little else but ride about from Place to Place." In early March 1766, before he took over the plantation of his late father, Hutson feared planting would take up too much of his time. By summer he realized the error in his thinking: "I have employed a Skilfull person to manage my plantation for me so that it is rather an Amusement to me than any Trouble."[72]

SLAVEHOLDING, irreligiosity, greed, and a leisured lifestyle all influenced the attitudes of lowcountry elites, and each contributed to the emergence of a self-conscious ruling class. But kinship defined who belonged in Charleston's inner circle. Family connections—as much as wealth and political power—shaped class identity. Elites depended on members of the family network to secure business and planting partnerships. Conversely, they altered their familial worlds to advance their economic agenda. By blending their economic and familial lives, South Carolina elites formed a powerful ruling class with its own unique values.

The culture that Charleston's interrelated gentry created was informed by and remarkably similar to sibling relationships. Elites treated one another as equals, cooperated on personal and financial matters, and guarded one another's economic interests. Those inside Charleston's concentric circles of kin found themselves protected and advanced. Outsiders felt like Affra Coming: "Sheep in the midst of wolves."

CHAPTER FIVE

"The Long and Steady Attachment"
Politics and Kinship

When President Washington appointed Charles Cotesworth Pinckney minister to France in 1796, Pinckney immediately sought the advice of his brother-in-law and business partner, Edward Rutledge. Until they could determine what to do, the brothers-in-law agreed to keep the matter secret. They told only Pinckney's sister, Harriott Pinckney Horry, and Rutledge's wife, Henrietta Middleton Rutledge. After much consultation, Pinckney decided to accept the offer. Then, as one of his first acts as minister, he named his nephew Henry Rutledge as his personal secretary. Charles viewed his young nephew "in the light of a Son," and wanted to fulfill his educational responsibility to Henry by launching his career in public service. Taking on the boy also repaid a number of family debts: Henrietta and Edward Rutledge oversaw many of Pinckney's interests in Charleston, and Edward Rutledge and his brothers supported Pinckney throughout his long political career. All of this, of course, expanded the Pinckney-Rutledge political power base at the same time that it reinforced their ties to one another. The family culture of lowcountry elites demanded this kind of interweaving of politics and kinship. As he prepared his son for his new job, Edward Rutledge explained that government and family so coalesced that political service was an unavoidable family responsibility: "The family my Son from which you have descended; the style of your education; the long and steady attachment of your Uncle Pinckney towards you; [and] the early acquaintance which you have formed with public men . . . forbid the idea of private life."[1]

This interweaving of political activity and familial identity shaped the Carolina lowcountry from its founding beyond the turn of the nineteenth century. Lowcountry elites made political decisions in the context of family objectives, and used political appointments to advance their kin. At every turn, lowcountry politicians considered the familial implications of their public behavior and tried to use their political positions to benefit relatives. At the same time, men like Pinckney and Rutledge believed that they owed it to their families and to South Carolina to serve in political office. Indeed, among eighteenth-century South Carolina elites, kinship obligations made public service a duty. This duty, in turn, served the interests of Charleston's interrelated gentry families. The synergy between family and politics thus produced a circle with each propelling the other.

Throughout the eighteenth century, lowcountry elites believed that protecting themselves and expanding their authority over Carolina depended on keeping Charleston the center of political power. The gentry first wrested control over the province away from the proprietors in the early colonial era. Then, they imposed their will for local control over political processes in the royal period. Under British rule, lowcountry elites expanded their power within the Commons House of Assembly and the Royal Council, therefore enhancing their influence over the colony. In time, this localistic political focus even affected South Carolina's determination to support independence from Great Britain. Finally, the struggle for local power over state interests spilled into the backcountry in the late eighteenth century.[2] At every juncture, kinship played a critical role in lowcountry political culture.

Power, like class, grew out of the cooperation, interdependence, and exclusivity that governed interaction within the intragenerational kin group. In their effort to monopolize political power, Charleston's ruling families followed the same pattern that was set in their personal relationships and employed to ensure economic control over the region. Their ambitions knew no bounds. Political preeminence, like economic power, did not occur spontaneously. Rather, this power over South Carolina politics grew out of a deliberate, self-conscious effort on the part of interrelated elites to protect their own interests at the expense of others. The desire for political power and the means to acquire it came from the same source: siblings and kin. Concentric circles of kin bound together men of power who willingly shared offices and political favors. At the same time, they restricted entry into the political area only to those possessing the proper pedigrees. Once in office, politicians fulfilled two familial obligations: enhancing the power of their kindred and ensuring the failure of unrelated rivals.

Laying the Foundation

Far from detached from public life, family provided the foundation of South Carolina political culture from the point of colonization. During Carolina's initial settlement, individuals depended on their families' political connections to secure land grants, political appointments, and government subsidies for colonization. In 1663 Sir John Colleton, a wealthy Barbadian planter, approached a number of his English friends, including brothers John and William Berkeley, about seeking a land grant in Carolina from Charles II. Although John Colleton died before settling in South Carolina, his sons, Peter and James, played important roles in Carolina government throughout the proprietary period. Peter Colleton succeeded his father as lord proprietor and James served as governor of the colony. Stephen Bull similarly used his familial connections with the proprietors to obtain a series of appointments, including proprietary deputy of the Grand Council. The Bull family survived the collapse of the proprietary government and remained one of the most politically powerful families in Carolina until the American Revolution.[3] The Colleton and Bull families typified early Carolina politics and set the standards followed by generations to come.

As the first English ships sailed into Charleston Bay, a number of families were already developing the kin-based political coalitions that would dominate South Carolina throughout the colonial and early national eras. In the early eighteenth century, brothers-in-law William Rhett and Nicholas Trott amassed an amazing array of political appointments. During the last years of the proprietary government, Rhett was receiver of quitrents and, sometimes simultaneously, surveyor general of customs and Speaker of the Commons House of Assembly. Trott served at varying times as attorney general, vice-admiralty court judge, and chief justice. Rhett and Trott hardly stood alone in this manipulation of family connections for political gain. Of the ten men who served as proprietary deputies between 1681 and 1690, at least five enjoyed direct kin ties to either a proprietor or governor.[4]

Early in the colonial era, powerful men also started using their influence to punish people who threatened the advancement of their kin. In 1707, for example, Governor Robert Johnson charged Thomas Nairne with treason. Nairne's crime? As an agent for the assembly's Indian trade commission, he attempted to prosecute a man for violating trading regulations. Unfortunately, the illegal trader was the son-in-law of Governor Johnson. Although the law stood on Nairne's side, familial bonds proved stronger than Carolina's legal code.[5]

Nairne's experience revealed the power of family connections as well as the profound conflict between the colonist-dominated assembly and the lord proprietors. Generally speaking, the proprietary period proved especially tumultuous for Carolinians, and in the early years of the colony local elites and absentee proprietors routinely butted heads. From the beginning of colonization, the efforts of local gentry to protect and extend their families' economic and political power clashed with the proprietors' agenda. An interrelated group of Barbadian planters called the "Goose Creek Men" particularly resented proprietors' efforts to expand the colony in the 1680s.[6] In an effort to increase the population of the colony and their profits from it, the proprietors began recruiting French Huguenots and English dissenters. They also appointed Joseph Morton governor, hoping he might draw in other dissenters. Finally, and for Charlestonians most disturbing, the proprietors tried altering election procedures to give dissenters a greater political voice. A proposed redistricting plan established three counties, Colleton, Craven, and Berkeley, and designated them as new election districts. Together, Berkeley, which contained Charleston, and Craven elected ten representatives. Colleton, the area south of the Stono River where dissenters had begun settling, received the same number. While paying little attention to the religious implications of the proprietors' program, the Goose Creek men balked at the prospect of dissenter votes eroding their influence in colonial politics. The expansion of the electorate and the reapportionment of the assembly clearly threatened the Goose Creek men's power and limited the availability of opportunities for their relatives. Outraged at this challenge, local elites railed against the proprietors "innovations." Religion, however, remained of secondary concern in the conflict. Rather, opposition centered around feared political marginalization and the shifting locus of power within the colony.[7]

The debates over the Fundamental Constitutions in the late seventeenth century similarly illustrate the nature of the divisions between the proprietors and colonists. The Fundamental Constitutions, a collaborative effort between Anthony Ashley Cooper and John Locke, was an elaborate blueprint for organizing the colony. It covered issues as wide ranging as landownership, government, and religion. In the minds of resident elites, however, the plan represented a direct challenge to family opportunities and diminished their power vis-à-vis the proprietors. Just as in the struggle over the proprietors' dissenter expansion program, local elite opposition to the Fundamental Constitutions reflected kin interest rather than a divergent ideological perspective. In both cases, the primary objective remained the preservation of local, familial power. The ultimate rejection of the Fundamental Constitutions strengthened the power of the residents and marked the further passage of power from the proprietors to the colonists.[8]

Throughout the proprietary period, local elites' struggle to acquire political dominion over the colony did not grow out of any coherent political philosophy. Instead, the desire to promote family interests lay at the heart of this localistic agenda. As they cooperated to undermine the power of the proprietors, interrelated local elites also tried to expand the jurisdiction of the institutions over which they presided. Within the assembly they seized the rights to control the membership, elect the speaker, and introduce legislation.[9] Local elites then used these new powers to secure political positions for kinsmen and pass laws to promote family interests. By the turn of the eighteenth century, political favors and appointments, land grants, legal training, and election to public office all flowed from kinship connections. Both the absentee proprietors and local elites recognized this system and encouraged its expansion. Despite their divisions over legislative apportionment and governmental structures, both the proprietors and colonists embraced the ties between kinship and politics. Indeed, the debates between residents and proprietors often came down to whose relatives benefited most. In the end, the resident planter-merchant families carried the day.

The transition from proprietary to royal government only superficially affected the relationship between kinship and politics. By the time the proprietary government collapsed in 1719, an increasingly interrelated group of planters and merchants had already begun to monopolize many of the colony's political offices and were busy expanding familial control over the provincial government. Although changes occurred in the structure and composition of South Carolina's government after it came under royal control, the pattern of family-based politics continued. A few prominent political families disappeared after the revolt against the proprietary government and a few new families replaced them. But while names changed, the relationship between kinship and government remained the same.

Keeping It All in the Family

During the early royal period, members of the gentry continued this campaign to promote their political influence over the colony. Simultaneously, they worked to foster political stability within Carolina. And they succeeded on both accounts. Between the 1730s and the 1750s, Charleston enjoyed a relatively stable political climate. No factional divisions existed, no sectional tensions divided the colony, and no one challenged the power of the elite families. The British crown's policy of salutary neglect only aided the growing power of these kin networks. Freed from the "intrusions" of the proprietors and crown, lacking any significant challenge from outside their class, and fueled by an expanding economy, lowcountry gentry families grew more powerful and more exclusive with each passing year.

The infusion of family objectives into lowcountry political culture occurred so routinely that, by the midpoint of the century, most political leaders in Charleston found themselves surrounded in office by relatives. The Middleton men typified the power of kin-based political networks in eighteenth-century South Carolina. During the middle of the century, Arthur Middleton held a number of important public offices, including an extensive period of service in the assembly, before going on to sign the Declaration of Independence. During his lifetime other Middleton family members in the assembly included his brothers, his father, both his grandfathers, his father-in-law, and six of his brothers-in-law.[10] The Middleton case was far from unusual. Brothers and other relatives typically served in political capacities together. In fact, the politician who served without family members stood out in colonial South Carolina. Lowcountry colonists grew so accustomed to such kin-based political coalitions that few ever questioned the nepotism pervading Charleston's public life.

The Lowndes brothers' monopoly over the provost marshal's office, for example, neither surprised nor concerned lowcountry colonists. Left alone in South Carolina after their father's suicide and their mother's return to St. Kitts, brothers Charles and Rawlins Lowndes understood the importance of broadly defined kin connections. Their father, Charles Lowndes, left his children very little money or land. Nevertheless, they received a legacy that in South Carolina was more precious than money: important friendships and familial ties throughout the Atlantic world. The brothers grew up in the home of their guardian, Provost Marshal Robert Hall, and parlayed that relationship into lifelong public careers. In 1745 Rawlins Lowndes succeeded Hall as provost marshal, the chief law enforcement officer in the colony. After his election to the assembly in 1749, Rawlins turned the provost's office over to Charles. The Lowndes brothers went on to monopolize that office for over fifteen years. Whenever one obtained a more prestigious political position or traveled to Europe on business, the other promptly stepped into office. From the provost marshal's office, Rawlins and Charles also launched themselves into various other political positions, including seats in the assembly.[11]

Similarly, William Bull II and his brother-in-law Henry Middleton shared the speakership of the assembly during the mid-eighteenth century. When health problems forced William II's resignation as speaker in 1747, Henry Middleton succeeded him. The following year Middleton's wife, Mary Henrietta Bull Middleton, fell ill and Henry resigned the speakership to care for her. Bull, now recovered, resumed his former position.[12] This sharing of political office was part of a long pattern in the Bull family. William Bull II first entered the Commons House of Assembly in 1736, and his younger brother Stephen joined him the following year. In 1738 Stephen and William's father, William Bull I, became lieutenant governor and acting governor of the colony after having sat on the Royal Council throughout the 1720s and 1730s. From 1738 until the outbreak of the American Revolution, a member of the Bull family held the lieutenant governorship, with only brief interruptions.[13]

The Wright siblings illustrate how sibling ties exerted a comparable influence over South Carolina's judicial system. Charles and James Wright both served as justices of the peace and grand jurors of St. Peter's parish. Their sister married James Graeme, the chief justice of South Carolina, and another brother became governor of Georgia.[14]

This pattern of shared political power continued throughout the eighteenth century. During the ratification of the Constitution, Charles Cotesworth Pinckney, his brother Thomas, and their cousin Charles Pinckney enjoyed the benefits of cooperating in public office. Charles and Charles Cotesworth attended the Constitutional Convention while Thomas served as governor of South Carolina. Charles Pinckney later succeeded Thomas as governor of the young state, while Thomas and Charles Cotesworth traveled to England and France as U.S. ministers.[15]

Hugh, John, and Edward Rutledge typified the political power shared by siblings in the eighteenth-century lowcountry. The Rutledge brothers served throughout the late eighteenth century in the state legislature, the governor's office, the U.S. Congress, and the Supreme Court. During the 1780s and 1790s, Hugh Rutledge acted as Speaker of the South Carolina House of Representatives, and both John and Edward won terms as governor. Hugh served as Speaker of the Commons House of Assembly, judge of the Court of Admiralty, and judge of the Court of Equity. Over his long career John Rutledge was South Carolina's attorney general, delegate to the first Continental Congress, head of the state militia during the Revolution, president of South Carolina, governor of South Carolina, U.S. congressman, Supreme Court justice, and chief justice of South Carolina. The third Rutledge brother, Edward, signed the Declaration of Independence, attended the first and second Continental Congresses, helped draft the state constitution of 1790, served in the South Carolina House of Representatives, and became governor. In the early national era, John was chief justice of South Carolina, Edward was governor, and Hugh was speaker of the House of Representatives. The Rutledge brothers' political base also included their sister Sarah's husband. In 1782 when his term as governor of South Carolina expired and the state constitution forbade his reelection, John Rutledge turned over the governorship to his brother-in-law John Mathews.[16]

Marriage intensified the connections between elites and helped solidify their political preeminence in South Carolina. Countless men forged powerful political alliances through careful marriage choices.[17] When, for example, John Drayton married Margaret Glen in 1752, he linked himself politically and personally with her brother, Governor James Glen. The same year Margaret married John Drayton, her brother recommended him for service on the Grand Council. When a vacancy occurred in 1754, Glen appointed Drayton. The brothers-in-law also cooperated on child-rearing strategies, planting decisions, and a host of other public and private matters. Drayton no doubt courted Margaret Glen with these kinds of perks in mind, since he was the widower of Charlotta Bull, the sister of Lieutenant Governor William Bull. If James Glen thought his sister's marriage opportunistic, he could hardly afford to say anything. He had, after all, secured his appointment as royal governor of South Carolina only because his sister Elizabeth married the Earl of Dalhousie who, after the wedding, used his influence in London to aid his new brother-in-law. In some cases, politics overtly guided marriage choices, and shaped the political climate of the lowcountry. When William Bull I, whose family members owed their political careers to the proprietors, married Mary Quintyne, an heiress of the Quintyne family of Barbados and Carolina, their union provided a much-needed bridge between the Goose Creek families and the proprietors.[18] The political payoffs of such marriages were undeniable.

Connections shared between brothers and kinsmen of the same generation and enhanced by careful marriages became the primary tools in acquiring and protecting political power. At the same time, interrelated political leaders also extended their connections vertically into the next generation. The political agendas of families included the training and incorporation of each new generation into the colonial and later state and national governments. Uncles, elder brothers, and other relatives helped fathers place their sons in political offices. Older kinsmen worked hard to ensure the success of younger relatives and thereby carry their power into the next generation at the same time that they diligently pursued political coalitions within their own generation.

The most successful political leaders immersed themselves in elaborate kin networks and surrounded themselves with relatives in office. They acquired power by depending on and supporting a wide array of politically active kinsmen. Furthermore, the reliance on family continued long after an individual launched a political career. Elder statesmen and newly elected representatives alike welcomed the advice of trusted kin. Even the most established political leaders rarely reached important decisions without consulting family members. As Ralph Izard debated leaving Congress in 1789, he sent a potential letter of resignation to his son-in-law Gabriel Manigault with instructions to present it to the governor of South Carolina only if Gabriel approved of the contents.[19]

As they married one another, raised each other's children, and developed lifelong patterns of interdependence, interrelated lowcountry elites created a culture predicated on mutuality and cooperation. The men who controlled South Carolina knew that their authority derived from their relatives, so they cooperated with one another for the advantage of the larger kin network. In this way, the value system that transformed gender relations also guided the political culture of the lowcountry.

At the same time elites treated unrelated outsiders ruthlessly for one important reason: exclusivity mattered just as much as cooperation. Lowcountry elites helped each other by quelling external competition. Voting procedures, legislative apportionment, and office-holding qualifications all heavily favored lowcountry elites and reinforced their political dominance of Carolina. The majority of the laws passed benefited members of the Charleston gentry and protected their interests. Lowcountry elite families dominated the assembly and courts. Indeed, elite family networks so effectively monopolized appointments and elected offices that those outside these kin groups found themselves essentially excluded from political life.

The Monopolization of Government

By the 1730s the tumultuous lowcountry had begun to stabilize, and kin networks were entrenched in every facet of lowcountry government. Among other things, Charleston's interrelated gentry kept careful watch over the judiciary. During the colonial era, all Carolina courts and administrative offices remained in Charleston, under the control of interrelated judges and lawyers.[20] All civil and criminal trials took place in Charleston, and all land grants, deeds, and other legal transactions had to be processed there. If backcountry plaintiffs and witnesses failed to make the difficult trip into Charleston for the adjudication of lawsuits, judges simply dismissed their cases. Since the courts were all housed in the city, the lawyers congregated there as well. And many came from the same families. As one observer noted, "All the attorneys centre in Charleston, are acquainted with one another & practice on so liberal a footing as only to adopt so much of the english practice as suits their cases & convenience."[21]

Although distinctly irreligious for most of the eighteenth century, Charleston's gentry nevertheless sought to monopolize church offices as well. A group of interrelated families—the Broughtons, Cordes, Guerards, Lejaus, Harlestons, Mazycks, Ravenals, Balls, and Keiths—dominated the vestry of St. John's Berkeley between 1720 and 1770. During that period, five Balls, six Broughtons, six Cordes, two Lejaus, two Guerards, four Harlestons, two Mazycks, and five Ravenals served as vestrymen and churchwardens. The Broughtons, Cordes, Harlestons, Keiths, and Ravenals served 146 of the 236 total terms on the vestry.[22]

While some families sought dominion over clerical matters, others showed even more aggression in gaining a hold over civil government. In particular, South Carolina's Royal Council caught their eye, although, truth be told, it became only the first among many governmental bodies that fell under the control of Charleston's interrelated gentry.[23] Between 1720 and 1763 the Board of Trade named forty-nine men to the Royal Council. Membership in this body of royally appointed local men hung on family and class connections. Almost all the members were prominent merchants or large planters, so they had great wealth in common. Estate records remain for only seventeen of the forty-nine, but each one's estates were valued at over £9,000. On average, they owned seventy-two slaves and 7,750 acres of land. Wealth alone, however, did not fully determine their selection. Many of the wealthiest Carolinians, including supposedly the richest man in South Carolina, Gabriel Manigault (1704-81), never secured an appointment on the twelve-man council. Personal connections, along with wealth, shaped council appointments. Two groups—one of families, the other of business partners—dominated the membership of the council. The intermarried clan of the Blake, Bull, Drayton, Fenwicke, Izard, and Middleton families held 38 percent of the councillor positions (nineteen of forty-nine) during the entire royal colonial period.[24] Furthermore, the Bull, Drayton, Middleton, and Blake families also included every governor of South Carolina between 1725 and 1756. When James Glen arrived largely unattached to local political elites, John Drayton married his sister, thus allying Glen with the group.[25] Influence with the royally appointed council and governor served to advance these elites' position within the colony and cement their bonds to relatives abroad. Such connections on both sides of the Atlantic strengthened the hand of power-seeking colonists. Their administrative influence, coupled with their presence in legal and clerical matters, made lowcountry elites a force to be reckoned with.

Legal, ecclesiastical, and administrative authority did not, however, satiate the appetites of these elites. Although lowcountry elites used their kin ties to acquire positions in courts and church offices and on the Royal Council, nothing proved more desirable or more useful in their acquisition of power than the Commons House of Assembly. Kin-based political coalitions dominated South Carolina's assembly in the colonial era. Between 1720 and 1760, for example, twenty-one men represented St. George's Parish in the assembly. Nearly half were either Izards or Warings, and three others were related through marriage to the two families.[26]

Saint George's typified the ways in which membership in the colonial assembly remained intricately connected to kinship. The more immersed in Charleston's elaborate kinship networks, the greater the political influence. Individuals who were connected horizontally (within their own generation) and vertically (across generations) to politically active kin held the advantages. Of the 383 men who sat in the assembly between 1721 and 1760, 63 percent were descendants of families arriving in Carolina before 1700, while only 28 percent were first-generation South Carolinians. Moreover, the vast majority of these first-generation assemblymen attained their seats by forming business partnerships with established planter-merchant families or marrying the kinswomen of prominent men.[27]

Lowcountry elites not only controlled their own region, but they also expanded their influence throughout the colony by placing relatives as the virtual representatives of outlying areas. Elite Carolinians considered virtual representation neither irregular nor unfair so long as they benefited from it. In other words, the street ran only one way. Charleston's elites routinely represented outlying parishes, but the parishes within Charleston never elected men who lived outside the city.[28] Virtual representatives in the assembly were based in Charleston and belonged to the city's interrelated gentry. This interrelated gentry therefore maintained a disproportionate number of representative seats in the lower house. As a result, they exercised an enormous amount of power in the assembly.

Prince Frederick's parish, located in the northwestern corner of the colony, illustrates the excessive power of the lowcountry on a variety of levels. The parish, even as it grew ever larger, acquired no more seats or influence, since population did not determine representation in the assembly. Furthermore, between 1721 and 1760 eight of the seventeen men elected were residents of Charleston, while only six lived in Prince Frederick's. Even those few legitimate representatives of Prince Frederick's were excluded from any real power within the colony. The real business of the assembly took place in committees. Those who failed to secure appointments on these committees still voted on at-large issues, but never set the agenda and rarely exercised significant power in the body. Of the six residents of Prince Frederick's who were elected, only one actually filled a position of power on a committee within the assembly. Of the Charlestonians who sat for the parish, all but one held positions of power.[29]

As they took more and more seats in the assembly, lowcountry families gradually expanded the rights of the body. Between 1719 and the 1760s, the assembly secured or in some cases assumed the right to determine qualifications for membership, censure and expel members, regulate voting requirements and districts, settle disputed elections, limit the franchise, influence the frequency of elections and sessions, and apportion representation.[30] Any one of these rights alone could have shifted the locus of power in the colony. Collectively, they rendered these interrelated assemblymen virtually invincible. Moreover, many of these measures, like settling disputed elections and expelling members, provided elites with opportunities to secure political positions for their kin and censure their opposition.

Throughout the colonial period, as they amassed more power within the assembly and insisted on more rights for the assembly, Charleston's representatives grew increasingly insular and interrelated. Many representatives were business partners and old school friends, and most belonged to the same extended families. Assemblymen saw the legislature as an extension of their kin connections, which shaped the way they conducted business. As one lowcountry visitor observed, during legislative sessions "the members conversed, lolled, and chatted much like a friendly jovial society."[31]

In many ways the "tangled cousinry" of the South Carolina Assembly paralleled the Virginia House of Burgesses. While 630 men sat in the House of Burgesses between 1720 and 1776, only 110 ever held any real position of power, and over half were related to Virginia's great families. The powerful members of the Burgesses included eleven members of the Randolph family, nine Carters, eight Beverleys, and six Lees.[32] Both the Virginia Burgesses and the South Carolina Assembly experienced continuity of leadership heavily dominated by family networks, witnessed a relative absence of factionalism, and shared a limited willingness to welcome new members. But while Virginians allowed in new members who served time in local courts and expressed the right religious attitudes, Carolinians cared mostly about pedigree. Whereas prior experience in local government and courts mattered a great deal to Virginians, South Carolinians with no experience at all could sit in the assembly, provided they possessed the right family connections. Indeed, virtually no one held power in the South Carolina Assembly without familial connections.[33]

Charleston elites exercised greater exclusivity in their assembly than their Chesapeake neighbors in part because they lived in closer proximity to one another. Charleston was, after all, a city. Elite men worked in counting houses with their relatives and lived within walking distance of scores of kinsmen. They encountered one another sometimes daily, and the level of intermarriage between groups exceeded the gentry of Virginia. They therefore possessed more opportunities and a greater desire to coordinate political behavior. Since many of Charleston's most powerful merchants cooperated with one another in business dealings and shared a common economic agenda, few political conflicts erupted. And because elite South Carolinians were so interrelated and their economic lives so interwoven, they saw themselves as part of an elaborate kin network. Ultimately their homogeneity and identity as part of these powerful families bound them together. Their desires to protect their interests over unrelated outsiders overrode personal tensions between specific families.

Similar patterns emerged within the merchant communities of Philadelphia, Boston, and New York. Families in these areas, however, never developed as intense a monopoly over public life as Charlestonians attained, and they experienced increased factionalism after the middle of the eighteenth century.[34] In these cities, as in Charleston, politics remained closely connected to kinship. But because powerful families in these regions did not intermarry as frequently as Charlestonians, they often formed competing factions rather than a homogeneous whole. In Philadelphia, for example, exogamous marriage patterns, along with greater ethnic and cultural diversity, yielded divisions between powerful families who then competed with one another in the political arena.[35] Conversely, in South Carolina the interconnectedness of the planter-merchant elite enabled them to avoid internal divisions.

Not distracted by interfamily rivalries, lowcountry elites could concentrate on protecting their own interests and removing outside threats to their authority. Individuals whose ideas did not mesh with those of the gentry sometimes found themselves barred from speaking or even sitting in the assembly. In the late colonial period the assembly tried raising the property qualifications for its members, in order to ensure that only the largest landowners could control politics.³⁶ The legislature even structured the tax system to protect their families' interests. They assessed land taxes at a flat rate so that the rich and improved lands of the lowcountry cost no more than the unimproved lands in the backcountry. The assembly also increasingly assumed responsibility for key political appointments, which the members doled out to relatives—thereby monopolizing power both within and outside the legislature.

The numbers speak for themselves. Between 1730 and 1775, thirty-seven men held significant positions of power within the assembly.³⁷ Of those thirty-seven, twenty-six (70.3 percent) represented the Charleston area at one time or another. Among the eleven important men representing outlying areas, five actually lived in Charleston, and three others held positions of power for less than three terms. In effect, only three of thirty-seven (8.1 percent) positions of significant power were held by men outside the lowcountry.³⁸

Not only did Charlestonians control most of the seats in the assembly and most of the power, but they also stayed in power for a long time. Between 1730 and 1775, thirty men served in the legislature for more than ten years. Ten of the thirty represented parishes outside the lowcountry.³⁹ But of those ten, only two, George Powell and James Parsons, served in the first rank of power, that is, on the assembly's most important committees. None of the other eight ever reached the first ranks of power despite years of service. Tacitus Gaillard sat in the assembly for eighteen years and only once served on a committee of the second rank. Together the ten backcountry representatives amassed almost 150 years of service to the assembly, yet they held positions of power in the first rank for only eight sessions, seven of which were secured by one man, James Parsons. Half of them served in secondary positions of power less than four times over their entire careers.⁴⁰ On the other hand, twenty of the assemblymen who served more than ten years represented the Charleston area. Of these, only five failed to reach the highest rank of power, and at least in one case there is reason to believe this was by choice.⁴¹ The remaining fifteen served an average of over nine years in the highest ranks of power. Conversely, representatives outside the Charleston area served on average less than one term in positions of power.

In South Carolina, a few interrelated lowcountry families held the keys to public offices. Almost no one reached the highest ranks of power without connections to them. A cursory look at backcountry representatives indicated a near absence of similar kinship patterns. Backcountry assemblymen tended to be first generation representatives and served without kinsmen around them. Although backcountry assemblymen may have had the wealth and time to serve in the assembly, they lacked the essential key to real power: kinsmen within the assembly to support their committee involvement. Clearly family, as much as wealth or education, determined who was and who was not at the nexus of political power, just as it determined membership in the elite class.

Threats to Family Empires

These political empires proved so sound that Charleston's interrelated gentry seldom faced challenges from outside their ranks. When they did encounter rivals, members of Charleston's interrelated gentry quickly rose to protect their common interests and silence their opposition. Indeed, by the late eighteenth century the political dominance of South Carolina by tidewater family networks seemed utterly incontestable. The desires of the elites, the preponderance of extended families, South Carolina's racial and legal system, and eighteenth-century cultural values all contributed to the persistence of interrelated kin networks that dominated public life.

Deference no doubt played some role in this, although it is never easy to determine where deferential behavior ended and coercion began. Whether outsiders willingly deferred to the "better sort," or Charleston's powerful families intimidated them into submission, the result was the same: few challenges were ever leveled.[42] And certainly, the interconnected system of political, economic, and social power could easily quash any challenges that might have arisen. Interrelated elites monopolized the political system, they dominated agriculture and trades in the colony, and they held the keys to inclusion in the elite class. The same men who exercised power in the assembly ran the counting houses in town. The planters who grew rice and merchants who traded slaves sat on the Royal Council. Unconnected men who depended on these merchants and planters for their livelihood dared not challenge their political preeminence.

Still, even minor challenges produced sharp, immediate reactions. In one instance, lowcountry elites, angered by the anti-elite preaching of minister William Tennent, added a clause to the state constitution prohibiting members of the clergy from serving as governor, lieutenant governor, or member of Congress or the Privy Council.[43] As one observer explained, they "fixed on him & his cloth a political silence forever," because he "opposed with great eloquence . . . the attempts that were made to establish hierarchy."[44]

Political challenges, no matter how informed by deference, all produced similar reactions. In the election of 1768, backcountry regulators and a group of mechanics from Charleston nominated, for the first time, their own slate of officers. Their choices were all men of rank, and thus not a direct challenge to lowcountry elites. Still, the mere organization and political participation of artisans, while it validated the deferential political framework, nonetheless troubled elites. Henry Laurens lamented this change: "We are become very important in this Town in the Electioneering business.... Therefore if you hear that I am no longer a Parliament Man, let not your Excellency wonder, for I walk on in the old road, give no Barbacu nor ask any Man for Votes." In reaction to this perceived threat to their political power, lowcountry families became increasingly defensive and conservative.[45]

The only significant challenge to lowcountry families' political dominance came from migrants into the backcountry. Between 1765 and 1767 new boundary lines were drawn in the backcountry, near present-day Anderson and Abbeville counties, which opened up the Carolina backcountry to white settlement. The extension of colonial boundaries coupled with a general security from Indian wars yielded tremendous growth of backcountry settlements. By the late 1760s three-quarters of the population of South Carolina lived in the backcountry. But the lowcountry still maintained 86 percent of the colony's taxable wealth and just over half of the assembly seats.[46]

The growth of the backcountry and the tidewater's persistent refusal to share power precipitated conflict between the two regions. The regional struggle exploded in 1767 after the new governor, Lord Montagu, pardoned a number of men convicted of breaking into houses and stealing horses in frontier communities. Backcountry farmers called "regulators," headed by Charles Woodmason, petitioned the governor to overturn these pardons. Then, their grievances moved beyond the issue of pardons. Angered by their region's continued political marginalization, the regulators petitioned the assembly for adequate schools, jails, and courts. Even though they composed the majority of the colony's population, backcountry settlers were still required to travel to Charleston to avail themselves of all judicial services and political activities. Finally, and most disturbingly, regulators demanded a reassessment of apportionment in the assembly, where the backcountry remained grossly underrepresented.[47] Despite the reasonable appeals for representational equity, powerful tidewater families refused to loosen their grip on the assembly. In the late 1760s and early 1770s they reluctantly sent two companies of rangers to police the backcountry, replaced the centralized office of provost marshal with a new system of local sheriffs, and established circuit courts to better serve the backcountry. But they firmly resisted reapportioning the legislature.[48]

This refusal to equitably share control of the state with the backcountry continued throughout the late eighteenth century. By 1790, the Charleston district comprised only 11 percent of the state's population, but elected 47 percent of the state representatives and 45 percent of the senators. (The backcountry did not achieve representational parity until the early nineteenth century.) Lowcountry elites remained intent on holding on to their power and even resorted to duplicity to do so. In 1790, during the state constitutional convention, lowcountry politicians agreed to move the state capital from Charleston to Columbia. Backcountry residents hoped that physically separating the capital from Charleston would wrest control of the state from lowcountry elite families. But they were sorely disappointed. Moving the capital did little to ameliorate the power imbalance in state politics: many lowcountry leaders simply ignored the fact that Columbia now served as the seat of state government, going so far as to replicate state offices in Charleston.[49]

Family identity played an important role in this regional conflict. Sharing power within the lowcountry posed few problems for the gentry class because they were able, quite literally, to keep things all in the family. Younger relatives, new husbands, and distant kin could be welcomed into the power nexus because they posed no significant threat to established kin groups. On the contrary, they served to extend influence in political life. Sharing power with unrelated backcountry settlers was another matter entirely. The vast majority of backcountry settlers migrated from Pennsylvania, North Carolina, and Virginia, and so the two regions shared virtually no family connections with one another. The powerful families that emerged in the west in the early nineteenth century and whose names are associated with antebellum leadership in the backcountry—the Calhouns, Andersons, Hammonds, Hamptons, and Pickens—traced their roots through the Shenandoah Valley. In fact, the Anderson, Pickens, and Calhoun families all moved into the Carolina frontier in the late eighteenth century from the same county in Virginia. Few lowcountry elites migrated to the frontier or married into backcountry families. Instead, they remained in the tidewater, immersed in their concentric kin circles, detached from and disdainful of western residents. The absence of familial connections contributed to the tidewater elites' skepticism and fear of rising backcountry elites: they were outsiders who threatened family power. Backcountry planters posed a significant political and economic challenge to tidewater supremacy as they increasingly rivaled Charleston's elites in both number and wealth. Not wanting to aid potential rivals of members of their kin group, tidewater politicians therefore resisted at every turn backcountry demands for political inclusion and an equitable share in state government. Their resistance proved insurmountable. Although backcountry settlers forced some concessions, the close of the eighteenth century saw no significant transformation in the political behaviors of these lowcountry elites and no dramatic shift in the locus of power in South Carolina politics.

The Revolution in Charleston

By the time backcountry migrants leveled these largely unsuccessful challenges, Charleston's planter-merchants had already weathered their darkest days: the war for American independence. South Carolinians experienced the full force of the brutality and viciousness of the Revolutionary War.[50] After the fighting ended, Governor John Rutledge insisted, "The good People of this state have not only felt the Common Calamities of War, but from the Wanton and Savage manner in which it has been prosecuted they have experienced such severities as are unpractised and will Scarcely be Credited by Civilized Nations." And, as Reverend Archibald Simpson surveyed the lowcountry in 1783–84, he found it in utter shambles: "Robberies and murders are often committed on the public roads. The people that remain have been peeled, pilaged, and plundered . . . [and] a dark melancholy gloom appears everywhere."[51]

In the face of such troubles, lowcountry residents turned to their kin.[52] Indeed, for South Carolinians the Revolutionary era cannot be understood apart from familial experiences. Brothers, cousins, and other members of the kin group enlisted and fought and sometimes died together. Lines between patriot and loyalist frequently took shape according to family membership. And the general reliance on kinship networks that characterized the lives of early-eighteenth-century Charlestonians expanded during the War for Independence.

In letters to one another, South Carolinians frequently discussed the Revolutionary War in familial terms. After the fall of Charleston, Governor John Rutledge lamented that "neither the Tears of Mothers, nor the Cries of Infants could excite in their Brests, pity or Compassion." Francis Kinloch wrote his guardian, Thomas Boone, that "such scenes have been perpetuated of Officers whom I could Name, & whose families are amongst the first in Great Britain, as would make you, and every worthy Englishman blush for the degeneracy of the Nation." Oliver Hart and his brother believed that the Revolution, "is the Legacy we mean to bequeath to our Posterity; In the Enjoyment of which our Children's Children to the last stages of Time, will rise up and call us blessed."[53] But family was far more than simply a rhetorical device. Kin played critical roles in practical reactions to war and in the intellectual construction of the American patriot movement.

Family membership frequently determined political allegiances as brothers and cousins joined or resisted the Revolutionary cause together.[54] The first blood of the American Revolution in South Carolina was drawn near Ninety-Six when Patrick Cunningham, a loyalist, seized a wagon train carrying gunpowder in an attempt to force Carolina patriots to free his brother who was imprisoned for sedition. Brothers Gabriel and Joseph Manigault joined the militia together just days after Gabriel returned from Europe. Upon their return from studying abroad Charles Cotesworth and Thomas Pinckney also took up the patriot cause together. Both served as captains in the South Carolina militia and the Continental army. In 1778 they went together on an expedition to St. Augustine and joined the assault on Savannah. British soldiers captured and imprisoned the brothers during the occupation of Charleston. When they were exchanged in 1781 they fled to Philadelphia with other kin. The Fenwick brothers embraced and abandoned the American cause together. The elder brother, Edward Fenwick, Jr., never seemed quite able to determine his loyalties during the Revolutionary War. In 1778 and 1779 he served as colonel in the Carolina militia, but deserted in 1779 to join the British. His brother Thomas also joined the militia and, along with Edward, deserted when the British invaded Carolina.[55]

Revolutionary political leadership followed the same path of sibling and kin-based allegiances. South Carolina's delegates to the First Continental Congress, for instance, were closely related. The 1774 delegation included brothers John and Edward Rutledge, Henry Middleton (Edward Rutledge's father-in-law), Christopher Gadsden (father-in-law of Andrew Rutledge, brother of John and Edward), and Thomas Lynch.[56]

Although many men formed loyalist or patriot allegiances based on family identity, the Revolutionary War also divided some Carolina families, both geographically and ideologically. The war caught two generations of the Manigault family on opposite sides of the Atlantic, although they were united in the patriot cause. Gabriel Manigault wrote his grandson and namesake in London about the flood of loyalists out of the state and back to England. The movement worked both ways, for the younger Gabriel responded, "In a short time I shall be almost the only Carolinian in London."[57] Although he remained in England during the early stages of the crisis, Gabriel kept in close contact with his friends and family in Carolina, and groomed himself for patriot service. He and John Laurens in particular spoke of the necessity of "Young Americans now, to qualify themselves for the Service to their Country."[58]

While the Atlantic divided Gabriel Manigault from his family, other relatives found themselves torn apart by ideology. As the colonists and the mother country went to war, so too did the powerful Bull family. Lieutenant Governor William Bull, for example, refused to renounce his allegiance to the crown. When the Provincial Congress formed the Council of Safety and granted it executive powers on 14 June 1775, the Revolutionary government relied on family ties to avoid blatantly offending Bull: the Congress sent as messengers two of his nephews, Stephen Bull and William Henry Drayton, who were among Carolina's strongest revolutionaries.[59] Mary Hutson Peronneau found herself torn between her loyalist husband and her patriot siblings. Ultimately she decided to remain in Carolina with her siblings even though her husband, Arthur Peronneau, fought for the British—demonstrating that in some cases the pull of sibling loyalty overrode marital connections. Peronneau reached her decision only after much anguish and heartache. Mary's brother compared the grief that accompanied such family separations to the biblical expulsion of Adam and Eve from the garden of Eden.[60]

Loyalism was quite common in Carolina, especially in the frontier regions.[61] While preaching in the backcountry in late 1775, Oliver Hart encountered so many outspoken opponents of the growing estrangement between the colonies and England that he feared they would never be moved on the subject of American rights. One man informed Hart after a sermon that he would never raise arms against his government and that he strongly disapproved of the tactics of lowcountry political leaders. Further, he insisted that he and his neighbors received threats because of their loyalty to Britain. Despite the intimidation, the man remained so resolute in his convictions that Hart found little reason to believe backcountry settlers would ever "be brought to have a suitable regard to ye Interest of America."[62]

Both loyalists and patriots employed threats and intimidation to garner support for their cause, and, because family played such a powerful role in political identity, they used family as a bargaining chip in these tactics. In the early stages of the war, patriots seized loyalists' estates and threatened loyalist families until they fled the colony. Similarly, the British targeted patriot families for retribution during the occupation of Charleston. After the fall of the city, relatives of active patriots often faced imprisonment, forced exile, and the confiscation of their estates. One general ordered his men to "take particular care, that the familys of those who have joined the enemy are not suffered to remain on their plantations but sent off immediately."[63]

While they feared British retribution for treason during the occupation, elite South Carolinians also worried that the war would destroy their carefully constructed social order. In particular, they feared a violent uprising within the slave community. Rumors of slave insurrections swept the colony during the early stages of the war, and many patriots believed that the British government acted as a co-conspirator in these plots to unseat local white rule. Even when fears of a violent slave rebellion dissipated, elites remained apprehensive that the ideology of the Revolution would dismantle their social order, particularly by challenging slavery. By war's end, they had determined that the Revolution would have to be confined to serve the interests of the "better sorts" and refrain from challenging racial and class hierarchy in any significant way. Despite their plans, after the Revolutionary War, elite Carolinians faced the first serious external criticism of their hierarchical society. They were forced to consider the implications of their social order and construct a new defense of it.[64]

Gender similarly received fresh attention in the Revolutionary era, as women filled new roles during the war.[65] Women found themselves pushed, metaphorically and physically, outside their homes. In the first place, the trauma of war forced them to assume full control of family houses, businesses, and plantations. War also caused women to expand their financial and emotional reliance on their kin.[66] Women fleeing the city after the British occupation frequently traveled with kin, moved temporarily into the homes of family members in the countryside, and oversaw the care of young people separated from their parents because of the war. Harriott Pinckney Horry gathered her kin at her Santee River Plantation when the British marched on Charleston in 1780. The group included Harriott's mother, Eliza Pinckney, Harriott's sister-in-law Sally (Sarah) Middleton Pinckney, Sally's sisters, Henrietta Middleton Rutledge and Hester Middleton Drayton, the wives of several other prominent patriot leaders, and all these women's children. During the war, Rebecca Brewton Motte's three daughters and the widow of Rebecca's nephew lived together at her plantation, St. Joseph. In letters to her brother Gabriel, Anne Manigault assured him that the women in her family remained safe and together, and told him how, along with her grandmother, aunt, and cousins, she had fled Charleston for the safety of the countryside. Occasionally, men worked with women in coordinating these evacuations. As brothers-in-law Isaac Hayne and Richard Hutson prepared to join the war effort together, they moved the women in their family, including Hayne's sister-in-law Mary Peronneau and his wife, Elizabeth Hutson Hayne, out of harm's way. When Elizabeth died and Isaac became a prisoner of war, Peronneau took charge of their four children and escorted them to British headquarters to plead unsuccessfully for their imprisoned father's life.[67]

Ironically, while many women found themselves expelled from their homes and forced to endure great hardships as a result of war, other women enjoyed greater legal latitude during the Revolutionary era. The case of loyalist wives is particularly revealing in this context. Occasionally, the wives of avowed loyalists renounced their husbands' actions and sided with the patriot cause. When that happened, the South Carolina government treated them like widows and allowed them to independently retain one-third of the family holdings.[68] The question of sincerity invariably arises here. Were wives genuinely differing from husbands in their political ideology? Or did women manipulate this legal loophole in order to maintain part of their estates? Patriots understandably wanted to encourage support for their cause. But allowing wives a political voice—even if it was to promote the patriot agenda—set a troubling precedent by potentially undermining the subordination of wives to patriarchs. Lowcountry patriots faced a difficult choice in this matter. They could discourage support by overturning the law granting dissident wives a widow's third, or they could encourage challenges to patriarchy by recognizing women's independent political identity.

For most women, war proved more physically dangerous and financially disruptive than personally liberating. Even Eliza Pinckney suffered fiscally, despite all her careful plans. Before the war Eliza controlled, by her own conservative accounting, "a fortune sufficiency to live Genteely in any part of the world, that fortune too in different kinds of property, and in four or five part of the Country." During the war, patriots seized her cattle and timber, and British troops occupied four houses she owned. Consequently, she found herself unable to repay even minor debts.[69]

Both women and men suffered as the fighting dragged on and South Carolina's situation worsened. And in response to the gravity of their situations, Carolinians turned more and more to their siblings and kin for financial and moral support. Brothers-in-law Isaac Motte and William Drayton infused their war letters with discussions of family responsibilities. After the fall of Charleston, Isaac Motte was forced to flee to Philadelphia. In his time of peril, he turned to his brother-in-law William Drayton. Motte suffered such heavy losses that he could scarcely provide for his family. More troubling, he reported, "My Brother Jacob and all my Relations . . . are Prisoners." Financially strapped, Motte relied on Drayton to assume responsibility for his debts abroad and loan him money. He also asked Drayton to fulfill one of his familial obligations. Before the war broke out, Motte agreed to support his other brother-in-law William Smith, as Smith traveled in England. After his losses in Charleston undermined his ability to do so, Motte asked Drayton to provide financial and emotional support for Smith.[70]

Even after the fighting ended, the demand for such aid from kin continued. In particular, Carolina loyalists needed their relatives to help them negotiate the difficult process of reclaiming their confiscated estates.[71] They also tried to reconstruct ties with their patriot kin and friends who possessed the power to get the petitions for their estates granted. Political conservatives in the state, eager to rebuild connections to the thriving markets in London and derail the radical impulses of the Revolution by reasserting traditional elite culture, answered the appeals. Restoring the ties of family and friendship between political conservatives in Charleston and exiled loyalists facilitated both a return to lucrative foreign markets and a revivified elite solidarity in the lowcountry. Elites in the 1780s and 1790s were therefore able to regain the wealth that the war had compromised and thwart the challenges to their control that had grown out of the radical, democratizing impulses of the Revolution.

The American Revolution was, after all, about far more than a war for independence. John Adams, Thomas Paine, and a host of other patriots insisted that the real revolution was in men's hearts and minds: in the ways they envisioned themselves and governed their society. Thus, the Revolution ushered in a new political culture and social ideology in America.[72] Among other things, the ideology of the Revolution rejected patriarchy and deference as acceptable models for political culture. But men continued to embrace patriarchy as the preferable system for household governance. Wives and daughters remained outside the framework of this political philosophy. Slaves and propertyless white men could not, under this theory, exercise virtue and were thus denied inclusion in the body politic.[73] The brotherhood of Revolutionary political rhetoric and theory, then, applied only to property-holding white men.

South Carolina politics had long operated, within the governing elite, under an unspoken sibling model of cooperation and equanimity. At the same time, this ruling elite excluded unrelated rivals and exploited African slaves in order to promote their status and class solidarity. So embracing a political philosophy that required equality—but only among a select few—did not require a radical transformation in lowcountry political culture.

Charleston's elites held on to their power in the wake of the Revolution, but not without a great deal of opposition and struggle, as new challenges arose both within South Carolina and without. Slavery in the age of the Revolution provoked difficult new questions, both within the slave quarters and from northern states outlawing the institution. Backcountry settlers, artisans, and small farmers rejected deferential political behavior and boldly insisted on a greater voice in the new state.

While new challenges threatened the elite-dominated social and political order in South Carolina, the close of the eighteenth century saw little dramatic change in the political actions of lowcountry elites. The War for Independence did, in the short term, influence family life within the elite class by encouraging a renewed reliance on siblings and kin. Elites experienced once again the logistical and practical needs for extensive kin networks, and relatives were brought closer together by the turbulence of war. Once the war ended, the gentry saw threats to familial and class identity leveled from new corners, and became convinced that the ideological implications of the Revolution required a vigorous reassertion of the old order.

Lowcountry elites effectively delayed the move of significant numbers of nonelites and backcountry residents into the political system because of their long tradition of protecting kin and class interests against outside threats and through their remarkable cohesion. The structure of South Carolina political systems, which privileged Charleston and its gentry leaders over other regions and residents, also aided them in this conservation of local, elite control. These factors—the traditions, the self-conscious commitment, and the logistics—enabled Charleston's interrelated gentry to keep their power despite the disintegration of deferential politics throughout America. For a generation or more after the Revolution, Charleston's ruling class resisted the radicalism of the Revolution and continued to monopolize political power in the state.

A New Republic and New Complications

Lowcountry elites carried their kinship ties, their class solidarity, and their quest for power into the new republic. In fact, in the early national period, the lowcountry planter-merchants' desire to protect familial interests spread beyond the borders of South Carolina and influenced national politics as well.[74] In the spring of 1787 South Carolina, along with the other states, dispatched a delegation to Philadelphia to revise the Articles of Confederation. The South Carolina representatives seemed not unlike those from Pennsylvania, New York, or Virginia. The four men, three lawyers and a planter, were all experienced political leaders who had served the patriot cause. But John Rutledge, Charles Cotesworth Pinckney, Charles Pinckney, and Pierce Butler shared more than wealth and political experience: they were family. Charles Cotesworth Pinckney and Charles Pinckney were cousins; John Rutledge was

Charles Cotesworth's brother-in-law; and Pierce Butler's wife was a relative of the wives of John Rutledge and Charles Cotesworth Pinckney. All four knew and respected one another. They socialized together, shared political ideas and offices, and to varying degrees recognized one another as members of their extended family.[75]

Protecting their familial interests and those of the merchant-planter elites in the lowcountry numbered among the South Carolina delegates' greatest concerns during the convention. It was widely understood that the Pinckneys, Rutledge, and Butler all firmly supported an aristocratic republic, protection of property interests, expansion of trade and commercial ventures, and a strong central government. Once in Philadelphia they also led the fight for a fugitive slave act and the maintenance of the international slave trade, eventually returning to Charleston with much of what they wanted.

Ratifying the Constitution depended on the support of Charleston's political families. The lowcountry endorsed the Constitution in large part because of the efforts of Charles Cotesworth Pinckney, his brother Thomas, his cousin Charles, his brother-in-law Edward Rutledge, and Edward Rutledge's brothers Hugh and John. The Rutledge and Pinckney coalition, rooted in boyhood ties forged during their education in England, eventually shaped the political destiny of the state and the young nation. In the wake of the Revolution, the Rutledges and Pinckneys formed the most powerful political alliance in South Carolina. In 1787, while his brother Charles Cotesworth attended the Constitutional convention in Philadelphia with their cousin Charles and brother-in-law John Rutledge, Thomas Pinckney assumed the governorship of South Carolina. He strongly supported ratification and along with Charles Cotesworth Pinckney, Charles Pinckney, and the Rutledge brothers, ensured Carolina's acceptance of the Constitution.[76] The kinship connections of the South Carolina delegation to the Constitutional convention and the intermingling of the personal and the political that occurred during the ratification debates marked the culmination of a century-long pattern in South Carolina political culture: family considerations determined political action.

Of course, differences sometimes arose between members of the state's political leadership. Despite substantial common ground, political factions did emerge in early national Charleston, and members of powerful kin groups occasionally disagreed over political philosophy and struggled with personal rivalries. Sometimes the very interrelated nature of lowcountry elites presented problems within kin groups. In 1774 Charles Pinckney and his brother-in-law Miles Brewton stood for election to the First Continental Congress. Pinckney and

Brewton lost the race to Henry Middleton and Edward Rutledge, the father-in-law and brother-in-law of Charles Cotesworth Pinckney. Charles Cotesworth no doubt found himself torn between his cousin Charles and his in-laws. This difficulty was not unique to the early republic. Throughout his career as colonial lieutenant governor, William Bull II's loyalties were divided between the crown and his family in Carolina. Because of this "duality of roles," appointed colonial officials, particularly members of the Royal Council, often experienced similar conflicts between the crown's wishes and their families' needs.[77]

More often in post-Revolutionary Carolina, divisions occurred between rather than within kin groups. During the 1790s, four Federalist factions existed in Charleston, all based on kin connections. One included Ralph Izard and his sons-in-law William Loughton Smith and Gabriel Manigault. A second consisted of Josiah Smith, his brother George, and their business partners Daniel DeSassure and Edward Darnell. (DeSassure and Darnell also served as leaders of the Chamber of Commerce and directors of the branch of the Bank of the United States.) Brothers William and Jacob Read and Jacob's brother-in-law James Simons constituted a third group. Perhaps most important was the Pinckney-Rutledge faction.[78] Brothers William and Jacob Read maintained a long-running political and personal conflict with the Rutledge brothers. William referred to John Rutledge as an "Arrogant Puppy," and insisted he appeared "most industriously aiming at popularity by every way & means." The Reads did everything they could to thwart the careers of the Rutledges. In 1795 Senator Jacob Read numbered among those who rejected George Washington's nomination of John Rutledge as chief justice of the Supreme Court. Ralph Izard and his sons-in-law, longtime friends and kinsmen of the Rutledge family, rose to Rutledge's defense. Following the failed confirmation, Izard wrote Senator Read, expressing his dismay and disapproval: "I am of the opinion that no Man in the United States would execute the Office of Chief Justice with more ability, & integrity." The following year Ralph Izard criticized Read's character in a letter to Charles Cotesworth Pinckney: "When I think of his [Read's] vanity, pomposity . . . I fear that something, not perfectly respectable either to himself, or the State, may now & then escape from him."[79]

Still, political power brokers tried to keep these divisions to a minimum because they all knew that inclusion in political life required extensive kin connections. If a man alienated his kin, he lost the one irreplaceable requirement for political office. Even if he remained a wealthy gentleman, he faced little better chance of securing a position than an unconnected artisan or a backcountry farmer. Wealth and ability alone were not enough. Family was essential.

Therefore, individuals antagonized powerful relatives at their own peril. For their part, siblings and kin worked hard to avoid such conflicts because they brought discord and heartache into the family and undermined the power of the larger kin network. Elites much preferred to focus their scorn on outsiders rather than their own relatives.

Most of the time their interconnectedness pulled lowcountry elites together rather than tearing them apart. Despite infrequent internal divisions, elite families maintained a strong sense of unity and an impenetrable hold over political life in South Carolina by carefully blending egalitarianism and exclusivity. Within their own ranks, elites could be cooperative and supportive. But those outside the kin circle were threats, and their ambitions had to be stymied whenever possible.

THE APPLICATION of these values to political life doubtless seemed, from the perspective of lowcountry elites, like a roaring success. By perfecting the early American pattern of using family ties to acquire political power, they exercised greater cohesion and more authority than elites in other regions. Throughout the eighteenth century, a few interrelated families monopolized political life in South Carolina. In 1790, just as in 1690, kin ties offered the surest — and often the only — path to political power. Offices still passed from relative to relative. Kinship remained the dominant structure of these political networks, and essentially the same kin groups controlled South Carolina on the eve of the nineteenth century.

Wealthy Charlestonians spent the better part of the eighteenth century constructing this system. They transformed their family lives to promote their economic and political agendas and used their power to advance family status. Two ironies emerge. First, the elaborate systems of kinship, the commitment to kin and class solidarity, and the conservative, localistic agenda that ensured these elites' success in the eighteenth century contributed to their undoing in the antebellum era. And second, their power derived from attitudes rooted in sibling relationships: cooperation, mutuality, and loyalty. Thus, the same values that made Charleston's gentry exclusive and dominant also made them interdependent and egalitarian.

Conclusion

The bonds of "blood and friendship" that Eliza Lucas evoked with such passion in the 1740s referred to far more than simply some sentimental, emotional attachment.¹ It suggests nothing less than the model for class identity and culture among Charleston's interrelated planter-merchants. The "hidden family" of siblings and kin reveals the interconnections between the creation of class, economic and political developments, the construction of identity, the socialization of children, and the nature of gender relations in the eighteenth-century lowcountry. Furthermore, these family networks played a critical role in the future of those early Carolinians and holds powerful implications for scholars looking back at the past. For South Carolinians, the gentry's family values produced unanticipated consequences in the early nineteenth century. For historians, this study of siblings and kin points out the necessity of broadening the definitions of what family meant and how it functioned in the past.

More than anything else, Charleston's gentry wanted power. Siblings and kin made their goal a reality. Visiting patterns, estate settlements, business transactions, child rearing, legislative action, and expressive letters collectively testify to the importance of siblings and kin among lowcountry elites and helped them realize their ultimate ambition. Using their kin networks, these elites created their own "earthly paradise" along Carolina's shore. By the middle of the eighteenth century, Charleston's interrelated gentry presided over an elaborate, exploitive social order.

They did not realize until it was too late that they had actually built a house of cards. Intent on protecting and extending family interests at all costs, the gentry grew ever more insular and conservative. Few migrated out of the lowcountry. Those who remained generation after generation continued the pattern of familial and social cohesion—but with mixed consequences. Elite domination of businesses and politics, for instance, protected their power and excluded potential rivals. But it also limited the infusion of new ideas and new people into public life. While the majority of the planter-merchants of Charleston embraced the patriot cause during the War for Independence, they rejected most of the democratizing impulses of the Revolution. Despite growing appeals from small farmers and backcountry migrants for a voice in state government, the lowcountry gentry refused to loosen their grip on South Carolina politics.

Similarly, monopolizing education increased their insularity and prestige— but this too produced unintended results. By sending their relatives abroad to study, planters and merchants ensured that prominent young men received the finest European education while avoiding funding local schools and the risk of training competitors. The few educational opportunities available in Charleston, apprenticing with local merchants or reading law with established lawyers, also required inclusion in Charleston's concentric circles of kin. Both formal and informal education therefore protected elites' interests and increased the gulf between these families and other lowcountry residents.[2] At the same time, this left many of their less prosperous neighbors intellectually impoverished and the lowcountry out of step with the educational innovations of the early nineteenth century. Social events like horse races, plays, and concerts likewise offered forums for the display of elite wealth and power, while publicly expressing the distance between the planter-merchant class and those outside its ranks. These social institutions reinforced elites' sense of cohesion and superiority, which in turn left them exceedingly reluctant to change.

At the core of this inward-looking, reactionary culture lay an intense class identity fostered by bonds of kinship. These interrelated elites envisioned themselves as the best of the "better sort." Their kin networks brought them unrivaled wealth and power. Why should they change and risk their position? The bonds cemented by their familial networks and the great success derived from those connections left the gentry unwilling to accept new ideas and new blood into the ruling class. Their preoccupation with family status along with the sense of entitlement that accompanied inclusion in Charleston's "tangled cousinry" produced an aversion to the changes facing them in the antebellum era.

Familial adaptation and cultural cohesion affected both the gentry and the slaves whose labor produced their wealth. In the early colonial era, both whites and blacks in the lowcountry were forced to redefine their conceptions of family. Each group suffered from high mortality rates in the harsh lowcountry environment, and neither could build families like those from the world they left behind. People from Africa faced an added burden: the deliberate separation from family members perpetuated by slave traders. To varying degrees then, black and white migrants into the lowcountry had to reimagine what family meant and bring into the familial world individuals who might not otherwise belong. The scant evidence available simply precludes determining the degree to which white Carolinians borrowed this practice from (or lent it to) enslaved Africans. We do know that the gentry's determination to remain in close contact and their refusal to migrate out of the lowcountry fostered strong cultural conservatism not only within their own ranks but also within the slave communities they regulated. Elites did not leave the lowcountry often, nor, consequently, did their slaves. Limited migration was one of a number of factors that enabled slaves there to create a culturally cohesive community more heavily reliant on African traditions than slaves in other regions of eighteenth-century America.[3]

Ironically, while this cultural conservatism promoted greater autonomy among enslaved Africans, it contributed to the undoing of the master class. The choices elites made in the eighteenth century came back to haunt them in the early nineteenth century, and both their families and the state of South Carolina paid a heavy price for their conservatism. In particular, the interrelated gentry's aggressive support of strict racial rankings and the institution of slavery proved disastrous. In the early colonial era the lowcountry had committed itself to a slave-produced, staple-crop economy. By 1860 slaves represented half the total wealth of the lowcountry and had made the slaveholders there some of the richest people in the South.[4] But what made Charleston's gentry so wealthy in the eighteenth century put them on the wrong side of history in the antebellum era. Lowcountry slaveholders invested more and more money in slaves, and they spent more and more energy defending their peculiar institution against a growing onslaught of anti-slavery activism. Their desire to promote white solidarity in the face of mounting criticisms of slaveholding no doubt chipped away at their exclusivity. And their insistence on defending slavery at any cost pulled them into a devastating, futile war. In early 1861, near the very spot where African slaves first disembarked onto Carolina's shore almost two hundred years earlier, Governor Francis Pickens launched a war to defend the indefensible institution of slavery. Charleston went on to suffer great financial and physical hardships, like so many other areas of the South, for this reactionary stance. After defeat by the Union in 1865, economic and social decline quickly turned into utter collapse as slaveholding Charlestonians permanently lost the source of most of their wealth.

The economic crisis that derived from the destruction of slavery during the Civil War represented the most profound of many fiscal difficulties that gentry attitudes contributed to in the early nineteenth century. During the antebellum era, this flourishing commercial community began a long struggle against economic decline.[5] Some of this declension lay beyond the control of Charleston's planters and merchants. They lost out in the rice market to India and the old Southwest. And, in the early nineteenth century, tidewater elites watched up-country cotton planters surpass them.[6] Still, much of this economic decline came at their own hands. Lowcountry Carolinians rejected most of the economic and social transformations that swept through America in the early nineteenth century. When, for example, a railroad company tried in 1814 to link Charleston to the growing commercial economy of the nation, city leaders refused to allow the company to lay tracks to the wharves—they insisted the line stop at the city limits.[7] Such obstinacy meant that Charleston lost out on the international shipping business to more receptive southern port towns like New Orleans and Mobile. Whenever Charlestonians seemed unprepared or unwilling to immerse themselves in the market economy, other cities happily took their place. Not surprisingly, then, between 1800 and 1860 Charleston fell from the fifth largest city in America to the twenty-second. To be sure, complex financial issues played more active roles in the economic diminution of the lowcountry. But family, by helping to produce a conservative ruling class, laid the cultural foundation for resistance to change and, consequently, economic decline.

Political influence followed a similar path. As the state's economic base shifted to the up-country in the early nineteenth century, so did political power.[8] Lowcountry elites successfully forestalled the egalitarian implications of the American Revolution in the last decades of the eighteenth century. But in 1808 they were finally forced to reapportion the state legislature and recognize the growing influence of up-country cotton planters in representative government. By the mid-nineteenth century the Pickens, Calhouns, and Butlers of the up-country seized the political momentum and began to eclipse lowcountry politicians on both the state and national scenes. Lowcountry elites, who shared few familial connections (and no desire to build more) with these backcountry politicians, offered little effective resistance as they watched their greatest fears come to pass. Perhaps, they slowly realized, their "earthly paradise" was a "damned fraud" after all.

Of course, the most important thing about the power of the lowcountry gentry was not how quickly it slipped away in the early decades of the nineteenth century, but rather how it was crafted and secured throughout the eighteenth century. In Charleston, family supplied the motivation and the means for creating elite identity. It also provided the foundation for the gentry's social ethos. Members of this interrelated elite class embraced the same attitudes of cooperation, mutuality, and loyalty that governed sibling connections between children. Gender relations, political and economic developments, and class identity all stemmed from the same core cultural values. Members of this interrelated class operated as equals, sharing financial resources, political offices, child-rearing responsibilities, and decision-making power. Over time they became mutually dependent and shared reciprocal responsibilities. They focused less on individual gain and more on the success of the whole kin network. Within the inner circle, elites protected and respected each other. They quickly resolved internal disputes and easily overwhelmed unrelated rivals. Disregarding most gender and age rankings within their sibling sets and blurring familial lines inside their class, elites paradoxically intensified their enforcement of class and race distinctions outside their ranks. In fact, the cooperative ethos pervading their own circles allowed the gentry to more ruthlessly control and exploit poorer whites, African Americans, and Indians. Rooted in the intimate bonds of sibling relations, the Carolina gentry built their empire on a seemingly contradictory combination of cooperation and exclusivity. They would have been the first to recognize that the culture they inhabited and the great power that they came to wield flowed from these blood ties and emotional bonds.

THE EXPLANATORY POWER of siblings and kin is not, however, limited by the boundaries of South Carolina. First, the South Carolina example discloses a great deal about kinship and elite culture in eighteenth-century America. South Carolina's planter-merchants more fully realized what elites throughout eighteenth-century America haltingly achieved: cooperative monopolization of public life and rigid control over those outside their ranks. Charlestonians, bound by elaborate kinship ties, behaved very much like wealthy, powerful families in other regions of North America. All along the Atlantic seaboard, early Americans manipulated family connections to acquire political power. Elites in New England, the Mid-Atlantic, and the Chesapeake Bay assumed the lion's share of political offices, and used their public positions

Conclusion 145

to advance family status.⁹ Kin-based businesses also developed in other colonies. Among Massachusetts merchants, family formed the core of economic activity. Since there were few banks, insurance companies, or other financial institutions, relatives provided the credit and connections for business ventures.¹⁰ Merchants in Philadelphia and New York entered into financially motivated marriages and used kin ties to secure contacts and credit abroad. In the Chesapeake, family connections allowed planters to expand their lucrative tobacco culture.¹¹

South Carolinians did these same things—they just did them better. Consequently, they surpassed the gentry in these areas in both the scope and the longevity of their power. Prominent families in eighteenth-century Boston, New York, and Philadelphia failed to match the level of cohesion among Charleston's elites. Although elites in these cities married within their class, cooperated in business ventures, and often shared common political agendas, they remained more culturally and ideologically divided. As a result, they split into family-based factions rather than forming a homogeneous whole. The lowcountry lacked the cultural pluralism of Philadelphia or the religious idealism of New England, which tempered elite ambitions in those regions. Unlike their far-flung plantation neighbors in Virginia or Georgia, Charlestonians lived in a concentrated city and did not have to overcome geographic obstacles in the construction of their empires. Charleston provided a perfect hothouse environment for the creation of a unified, kin-based elite class. Most elites maintained houses in town and lived within walking distance of many of their relatives. They saw one another sometimes daily, so they could efficiently coordinate everything from cousin marriages to political strategies. No ethnic or religious cleavages split them apart. Neither religious ideals nor cultural values offered significant restraints on their behavior. Charleston's elites were wealthier than most other colonists, more closely interrelated, and more single-minded in their desires. They possessed the kin ties and the homogeneity and the cultural values to make the Carolina lowcountry the most insular, exclusive area in eighteenth-century America. But they accomplished this by employing practices common to elites throughout eighteenth-century America.

Kinship was not, however, the exclusive dominion of elites. It provides explanatory power far beyond the great houses of the eighteenth century and calls into question some of the fundamental assumptions about the nature of early American society. First, the sibling and kin universe demonstrates the interconnections between family and society while blurring the traditionally exaggerated lines between "public" and "private." By moving the definition of family outside the conjugal household, we can see clearly that kinship ties played critical roles in economic, governmental, and legal activities. Conversely, these supposedly public matters influenced, among other things, marital and child-rearing decisions. Viewed from this perspective, the lines between public and private blur, even disappear.[12] And more of the eighteenth-century world as early Americans knew it is revealed.

Collapsing public and private categories necessarily complicates our understanding of male and female. If the private is public and vice versa, what happens to women's sphere? And if sisters and brothers act as relative equals, what becomes of the paradigm of gendered power and female subordination? The "hidden family" model establishes that women were not simply deferential victims of patriarchal authority in their households. Women also acted as equal partners with their sisters, brothers, and kindred. By moving women from being the objects of patriarchal authority to acting as creators of kinship networks, one can more fully uncover the emotional reality of women's lives. What has often been considered women's private world was actually intricately intertwined with men's public life. Furthermore, the attitudes of cooperation and mutuality so often ascribed to women in the eighteenth century actually pervaded the whole kin group, male and female.

As this expanded conception of family further illuminates the complexity of women's lives, it also forces a rethinking of deeply ingrained assumptions about power—particularly patriarchal power—within households. Put plainly, this perspective on family indicates that patriarchy did not exercise the pervasive influence scholars often assume. Not only did these horizontal relationships provide an alternative familial experience; siblings and kin also complicated patriarchal authority within households. Siblings and kin, by and large, ignored the deferential-patriarchal model of interaction. Women formed egalitarian relationships with their brothers and sisters and exercised great influence within the kin network. Siblings interfered with parental authority over young children's socialization and education. At various stages during the life course, including childbirth, visits, and the coordination of marriages, siblings and kin interceded in and even prevailed over the patriarchal household. Clearly then, patriarchy and deference did not exert an unmitigated or pervasive influence over households and communities.[13]

Moreover, patriarchal authority did not, as many historians have argued, simply give way to individual autonomy in the late eighteenth century.[14] The South Carolina example indicates that people did not blindly defer to the demands of family patriarchs. Nor, on the other hand, did they behave as independent individuals. Instead, when making key life decisions about everything from education to marriage to inheritance, they sought the advice and considered the needs of their siblings and kin. Throughout the life course they carefully balanced individual desires with familial concerns. The sibling-kin group thus circumscribed the personal ambitions of individuals and checked the authority of patriarchs.

In sum, most historians studying early America envision public and private, male and female, and deferential and autonomous as distinct, even disjunctive categories. Sibship and kinship force us to rethink these perceived polarities by revealing a third force in personal and social behavior. This alternative pattern of interaction goes beyond simply adding to the story—it forces a retelling of it.

So, too, do siblings and kin require a reassessment of family history. Indeed, it is past time to embrace the multiplicity of family experiences in our history. For most of our past (as today), Americans have not defined family strictly—or in some cases even primarily—as the conjugal household. Who is included in the family and what the family does for the individuals it brings together shifts over time according to societal needs and abilities. By subscribing to an essentially static definition of family, historians contribute to the divorce of family from other areas of inquiry. In fact, family, in all its myriad forms, has historically formed the core of society. In the case of eighteenth-century South Carolina, the intragenerational world of siblings and kin was so much the center of gentry life that one simply cannot understand their society without accepting their definition of family: what they often referred to as "all our relations." How precisely these ties shaped the lives of other people in other times—which requires a willingness to acknowledge diverse definitions of family—remains to be seen.

APPENDIX I

Estate Dispersal Patterns and Sibling and Kin Connections

Name	Date of Death	Sibs at Death	Bequests: Sp, Si, C, K	Executors: Si, K, Con	Total Number of Sibs/Kin Named
Ann Ball	1799	N	C, K	Con	2
Elias Ball	1751	N	C	other	0
Elias Ball	1758	N	C	K	2
Elias Ball	1788	N	C	Con	0
George Ball	1754	Y	Sp, Si	Si	2
John Ball	1764	Y	Sp, C	Si, K, Con	2
John Ball	1792	Y	Si, K	K	9
Joseph Ball	1769	N	Sp, C	K, Con	1
Joseph Ball	1787	N	Sp, C	K, Con	2
Judith Ball	1772	N	C, K	K	3
Lydia Ball	1783	N	C	K, Con	5
Sampson Ball	1766	N	K	K	5
Samuel Ball	17??	Y	Sp, Si	Con	2
Samuel Ball	1784	N	C, K	other	1
Daniel Blake	1780	Y	Sp, Si, K	Si, K, Con	6
Elizabeth Blake	1726	Y	Si, C	Con	3
Elizabeth Blake	1792	N	K	K	12
Joseph Blake	1700	Y	Sp, Si, C	Con	3
Joseph Blake	1751	N	C	Con	0
Barnaby Bull	1754	Y	C, K	Con	4
Hannah Bull	1797	Y	Si, K	other	12
John Bull	1767	N	Sp, K	Con	1
Mary Bull	1771	N	C, K	K	7
Stephen Bull	1749	Y	Sp, C	Si, Con	1
Stephen Bull	1770	N	C	K	1
Thomas Bull	1772	N	Sp, C	Con	0
William Bull	1755	Y	C, K	K	5
William Bull	1791	N	Sp, K	Con	4
Anne Drayton	1748	N	C	Con	2
John Drayton	1774	Y	Si, K	Si, K	5
Stephen Drayton	1734	Y	Si, K	Si, Con	4
Thomas Drayton	1724	N	Sp, C	other	0
Thomas Drayton	1761	Y	Sp, C, K	Si, Con	2
William Drayton	1790	N	Sp, C	K	1
Charles Izard	1744	Y	Sp, Si, K	Si, K	2
John Izard	1754	Y	Sp, C	Si	2
John Izard	1782	Y	Sp, Si	K, Con	2
Joseph Izard	1745	Y	Sp, C	Si	2
Magdaline Izard	1746	N	C, K	Con	2
Ralph Izard	1723	Y	Si, C, K	other	2
Ralph Izard	1745	Y	Sp, C	Con	0
Ralph Izard	1761	Y	C	Si, K	3
Thomas Izard	1754	Y	Si, K	Si	6
Walter Izard	1750	N	Sp, C, K	Con	8
Walter Izard	1788	Y	Si, K	Si	12
Henry Laurens	1792	N	C, K	K, Con	3
James Laurens	1784	Y	Sp, Si, K	Si, K, Con	10
John Laurens	1747	N	Sp, C	Con	0
Peter Laurens	1747	Y	Si, K	K	4
Anne Manigault	1782	N	K	K	5

(*continued*)

Name	Date of Death	Sibs at Death	Bequests: Sp, Si, C, K	Executors: Si, K, Con	Total Number of Sibs/Kin Named
Gabriel Manigault	1781	N	Sp, K	K, Con	6
Peter Manigault	1733	N	C	K, Con	2
Pierre Manigault	1729	N	C, K	Con	1
Arthur Middleton	1739	N	Sp, C	K, Con	1
Elizabeth Middleton	1784	Y	Si, K	K	18
Henry Middleton	1784	N	Sp, C	Con	0
Sarah Middleton	17??	N	C, K	K	26
Sarah Middleton	1798	N	C	Con	1
Thomas Middleton	1746	N	C	Con	0
Thomas Middleton	1767	Y	Sp, C	Si, Con	1
Charles Pinckney	1782	Y	Sp, C	K, Con	3
Deborah Pinckney	1789	N	C, K	K, Con	2
Hopson Pinckney	1794	N	Sp, C	K	1
Roger Pinckney	17??	Y	Sp, Si, C, K	Si, K	6
Andrew Rutledge	1755	N	K	K	4
Andrew Rutledge	1772	Y	Sp	Si, K, Con	2
Edward Rutledge	1800	Y	Sp, Si, C	Si, Con	2
John Rutledge	1750	N	Sp	Con	0
Sarah Rutledge	1792	N	C, K	Con	5
John Wragg	1780	N	K	other	2
Joseph Wragg	1751	Y	Sp, C	Con	1
Joseph Wragg	1751	Y	Si, K	Si	2
Judith Wragg	1767	N	C	Con	5
Judith Wragg	1783	Y	Si, K	Si, K	20
William Wragg	1780	Y	Sp, Si, C, K	Con	7

Sp = spouses; C = children; Si = siblings; K = other kin; Con = conjugal family members (spouses, children, parents)

"Other" refers to testators who chose only unrelated executors such as neighbors, friends, or business associates and did not select any family member to help oversee the estate.

APPENDIX 2

Most Powerful Members of the South Carolina Assembly, 1730–1775

Name	Years of Service	Sessions in 1st Rank	Sessions in 2nd Rank	Parish(es) Represented
George Austin	1741–42 1745–46 1749–51 1754–57	3	3	St. Philip's, St. Bartholomew
Othneil Beale	1731–36 1745–46	6	1	St. Philip's
Thomas Bee	1762–75	3	3	St. Paul's, St. Peter's, St. Luke's, St. Andrew's
Jacob Bond	1731–33 1736–39 1745–46 1748–54	3	7	Christ Church, St. Helena, St. Thomas & St. Dennis, St. Bartholomew
Miles Brewton	1765–68 1771–75	3	4	St. Philip's, St. Andrew's, St. Michael's
William Bull, Jr.	1736–49	8	3	St. Andrew's, St. John's Berkeley, Prince William's, St. Bartholomew
Benjamin Dart	1761–62 1765–71	3	4	St. Andrew's, St. Michael's
John Dart	1735–45 1749–51 1753–54	7	7	St. Philip's, St. Helena
William Drake	1730–39	2	4	St. John's Berkeley, St. James Santee, St. John's Colleton
Christopher Gadsden	1757–75	11	6	St. Philip's, St. Paul's
James Graeme	1733 1742–45 1749–51	2	4	St. Helena, St. Philip's, St. George Dorchester
John Guerand, Jr.	1754–60	2	4	St. Philip's
Robert Hume	1731–33	3	0	St. Philip's
Henry Hyrne	1736–42 1761	2	4	St. Paul's, St. Bartholomew
Paul Jenys	1730–36	4	2	St. Philip's, St. George Dorchester
Thomas Lamboll	1754–60	4	3	St. Paul's, St. Andrew's
Henry Laurens	1757–72	8	4	St. Philip's, St. Michael's
John Lloyd I	1731–33	10	2	St. Philip's, St. Thomas & St. Dennis, St. James Goose Creek
Rawlins Lowndes	1749–54 1757–75	10	6	St. Paul's, St. Bartholomew
Thomas Lynch, Jr.	1752–75	6	9	Prince Frederick, St. James Santee, Prince George Winyaw
Gabriel Manigault	1733–35 1745–46 1748 1751–54	3	3	St. Philip's, St. Thomas & St. Dennis
Peter Manigault	1755–73	14	7	St. Philip's, St. Thomas & St. Dennis

(*continued*)

Name	Years of Service	Sessions in 1st Rank	Sessions in 2nd Rank	Parish(es) Represented
Isaac Mazyck	1736–51 1753–54 1757–70	18	9	St. Philip's, St. Thomas & St. Dennis, Prince George Winyaw, Prince Frederick, St. John's Berkeley, St. James Goose Creek
Henry Middleton	1742–48 1754–56	3	1	St. George Dorchester
James Parsons	1752–54 1760–75	6	12	St. Paul's, St. Bartholomew
Charles Pinckney (1699–1758)	1731–41	9	2	Christ Church, St. Philip's
Charles Pinckney (1732–82)	1754–75	8	12	Christ Church, St. Philip's, St. Michael's
C. Cotesworth Pinckney	1769–75	1	5	St. John's Colleton
John Rattray	1754–61	6	0	St. Helena, Prince William's
Andrew Rutledge	1733–42 1746 1748–54	10	6	Christ Church, St. John's Colleton
John Rutledge, Jr.	1761–75	3	12	Christ Church
Benjamin Smith	1747–70	13	5	St. Philip's, St. George Dorchester, St. James Goose Creek, St. John's Colleton
Thomas Smith	1751–54 1760–65 1769–72	3	6	St. Philip's, St. Paul's, St. Andrew's, St. Helena, St. James Goose Creek
Peter Taylor	1733–39 1742–45 1749–51 1757–62	8	7	St. James Goose Creek
Paul Trapier	1748 1751–54 1757–60	2	3	Prince George Winyaw
Benjamin Whitaker	1736–45	9	0	St. Philip's
William Wragg	1758–68	5	3	St. John's Colleton

SOURCE: This material comes from the data compiled by Jack Greene in *The Quest for Power: The Lower Houses of Assembly in the Southern Royal Colonies, 1689–1776* (Chapel Hill: University of North Carolina Press, 1963), 475–88.

APPENDIX 3

Longest-Serving Members of the South Carolina Assembly, 1730–1775

Name	Years of Service	Sessions in 1st Rank	Sessions in 2nd Rank	Parish(es) Represented
Thomas Bee	1762–75	3	3	St. Paul's, St. Peter's, St. Luke's, St. Andrew's
William Bull, Jr.	1736–49	8	3	St. Andrew's, St. John's Berkeley, Prince William's, St. Bartholomew
Thomas Cordes, Sr.	1733–42, 1745–46, 1748	0	5	St. John's Berkeley
John Dart	1735–45, 1749–51, 1753–54	7	7	St. Philip's, St. Helena
William Elliott, Jr.	1731–36, 1739–45, 1748	0	2	St. Andrew's, St. Paul's
Thomas Ferguson	1762–75	0	3	St. Andrew's, Prince William's, All Saints, St. Paul's
Christopher Gadsden	1757–75	11	6	St. Philip's, St. Paul's
Tacitus Gaillard	1749–54, 1762–75	0	1	St. James Santee, St. Matthew's, St. Stephen's, St. George Dorchester
David Hext	1736–51	0	5	St. John's Colleton, St. James Goose Creek, Prince Frederick, St. Philip's
Henry Laurens	1757–72	8	4	St. Philip's, St. Michael's
Rawlins Lowndes	1749–54, 1757–75	10	6	St. Paul's, St. Bartholomew
Thomas Lynch, Jr.	1752–75	6	9	Prince Frederick, St. James Santee, Prince George Winyaw
Peter Manigault	1755–73	14	7	St. Philip's, St. Thomas & St. Dennis
Anthony Mathewes	1733–42, 1746–47, 1749–51	0	2	St. Bartholomew, St. John's Colleton
Isaac Mazyck	1736–51, 1753–54, 1757–70	18	9	St. Philip's, St. Thomas & St. Dennis, Prince George Winyaw, Prince Frederick, St. John's Berkeley, St. James Goose Creek
Thomas Middleton	1742–48, 1752–54, 1756–62	1	2	St. James Goose Creek, St. Bartholomew, Prince William's, St. Michael's
William Moultrie	1761–73	0	1	Prince Frederick, St. Helena, St. John's Berkeley
David Oliphant	1761–75	0	3	Prince William's, St. James Santee, St. George Dorchester
James Parsons	1752–54, 1760–75	6	12	St. Paul's, St. Bartholomew
Charles Pinckney (1732–82)	1754–75	8	12	Christ Church, St. Philip's, St. Michael's

(continued)

Name	Years of Service	Sessions in 1st Rank	Sessions in 2nd Rank	Parish(es) Represented
George Gabriel Powell	1751–57 1761 1769–71 1773–75	1	4	Prince George Winyaw, St. Helena, St. David's
William Roper	1748 1757–71	0	3	St. Helena, Prince William's
Andrew Rutledge	1733–42 1746 1748–54	10	6	Christ Church, St. John's Colleton
John Rutledge, Jr.	1761–75	3	12	Christ Church
William Scott	1762–75	0	2	St. Philip's, St. Andrew's
Benjamin Smith	1747–70	13	5	St. Philip's, St. George Dorchester, St. James Goose Creek, St. John's Colleton
Thomas Smith	1751–54 1760–65 1769–72	3	6	St. Philip's, St. Paul's, St. Andrew's, St. Helena, St. James Goose Creek
Peter Taylor	1733–39 1742–45 1749–51 1757–62	8	7	St. James Goose Creek
William Williamson	1760–71	0	2	St. Paul's, St. Peter's
Thomas Wright	1740–47 1752–60 1762–66	0	7	St. Thomas & St. Dennis, St. John's Colleton, St. John's Berkeley

SOURCE: This material comes from the data compiled by Jack Greene in *The Quest for Power: The Lower Houses of Assembly in the Southern Royal Colonies, 1689–1776* (Chapel Hill: University of North Carolina Press, 1963), 475–88.

APPENDIX 4

Biographical Sketches of Key Figures

Harriott Pinckney Horry (1748-1830) was the only daughter of Eliza Pinckney, and the wife (and young widow) of Daniel Horry. Throughout her life, she remained deeply attached to her brothers, Charles Cotesworth Pinckney and Thomas Pinckney.

Alice DeLancey Izard (?-1832) was born into a prominent New York family. She married Ralph Izard (ca. 1741-1804) in 1767. Their children included Margaret Izard Manigault, Charlotte Izard Smith, Henry Izard (husband of Emma Middleton), Ralph Izard, Jr. (husband of Elizabeth Middleton), Anne Izard Deas, and Charlotte Georgina Izard Smith.

Henry Laurens (1724-92), one of South Carolina's most famous merchants, married Eleanor Ball (1731-70) in 1750 and thereby connected himself to the powerful Ball family. Eleanor Ball Laurens was the daughter of Elias Ball (1676-1751) and the sister of John Coming Ball (1714-64), Ann Ball Austin (1701-65), and Elias Ball (1709-86). Through his marriage, Henry formed economic and emotional ties to Eleanor's brothers and her brother-in-law, George Austin.

Gabriel Manigault (1704-81) settled in Carolina with his brother Pierre. By the time he married Anne Ashby Manigault (1705-82) in 1730, he was well on his way to becoming one of the wealthiest men in the colony.

Gabriel Manigault (1758-1809) was the eldest grandson and namesake of Gabriel Manigault (1704-81). Orphaned in his teens, he studied abroad before returning to Carolina and assuming responsibility for his brother, Joseph Manigault (1763-1842), and sister, Anne Manigault (1762-1811). Joseph and Gabriel remained deeply attached to one another until Gabriel's death.

Margaret Izard Manigault (1768-1824) was the eldest daughter of Ralph (ca. 1741-1804) and Alice DeLancey Izard. She married Gabriel Manigault (1758-1809) in 1785. Margaret was especially close to her sister Charlotte Izard (1770-92), who married William Loughton Smith.

Peter Manigault (1731-73), the only son of Gabriel and Anne Ashby Manigault, married Elizabeth Wragg (1736-73) in 1755. Peter and Elizabeth both died in 1773. They left behind their children, Gabriel, Joseph, and Anne, for Peter's parents to raise. Peter and Elizabeth named these children after their parents: Gabriel was Peter's father's name, Anne was his mother, and Joseph was named after Elizabeth's father.

Charles Pinckney (1757–1824) attended the Constitutional convention with his cousin Charles Cotesworth Pinckney and helped form a powerful political alliance with Charles Cotesworth and Thomas Pinckney in the late eighteenth century.

Charles Cotesworth Pinckney (1745–1825) and his brother, Thomas Pinckney (1750–1828), studied and lived in Europe together for most of their youth. In their early twenties, they returned to Carolina and began successful political careers. During the Washington administration, Thomas was named minister to Great Britain, and Charles Cotesworth assumed the same post in France. Charles Cotesworth first married Sally (Sarah) Middleton. When she died in 1784, he married Mary Stead.

Eliza Lucas Pinckney (1722–93), because of her planting successes and her revealing letterbook, became one of colonial South Carolina's most famous residents. In the early part of her letterbook, she spoke often of her siblings, Thomas, Polly, and George Lucas. In 1744 she married Charles Pinckney (ca. 1699–1758) only a few months after his first wife's death. Three of their children survived into adulthood: Charles Cotesworth Pinckney, Harriott Pinckney Horry, and Thomas Pinckney.

Harriott Pinckney (1776–1866) was the niece and namesake of Harriott Pinckney Horry. After her mother, Sally Middleton Pinckney, died in 1784, Harriott's father, Charles Cotesworth Pinckney, sent Harriott and her sisters, Maria Henrietta and Eliza, to live with their aunt, Harriott Horry. In her youth, Harriott corresponded regularly with her cousin, Thomas Pinckney, Jr. (1780–1842), the son of her uncle, Thomas Pinckney.

Andrew Rutledge (?–1755) migrated to Carolina in the 1730s with his brother John Rutledge (?–1750). Andrew married the widow Sarah Boone Hext (?–1743) shortly after his arrival in the colony. John married Sarah's fourteen-year-old daughter (thus his brother's stepdaughter), also named Sarah Hext (1724–92), in 1738. The brothers served in the General Assembly together and, thanks in no small measure to their marriages, amassed significant wealth and prominence in the colony. John and Sarah's children included John, Hugh, and Edward Rutledge.

John Rutledge (1739–1800) and his brothers, Hugh Rutledge (ca. 1745–1811) and Edward Rutledge (1749–1800), formed one of the most politically powerful sibling groups in South Carolina. In early national South Carolina,

Edward was governor of the state, John the chief justice, and Hugh the Speaker of the House. Edward married Henrietta Middleton in 1774 and became the brother-in-law of Charles Cotesworth Pinckney, who married Henrietta Middleton's sister Sally.

William Loughton Smith allied himself with the powerful Izard family when he married Charlotte Izard in 1786. Although she died in 1792 and he remarried (to Charlotte Wragg in 1805), he remained closely attached to the Izards, especially his mother-in-law, Alice DeLancey, and sister-in-law Margaret Izard Manigault. Charlotte Izard's youngest sister was born the same year Charlotte died. Alice and Ralph Izard named their last child Charlotte Georgina Izard, after her dead sister. She eventually married Joseph Allen Smith, the stepbrother of William Loughton Smith.

NOTES

INTRODUCTION

1. Eliza Lucas to George Lucas, 1 June 1742, in Elise Pinckney, ed., *The Letterbook of Eliza Lucas Pinckney* (Columbia: University of South Carolina Press, 1997), 49. For the latest word on Eliza Lucas Pinckney, see *South Carolina Historical Magazine* 99 (July 1998), which was devoted to her.

2. I have not limited my definition of family to mean only members of the conjugal household, for the simple reason that eighteenth-century Carolinians did not define family that way. In their minds, family had a much broader and more amorphous meaning—it included a wide array of consanguineous and affinal relatives. Where appropriate, I have distinguished relationships between husbands and wives and parents and children by referring to those family ties as conjugal or patriarchal.

3. *Patriarchy* has been a charged and complicated term among early American scholars, and its meaning and explanatory power have created significant debate. Patriarchal values shaped both the political culture of early America and the relationships between masters and their servants and slaves throughout British North America. In this work I use the term primarily to describe the power that male heads of households exercised over their wives and children.

4. For psychological theories on sibling relations, see Stephen Bank and Michael Kahn, *The Sibling Bond* (New York: Basic Books, 1982); Victor Cicirelli, *Sibling Relationships across the Life Span* (New York: Plenum Press, 1995); Michael Lamb and Brian Sutton-Smith, eds., *Sibling Relationships: Their Nature and Significance across the Life Span* (Hillsdale, N.J.: Lawrence Erlbaum Associates, 1982); Judy Dunn and Carol Kendrick, *Siblings: Love, Envy, and Understanding* (Cambridge: Harvard University Press, 1982); and Judy Dunn and Frits Boer, eds., *Children's Sibling Relationships: Developmental and Clinical Issues* (Hillsdale, N.J.: Lawrence Erlbaum Associates, 1992).

5. I use the term *public* to refer to legal, political, and economic matters that were transacted in the larger community. Public is thus distinguished from the private, emotional, day-to-day lives of individuals, particularly their relationships within families. Ultimately, however, the larger point of this work is that the lines between public and private were so often transgressed in eighteenth-century South Carolina as to render the distinction impractical.

6. The first colonists in Carolina named the city they founded *Charles Town*, after

England's reigning monarch. In correspondence throughout the eighteenth century, residents sometimes rendered the two words as one, calling their home *Charlestown*. In the wake of the American Revolution and the evacuation of the British from the city, Carolinians renamed it *Charleston*. For purposes of continuity, I always refer to the city as *Charleston*.

7. See, for example, Philip Greven, *Four Generations: Population, Land, and Family in Colonial Andover* (Ithaca: Cornell University Press, 1970); Jan Lewis, *The Pursuit of Happiness: Family and Values in Jefferson's Virginia* (New York: Cambridge University Press, 1983); Carol Shammas, "Anglo-American Household Government in Comparative Perspective," *William and Mary Quarterly* 52 (January 1995), 104–44; and Daniel Blake Smith, *Inside the Great House: Planter Family Life in Eighteenth-Century Chesapeake Society* (Ithaca: Cornell University Press, 1980). When siblings and kin do appear in scholarly works, they are usually relegated to positions of secondary importance. See David Jordan, "Political Stability and the Emergence of a Native Elite in Maryland," in Thad Tate and David Ammerman, eds., *The Chesapeake in the Seventeenth Century: Essays on Anglo-American Society* (New York: W. W. Norton, 1979), 243–73; Jacob Price, *Perry of London: A Family and a Firm on the Seaborne Frontier, 1615–1753* (Cambridge: Harvard University Press, 1992); Cynthia Kierner, *Traders and Gentlefolk: The Livingstons of New York, 1675–1790* (Ithaca: Cornell University Press, 1992); Allan Kulikoff, *Tobacco and Slaves: The Development of Southern Cultures in the Chesapeake, 1680–1800* (Chapel Hill: University of North Carolina Press, 1986); and Philip Greven, *The Protestant Temperament: Patterns of Childrearing, Religious Experience, and the Self in Early America* (New York: Knopf, 1977). This problem affects other disciplines, such as anthropology, as well. See Ladislav Holy, *Anthropological Perspectives on Kinship* (London: Pluto Press, 1997), and Ranya Rapp, "Toward a Nuclear Freeze? The Gender Politics of Euro-American Kinship Analysis," in Jane Fishburne Collier and Sylvia Junko Yanagisako, eds., *Gender and Kinship: Essays toward a Unified Analysis* (Stanford: Stanford University Press, 1987), 119–31.

8. Historians are not alone in slighting siblings and kin in their research. Psychologists, until quite recently, have been preoccupied with a mother-child dyad in both clinical research and psychological theory. If siblings are studied at all, it is only in the context of rivalry for maternal attention or the effect of birth order or difference in age on personality development. Both reflect the assumption that the mother is the center of family dynamics and individual child development. More recently, however, a few scholars have started to move beyond this dyadic approach and take siblings seriously. They have discovered not only that siblings exert a profound influence over one another but that the nature of sibling ties differs dramatically from that of parent-child relationships, since siblings are governed by equality and interdependence. See Bank and Kahn, *Sibling Bond;* and Lamb and Sutton-Smith, *Sibling Relationships*.

9. Much has been made recently about birth order studies and personality development, especially after the publication of Frank Sulloway's *Born to Rebel: Birth Order,*

Family Dynamics, and Creative Lives (New York: Pantheon Books, 1996). Sulloway's work, while impressive in its scope, is so informed by Darwinian theory that it tends to deny human agency. In eighteenth-century South Carolina, no discernible personality developments or patterns of sibling relations seemed to flow from birth order. Only in cases of significant age discrepancies did siblings mention or seem to honor birth order or age differences. While their sibling connections were often complicated, the complexity derived from individual circumstances rather than inherent, biologically influenced tendencies for rivalry or personality differences.

10. For a fuller discussion see Richard Bushman, *The Refinement of America: Persons, Houses, Cities* (New York: Knopf, 1992).

11. Historians of the African-American experience have produced far more research on the impact of kinship among enslaved Africans, with far less evidence, than scholars studying Europeans in the Americas. Important recent works on African-American culture and community in early America include Gwendolyn Midlo Hall, *Africans in Colonial Louisiana: The Development of Afro-Creole Culture in the Eighteenth Century* (Baton Rouge: Louisiana State University Press, 1992); Kimberly Hanger, *Bounded Lives, Bounded Places: Free Black Society in Colonial New Orleans* (Durham, N.C.: Duke University Press, 1997); Kulikoff, *Tobacco and Slaves;* Jon Sensbach, *A Separate Canaan: The Making of an Afro-Moravian World in North Carolina, 1763–1840* (Chapel Hill: University of North Carolina Press, 1998); and especially Philip Morgan, *Slave Counterpoint: Black Culture in the Eighteenth-Century Chesapeake and Lowcountry* (Chapel Hill: University of North Carolina Press, 1998).

12. For regional comparisons see Robert Gough, "Close-Kin Marriage and Upper-Class Formation in Late Eighteenth-Century Philadelphia," *Journal of Family History* 14, 2 (1989), 119–36; Peter Dobkin Hall, "Family Structure and Economic Organization: Massachusetts Merchants, 1700–1850," in Tamara Hareven, ed., *Family and Kin in Urban Communities, 1700–1930* (New York: New Viewpoints, 1977); Smith, *Inside the Great House;* and Kulikoff, *Tobacco and Slaves.*

13. Robert Gross, *The Minutemen and Their World* (New York: Hill and Wang, 1976); Bill Boller, "Kinship and Culture in the Mobilization of Colonial Massachusetts," *Historian* 57 (Winter 1995), 291–302; Jack Greene, "Foundations of Political Power in the Virginia House of Burgesses," *William and Mary Quarterly* 16 (October 1959), 485–506; Donn M. Kurtz II, *Kinship and Politics: The Justices of the United States and Louisiana Supreme Courts* (Baton Rouge: Louisiana State University Press, 1997); Paul Goodman, "The Social Basis of New England Politics in Jacksonian America," *Journal of the Early Republic* 6 (Spring 1986), 23–47; Edward E. Baptist, "The Migration of Planters to Antebellum Florida: Kinship and Power," *Journal of Southern History* 62 (August 1996), 527–54; Paul Johnson, *A Shopkeeper's Millennium: Society and Revivals in Rochester, New York, 1815–1837* (New York: Hill and Wang, 1978); Kenneth Minkema, "Hannah and Her Sisters: Sisterhood, Courtship, and Marriage in the Edwards Family in the Early Eighteenth Century," *New England Historical and Genealogical Register* 146 (Janu-

ary 1992), 35–56; Greven, *Protestant Temperament;* and Hanger, *Bounded Lives, Bounded Places.*

CHAPTER ONE

1. Eager to populate the area, the proprietors promised 150 acres of land to all free settlers over the age of sixteen years. Each healthy male brought along earned an additional 100 acres for the master.

2. Kinloch Bull, Jr., *The Oligarchs in Colonial and Revolutionary Charleston: Lieutenant Governor William Bull II and His Family* (Columbia: University of South Carolina Press, 1991), 9–10; Walter J. Fraser, *Charleston! Charleston! The History of a Southern City* (Columbia: University of South Carolina Press, 1989), 3.

3. Hyrne-Massingberd Papers, Lincolnshire Archives Committee, Lincoln, England. Reprinted in Roy Merrens, ed., *The Colonial South Carolina Scene* (Columbia: University of South Carolina Press, 1977), 16–23; Albert J. Schmidt, ed., "Hyrne Family Letters," *South Carolina Historical Magazine* 63 (July 1962), 150–57. South Carolina did not experience a "starving time" like the early settlers in Jamestown.

4. Edward Hyrne to Burrell Massingberd, 19 January 1701, Merrens, *Colonial South Carolina Scene,* 19.

5. This holds true primarily for the members of planter-merchant families. Materials detailing the motivations of nonelites simply do not exist in sufficient numbers to make any persuasive interpretations. The manuscript materials that have survived from the late seventeenth and early eighteenth centuries are almost exclusively those of elite white families. Clearly, this discussion about motivations of migration would not apply to the thousands of African slaves forced to come to the lowcountry, either. For more general analysis of early South Carolina, see Agnes Leland Baldwin, *First Settlers of South Carolina, 1670–1680* (Columbia: University of South Carolina Press, 1969); B. D. Bargar, *Royal South Carolina, 1719–1763* (Columbia: University of South Carolina Press, 1970); Stanley South and Michael Hartley, *Deep Water and High Ground: Seventeenth Century Low Country Settlement* (Columbia: University of South Carolina Press, 1980); Joseph Waring, *The First Voyage and Settlement of Charles Town, 1670–1680* (Columbia: University of South Carolina Press, 1970).

6. Timothy H. Breen, "Looking Out for Number One: The Cultural Limits on Public Policy in Early Virginia," in Breen, *Puritans and Adventurers: Change and Persistence in Early America* (New York: Oxford University Press, 1980). Darrett and Anita Rutman challenged this interpretation in *A Place in Time: Middlesex County, Virginia, 1650–1750* (New York: Norton, 1984), particularly in chap. 4, "Family, Friends, Neighbors." The Rutmans' quantitative analysis demonstrated a clear pattern of chain migrations and settlements among early Virginians. Once they arrived, new colonists typically settled in areas close to relatives or friends, so family identity and cultural patterns persisted between England and the colony. For more on the persistence of traditions

and cultural continuity during colonization, see Bernard Bailyn, *The Peopling of British North America* (New York: Knopf, 1987); David Grayson Allen, *In English Ways: The Movement of Societies and the Transferal of English Local Law and Custom to Massachusetts Bay in the Seventeenth Century* (Chapel Hill: University of North Carolina Press, 1980); Timothy H. Breen, "Persistent Localism: English Social Change and the Shaping of New England Institutions," *William and Mary Quarterly* 32 (January 1975), 3-28; and David Hackett Fischer, *Albion's Seed: Four British Folkways in America* (New York: Oxford University Press, 1989).

7. See, for example, Greven, *Protestant Temperament,* and Joan Cashin, *A Family Venture: Men and Women on the Southern Frontier* (New York: Oxford University Press, 1991).

8. The nineteenth-century business families who migrated into Rochester, New York, replicated elite Charlestonians' behavior. Over time Rochester elites intensified and expanded their kin connections in the same way as eighteenth-century Carolinians. Johnson, *A Shopkeeper's Millennium,* 25. Similar patterns were uncovered by Gail Terry in "Family Empires: A Frontier Elite in Virginia and Kentucky, 1740-1815" (Ph.D. diss., College of William and Mary, 1992); and by Baptist, "Migration of Planters to Antebellum Florida." See also John Waters, "Family, Inheritance, and Migration in Colonial New England: The Evidence from Guilford, Connecticut," *William and Mary Quarterly* 39 (1982), 64-86; and Richard Grassby, *The Business Community of Seventeenth-Century England* (Cambridge: Cambridge University Press, 1995).

9. Significant works concerning the South Carolina-West Indies connection include Richard Dunn, "The English Sugar Islands and the Founding of South Carolina," *South Carolina Historical Magazine* 72 (1971), 81-93; Jack Greene, "Colonial South Carolina and the Caribbean Connection," *South Carolina Historical Magazine* 88 (1987), 192-210; John Thomas, Jr., "The Barbadians in Early South Carolina," *South Carolina Historical and Genealogical Magazine* 31 (1930), 75-92; and Richard Waterhouse, "England, the Caribbean, and the Settlement of Carolina," *Journal of American Studies* 9 (1975), 259-81.

10. Thomas, "The Barbadians in Early South Carolina," 78; Richard Dunn, *Sugar and Slaves: The Rise of the Planter Class in the English West Indies, 1624-1713* (Chapel Hill: University of North Carolina Press, 1972), 111-16; Baldwin, *First Settlers of South Carolina, 1670-1680.* For 394 of these earliest settlers, no place of origin could be ascertained. Baldwin lists 146 settlers from the island colonies, 134 from England, and 10 from other mainland colonies.

11. Greene, "Colonial South Carolina and the Caribbean Connection," 192-210.

12. Eugene M. Sirmans, "The Legal Status of the Slave in South Carolina, 1670-1740," *Journal of Southern History* 28 (1962), 462-66; Dunn, *Sugar and Slaves,* 116.

13. Jack Greene, *The Quest for Power: The Lower Houses of Assembly in the Southern Royal Colonies, 1689-1776* (Chapel Hill: University of North Carolina Press, 1963); Dunn, *Sugar and Slaves,* 112; Robert Weir, *Colonial South Carolina: A History* (New York: KTO Press, 1983), 65. For more on the collapse of the proprietary government,

see M. Eugene Sirmans, *Colonial South Carolina: A Political History, 1663-1763* (Chapel Hill: University of North Carolina Press, 1966), 101-28; and J. Leitch Wright, Jr., *The Only Land They Knew: The Tragic Story of the American Indians in the Old South* (New York: Free Press, 1981). Wright discovered that the Goose Creek men also dominated the Indian trade during the same period. See also Kathryn E. Holland Braund, *Deerskins and Duffels: Creek Indian Trade with Anglo-Americans, 1685-1815* (Lincoln: University of Nebraska Press, 1994).

14. H. Roy Merrens and George D. Terry, "Dying in Paradise: Malaria, Mortality, and the Perceptual Environment in Colonial South Carolina," *Journal of Southern History* 50 (November 1984), 543-46. For more on the demographic and health issues in early South Carolina, see John Duffy, "Eighteenth-Century Colonial South Carolina Health Conditions," *Journal of Southern History* 18 (1952), 289-302; and John Duffy, "Yellow Fever in Colonial Charleston," *South Carolina Historical Magazine* 52 (1951), 189-97.

15. James Glen to Alexander Brodie, 22 September 1757, James Glen Papers, South Caroliniana Library, Columbia, South Carolina (hereafter SCL).

16. Cara Anzilotti, "'In the Affairs of the World': Women and Plantation Ownership in the Eighteenth-Century South Carolina Lowcountry" (Ph.D. diss., University of California, Santa Barbara, 1994), 61; Peggy Clark, "'That Cursed Sharp Woman': Sarah Cooke Rhett Trott," unpublished manuscript, presented at the 1997 meeting of the Southern Association of Women's Historians, Charleston, South Carolina.

17. Similar patterns occurred in the seventeenth-century Chesapeake where, according to Darrett and Anita Rutman, high mortality also fostered quick remarriage after spousal death. Rutman, *A Place in Time*, 113-20.

18. For more on the lives of blacks in the colonial South, see Cheryll Ann Cody, "Slave Demography and Family Formation: A Community Study of the Ball Family Plantation, 1720-1896" (Ph.D. diss., University of Minnesota, 1982); Allan Kulikoff, "The Origins of Afro-American Society in Tidewater Maryland and Virginia," *William and Mary Quarterly* 45 (1988), 226-59; Kulikoff, *Tobacco and Slaves;* Daniel Littlefield, *Rice and Slaves: Ethnicity and the Slave Trade in Colonial South Carolina* (Baton Rouge: Louisiana State University Press, 1981); Philip Morgan, "Black Life in Eighteenth-Century Charleston," *Perspectives in American History*, 1984; Sirmans, "Legal Status of the Slave in South Carolina"; and especially Peter Wood, *Black Majority: Negroes in Colonial South Carolina, from 1670 through the Stono Rebellion* (New York: Knopf, 1974); and Morgan, *Slave Counterpoint*.

19. Thomas Brett to Archibald Campbell, 23 November 1723, Brett Papers, Bodleian Library, Oxford. Reprinted in Brian J. Enright, ed., "An Account of Charles Town in 1725," *South Carolina Historical Magazine* 61 (1960), 13-18; miscellaneous correspondence, Schmidt, "Hyrne Family Letters," 150-57.

20. Anne Simons Deas, *Recollections of the Ball Family of South Carolina and Comingtee Plantation* (Charleston, 1909); Anzilotti, "In the Affairs of the World"; Edward Ball, *Slaves in the Family* (New York: Hill and Wang, 1998).

21. Early modern English scholars have conducted extensive work on this shift in marriage practices and ideals. Important examples include Lawrence Stone, *The Family, Sex and Marriage in England, 1500–1800* (New York: Harper and Row, 1977); Randolph Trumbach, *The Rise of the Egalitarian Family: Aristocratic Kinship and Domestic Relations in Eighteenth-Century England* (New York: Academic Press, 1978); and Mary Abbott, *Family Ties: English Families, 1540–1920* (London: Routledge, 1993).

22. Trumbach, *Rise of the Egalitarian Family*, 51.

23. Pinckney, *Letterbook*, xx; Anne Firor Scott, "Self-Portraits: Three Women," in Richard Bushman et al., *Uprooted Americans: Essays to Honor Oscar Handlin* (Boston: Little, Brown, 1979), 65; Thomas Dale to Thomas Birch, 17 November 1732, Thomas Dale Papers, SCL.

24. Trumbach, *Rise of the Egalitarian Family*, 35.

25. Ibid., 21–22.

26. For further analysis of the shifting meaning of incest see Robin Fox, *Kinship and Marriage: An Anthropological Perspective* (Harmondsworth: Penguin, 1967), chap. 2; Robin Fox, *The Red Lamp of Incest* (New York: Dutton, 1980); Burton Pasternak, Carol R. Ember, and Melvin Ember, eds., *Sex, Gender, and Kinship: A Cross-Cultural Perspective* (Englewood Cliffs, N.J.: Prentice Hall, 1997), chaps. 5 and 6; Sybil Wolfram, *In-Laws and Outlaws: Kinship and Marriage in England* (London: Croom Helm, 1987); Martin Ottenheimer, *Forbidden Relatives: The American Myth of Cousin Marriage* (Urbana: University of Illinois Press, 1996), chap. 1; and Vikki Bell, *Interrogating Incest: Feminism, Foucault, and the Law* (New York: Routledge, 1993).

27. Daniel Blake Smith's analysis of family life in the eighteenth-century Chesapeake revealed similar patterns. Smith, *Inside the Great House*, 247. See also Toby Ditz, *Property and Kinship: Inheritance in Early Connecticut, 1750–1820* (Princeton: Princeton University Press, 1986).

28. Grassby, *Business Community of Seventeenth Century England*, 330.

29. Ditz, *Property and Kinship;* Kulikoff, *Tobacco and Slaves*, 200–201; Smith, *Inside the Great House*, 247.

30. See, for example, Stone, *Family, Sex and Marriage;* Trumbach, *Rise of the Egalitarian Family;* Alan Macfarlane, ed., *The Diary of Ralph Josselin, 1616–1683* (London: Oxford University Press, 1976); and Keith Wrightson, *English Society, 1580–1680* (New Brunswick, N.J.: Rutgers University Press, 1982). A few historians challenge this orthodoxy and insist that, although limited in scope, kin did form an important part of family and community life in England. In particular, they point to the roles that kin played in the internal lives of one another and in the commercial enterprises of business families. Examples include David Cressy, "Kinship and Kin Interaction in Early Modern England," *Past and Present* 113 (November 1986), 38–69; and Alan Everitt, *Landscape and Community in England* (London: Hambledon Press, 1985).

31. See David Hancock, *Citizens of the World: London Merchants and the Integration of the British Atlantic Community, 1735–1785* (Cambridge: Cambridge University Press,

1995); Jacob Price, "The Trans-Atlantic Economy," and Richard Sheridan, "The Domestic Economy," both in Jack Greene and J. R. Pole, eds., *Colonial British America: Essays in the New History of the Early Modern Era* (Baltimore: Johns Hopkins University Press, 1984); Bernard Bailyn, *The New England Merchants in the Seventeenth Century* (Cambridge: Harvard University Press, 1955); Grassby, *Business Community;* and *William and Mary Quarterly* 54 (January 1999), John McCusker, guest editor.

32. Grassby, *Business Community*, 329.

33. *South Carolina Historical and Genealogical Magazine* 18 (January 1917), 13; Eliza Lucas to Mrs. Boddicott, 2 May 1740, in Pinckney, *Letterbook*, 7; Peter Manigault to Anne Manigault, 21 July 1773, "Letters Concerning Peter Manigault," *South Carolina Historical and Genealogical Magazine* 21 (1920), 40; Gabriel Manigault to Margaret Manigault, 6 December 1791, Manigault Family Papers, SCL.

34. Schmidt, "Hyrne Family Letters," 151.

35. Anzilotti, "In the Affairs of the World," 21.

36. Deas, *Recollections of the Ball Family of South Carolina and the Comingtee Plantation;* Eliza Lucas to Mrs. Boddicott, 2 May 1740, in Pinckney, *Letterbook*, 7. Eliza Lucas Pinckney has received a great deal of scholarly attention, particularly concerning her role in the development of indigo cultivation in South Carolina. For more on Lucas's family life, see Paula Treckel, "Eliza Lucas Pinckney: 'Dutiful, Affectionate and Obedient' Daughter," in Winifred B. Moore et al., eds., *Developing Dixie: Modernization in a Traditional Society* (Westport, Conn.: Greenwood Press, 1988); and *South Carolina Historical Magazine* 99 (July 1998). See also Cara Anzilotti, "Autonomy and the Female Planter in Colonial South Carolina," *Journal of Southern History* 63 (May 1997), 239–68.

37. George Lane, "The Middletons of Eighteenth Century South Carolina: A Colonial Dynasty, 1678–1787" (Ph.D. diss., Emory University, 1990); Langdon Cheves, comp., "Middleton of South Carolina," *South Carolina Historical and Genealogical Magazine* 1 (1900), 228–62; Peter Colleton Papers, SCL; Colleton Family Papers, SCL; Peter C. J. H. Easterby, ed., *Wadboo Barony: Its Fate as Told in Colleton Family Papers* (Columbia: University of South Carolina Press, 1952).

38. For more on the Pinckney brothers and their descendants, see Francis Leigh Williams, *A Founding Family: The Pinckneys of South Carolina* (New York: Harcourt, Brace, Jovanovich, 1978); Marvin Zahniser, *Charles Cotesworth Pinckney: Founding Father* (Chapel Hill: University of North Carolina Press, 1967); and George C. Rogers, Jr., *Charleston in the Age of the Pinckneys* (Norman: University of Oklahoma Press, 1969).

39. Mabel Webber, comp., "Dr. John Rutledge and His Descendants," *South Carolina Historical and Genealogical Magazine* 31 (1930), 7–25.

40. Eirlys M. Barker, "Pryce Hughes, Colony Planner, of Charles Town and Wales," *South Carolina Historical Magazine* 95 (1994), 302–13; Thomas Dale to Thomas Birch, 17 November 1732, Thomas Dale Papers, SCL.

41. Philip M. Hamer, George C. Rogers, Jr., et al., eds., *The Papers of Henry Laurens* (Columbia: University of South Carolina Press, 1980), vols. 1–2, *passim;* Walter Edgar,

ed., *The Letterbook of Robert Pringle* (Columbia: University of South Carolina Press, 1972); Ball Family Papers, SCL; Henry Laurens to Ross & Mill, 2 September 1768, *Papers of Henry Laurens,* vol. 6, 87–91.

42. Elias Ball (elder) to Elias Ball (younger), 7 April 1788, Ball Family Papers, SCL.

43. Ibid.

44. Peter Colleton to John More, 24 April 1684, Peter Colleton Papers, SCL; Carl Vipperman, *The Rise of Rawlins Lowndes* (Columbia: University of South Carolina Press, 1978).

45. Eliza Lucas to Thomas Lucas, 22 May 1742, in Pinckney, *Letterbook,* 39.

46. Anthony Gondy to "dear Brother," 28 May 1733, in R. W. Kelsey, ed., "Swiss Settlers in South Carolina," *South Carolina Historical and Genealogical Magazine* 23 (1922), 87.

47. Samuel Dyssli to [various family members], 3 December 1737, in Kelsey, "Swiss Settlers in South Carolina," 89–91.

48. Richard Waterhouse, "South Carolina Colonial Elites: Social Structure and Political Culture, 1670–1760" (Ph.D. diss., The Johns Hopkins University, 1973), 50.

49. Edmund Brailsford to Edmund Brailsford, miscellaneous letters, *South Carolina Historical and Genealogical Magazine* 8 (1907), 151–63.

50. Schmidt, "Hyrne Family Letters," 152.

51. Elizabeth Hyrne to Burrell Massingberd, 8 February 1702, in Schmidt, "Hyrne Family Letters," 153.

52. Elizabeth Hyrne to Burrell Massingberd, undated letter, in Merrens, *The South Carolina Scene,* 19–22; Schmidt, "Hyrne Family Letters," 152–53.

53. Elias Ball to Elias Ball, 7 April 1788, Ball Family Papers, SCL; Robert Colleton to Dr. Keith, 6 July 1751, Colleton Family Papers, SCL.

54. Thomas Brett to Archibald Campbell, 23 November 1723; Margaret Kennett to Thomas Brett, in Enright, "An Account of Charles Town in 1725," 13–18.

55. Margaret Kennett to Thomas Brett, undated letter; Margaret Brett to Mrs. Brett, 20 January 1725, in Enright, "An Account of Charles Town in 1725," 13–18.

56. For a different interpretation of kinship in eighteenth-century Virginia, see Smith, *Inside the Great House,* 230.

CHAPTER TWO

1. Analyses of cultural and social continuity include Bailyn, *Peopling of British North America;* Allen, *In English Ways;* Breen, "Persistent Localism"; and Fischer, *Albion's Seed.*

2. For more on New England family patterns, see Breen, *Puritans and Adventurers;* John Demos, *A Little Commonwealth: Family Life in Plymouth Colony* (New York: Oxford University Press, 1970); Greven, *Four Generations;* Kenneth Lockridge, *A New England Town, The First Hundred Years: Dedham, Massachusetts, 1636–1736* (New York: Norton, 1970).

3. Bank and Kahn, "Intense Sibling Loyalty," in Lamb and Sutton-Smith, eds., *Sibling Relationships*, 251–66. Their ideas are expanded in Bank and Kahn, *Sibling Bond*. See also Judy Dunn, *Sisters and Brothers* (London: Fontana, 1984), and Dunn and Kendrick, *Siblings: Love, Envy, and Understanding*.

4. Greven, *Protestant Temperament*, 155.

5. Cicirelli, *Sibling Relationships across the Life Span*, 6; Patricia Goldring Zukow, *Sibling Interaction across Cultures: Theoretical and Methodological Issues* (New York: Springer-Verlag, 1989), 1. Other important works moving beyond this mother-child dyad and investigating the power of sibling relations include Dunn and Kendrick, *Siblings: Love, Envy and Understanding*; Boer and Dunn, *Children's Sibling Relationships*; Lamb and Sutton-Smith, *Sibling Relationships*; and especially Bank and Kahn, *Sibling Bond*, a ground-breaking work that shifted sibling studies away from rivalry and birth order toward fuller explorations of the content and meaning of sibling interaction. Throughout her work, Judy Dunn argues that "if we are to understand children's development, and gain insights into ways to help them, we have to include siblings—as part of their family world—in that study." Boer and Dunn, *Children's Sibling Relationships*, xv.

6. Susan Merrell, *The Accidental Bond: The Power of Sibling Relationships* (New York: Random House, 1995), 12. See also Zukow, *Sibling Interaction across Cultures*.

7. In his study of religious temperament and family values, Philip Greven argued that moderate families "flourished best when nurtured and sustained by the connections of kinship." Greven, *Protestant Temperament*, 152–53. Analyses of the importance of kinship are rare, but include Marilyn Ferris Motz, *True Sisterhood: Michigan Women and their Kin, 1820–1900* (Albany: State University of New York Press, 1983); Nancy Grey Osterud, *Bonds of Community: The Lives of Farm Women in Nineteenth-Century New York* (Ithaca: Cornell University Press, 1991); Laurel Ulrich, *Goods Wives: Image and Reality in the Lives of Women in Northern New England, 1650–1750* (New York: Oxford University Press, 1980); and Joan Cashin, "The Structure of Antebellum Planter Families: 'The Ties That Bound Us Was Strong,'" *Journal of Southern History* 56 (1990), 55–70.

8. Members of the planter-merchant class of eighteenth-century Charleston differed sharply from their Chesapeake counterparts. In his study of Chesapeake planter families, Daniel Blake Smith argued that in the late eighteenth century family attention increasingly focused inward. Smith uncovered the importance of kinship in courtship, marriage (both as advisors and as potential spouses), socialization, education, and employment and found that "personal documents of brothers and sisters reveal warm, cooperative sibling relationships." Nevertheless, he argued that by the late eighteenth century, "kinship was not a controlling force in the social world of these planters." Smith, *Inside the Great House*, 178, 226.

9. For more on the problems of pregnancy and childbirth in early America, see Laurel Ulrich, *A Midwife's Tale: The Life of Martha Ballard, Based on her Diary, 1785–1812* (New York: Knopf, 1990); Ulrich, *Good Wives*; Darrett and Anita Rutman, "Now-Wives and Sons-in-Law: Parental Death in a Seventeenth-Century Virginia County," in Tate and

Ammerman, *Chesapeake in the Seventeenth Century;* and Lois Carr and Lorena Walsh, "The Planter's Wife: The Experience of White Women in Seventeenth-Century Maryland," *William and Mary Quarterly* 34 (October 1977), 542-71.

10. These figures are based on an analysis of sibling sets from eight lowcountry gentry families whose genealogical patterns could be fully and reliably charted over the course of the eighteenth century.

11. Journal of Anne Ashby Manigault, March-April 1758, Manigault Family Papers, South Carolina Historical Society, Charleston, South Carolina (hereafter SCHS); Henry A.M. Smith, comp., "Wragg of South Carolina," *South Carolina Historical and Genealogical Magazine* 19 (July 1918), 121-23.

12. Mary Pinckney to Margaret Manigault, 30 March 1797, Manigault Family Papers, SCL.

13. Ibid.

14. Journal of Anne Ashby Manigault, Manigault Family Papers, SCHS; William Read to Jacob Read, 29 December 1795, Read Family Papers, SCL.

15. William Read to Jacob Read, 26 February 1796, Read Family Papers, SCL.

16. See note 10, above.

17. Cheves, "Middleton of South Carolina," *South Carolina Historical and Genealogical Magazine* 1 (1900), 241-43.

18. Although birth order analyses have been a mainstay of sibling studies for years and have drawn sharp criticisms from many in the psychological community, Frank Sulloway's massive *Born to Rebel* breathed new life into the topic. See Introduction, note 9, above.

19. Sulloway, *Born to Rebel*, "Introduction," especially xv.

20. Joseph Manigault to Gabriel Manigault, 30 December 1786, Manigault Family Papers, SCL.

21. William Read to Jacob Read, 29 December 1795, Read Family Papers, SCL; Journal of Anne Ashby Manigault, Manigault Family Papers, SCHS; Henry Laurens to Matthias Holmes, 20 May 1763, *Papers of Henry Laurens,* vol. 3, 460-61; T. Boone to Margaret Colleton, 29 September 1773, Margaret Colleton Papers, SCL.

22. For comparisons see Daniel Scott Smith, "Child-naming Practices, Kinship Ties, and Change in Family Attitudes in Hingham, Massachusetts, 1641-1880," *Journal of Social History* 18 (1985), 541-65; Ulrich, *Good Wives*, 150-52; Kulikoff, *Tobacco and Slaves*, 245-49.

23. Alan Gallay, *The Formation of a Planter Elite: Jonathan Bryan and the Southern Colonial Frontier* (Athens: University of Georgia Press, 1989); Cheves, "Blake Family Genealogy," *South Carolina Historical and Genealogical Magazine* 1 (1900), 159-66; *The Papers of Henry Laurens;* George Lane, "The Middletons of Eighteenth-Century South Carolina" (Ph.D. diss., Emory University, 1990).

24. This pattern paralleled naming practices in the eighteenth-century Chesapeake where, according to historian Allan Kulikoff, "more than three-quarters of the children

born into large families . . . were named for blood relations." But one interesting distinction arises between the two regions. Chesapeake naming patterns favored members of the conjugal family rather than the extended kin group, whereas Carolinians concentrated on intragenerational kin when naming children. Kulikoff, *Tobacco and Slaves*, 249.

25. Ulrich, *Good Wives*, 152. Along with Allan Kulikoff, Laurel Ulrich and Jane Censer convincingly demonstrated the inaccuracy of the parental indifference interpretation. Ulrich, *Good Wives;* Jane Turner Censer, *North Carolina Planters and their Children, 1800–1860* (Baton Rouge: Louisiana State University Press, 1984). For a different interpretation of New England naming practices, see Smith, "Child-naming Practices."

26. Philip Greven made a similar argument—that kin gave children "a sense of attachment both to people and to places that would undergird their sense of self and the world for the rest of their lives." Greven, *Protestant Temperament*, 152–53.

27. Cicirelli, *Sibling Relationships across the Life Span*, 78.

28. See Barry Levy, "'Tender Plants': Quaker Farmers and Children in the Delaware Valley, 1681–1735" *Journal of Family History* 3 (1978), 116–35; Greven, *Protestant Temperament;* Smith, *Inside the Great House*.

29. Cicirelli, *Sibling Relationships across the Life Span*, 78. See also Merrell, *Accidental Bond;* and Victoria Bedford and Deborah Gold, eds., "Siblings in Later Life: A Neglected Family Relationship," in *American Behavioral Scientist* 33 (September-October 1989).

30. For more on early American educational practices see Lawrence Cremin, *American Education: The Colonial Experience, 1607–1783* (New York: Harper and Row, 1970); James Axtell, *The School upon a Hill: Education and Society in Colonial New England* (New Haven: Yale University Press, 1974); *History of Education Quarterly* 37 (Summer 1997), an issue that was devoted to education in early America and guest edited by Maris Vinovskis; and Michael Zuckerman, "Penmanship Exercises for Saucy Sons: Some Thoughts on the Colonial Southern Family," *South Carolina Historical Magazine* 84 (July 1983), 152–66.

31. Ralph Izard to Herman LeRoy, 25 May 1795; Anne Izard Deas, ed., *The Correspondence of Ralph Izard of South Carolina, 1774–1804* (New York: Charles S. Francis & Co., 1844); Cheves, "The Blake Family," *South Carolina Historical and Genealogical Magazine* 1 (1900), 153–66; "Izard Family," *South Carolina Genealogies* (Spartanburg: Reprint Company, 1983).

32. Ralph Izard to Edward Rutledge, 16 March 1789; Ralph Izard to Edward Rutledge, 16 March 1791; Ralph Izard to Edward Rutledge, 27 September 1791, Ralph Izard Papers, SCL.

33. Siblings and close kin held a solemn responsibility for their younger kin. When they abandoned that responsibility, an essential part of a child's upbringing was lost. After his son returned from an extended stay with his family in London, Edmund Brails-

ford complained that "he could not when he came to me read a chapter in the Bible." Brailsford deeply resented his family's failure to appropriately mentor his son. His disappointment attests to the importance of their job. Edmund Brailsford to Edmund Brailsford, *South Carolina Historical and Genealogical Magazine* 8 (1907), 158.

34. George Izard to Gabriel Manigault, 29 May 1804, Ralph Izard Papers, SCL; Edward Rutledge to Cambridge University Official, 15 June 1797, Edward Rutledge Papers, SCL; Stephen Moore to Frances Moore Bayard, 28 September 1769; Frances Moore Bayard to Stephen Moore, 24 November 1763, Stephen Moore Papers, SCL; Melvin Herndon, "Pinckney Horry, 1769–1828: Rebel without a Cause," *Georgia Historical Quarterly* 70 (Summer 1986), 232–53. Daniel Horry changed his name to Charles Lucas Pinckney Horry in the 1790s, and, from that point on, went by the name Pinckney Horry. Despite the best efforts of his uncles, Daniel (alias Pinckney) Horry became estranged from his family after he reached adulthood.

35. William Loughton Smith to Alice Izard, Ralph Izard Papers, SCL.

36. Eliza Lucas to George Lucas, undated, ca. 1742; Eliza Lucas to George Lucas, undated, ca. 1742, in Pinckney, *Letterbook*, 45, 52.

37. Eliza Pinckney to Charles Cotesworth and Thomas Pinckney, March 1760, *Letterbook*, 143; Edward Rutledge to unknown, 12 September 1789, Edward Rutledge Papers, SCL; Edward Rutledge to Sarah Rutledge, 8 October 1792, Edward Rutledge Papers, SCL.

38. Eliza Pinckney to Charles Cotesworth Pinckney, 9 June 1761; Eliza Pinckney to Charles Cotesworth Pinckney, March [1760]; Eliza Pinckney to Charles Cotesworth Pinckney, 7 February 1761, *Letterbook*, 171, 142, 158–59; John Rutledge, open letter, 9 September 1799, John Rutledge Papers, SCL.

39. Eliza Pinckney to Charles Cotesworth Pinckney, 15 April 1761, *Letterbook*, 167; Eliza Pinckney to Daniel Horry, Jr., 16 April 1782, *South Carolina Historical Magazine* 76 (1975), 167; Harriott Pinckney Horry to Daniel Horry, 28 February 1786, Harriott Pinckney Horry Letterbook, SCHS.

40. Richard Hutson to Isaac Hayne, 9 October 1773, Letterbook of Richard Hutson, Langdon Cheves Papers, SCHS.

41. Henry Laurens to Ross & Mill, 28 October 1767, *Papers of Henry Laurens*, vol. 5, 384–86.

42. Martine Segalen offers an interesting cross-cultural comparison to Carolina in "'Avoir sa part': Sibling Relations in Partible Inheritance Brittany," in Hans Medick and David Warren Sabean, eds., *Interest and Emotion: Essays on the Study of Family and Kinship* (Cambridge: Cambridge University Press, 1984), 129–44. Segalen found that while parent-child relations were "rather cold and characterized by respect," sibling relationships tended to be more affectionate and gregarious. Segalen, "Avoir sa part," 133.

43. John Drayton to James Glen, 24 December 1769; James Glen to John Drayton, 5 April 1768, James Glen Papers, SCL; W. Stitt Robinson, *James Glen: From Scottish*

Provost to Royal Governor of South Carolina (Westport, Conn.: Greenwood Press, 1996), 127.

44. Peter Manigault to Andrew Rutledge, 26 February 1754, Manigault Family Papers, SCL; William Drayton to Peter Manigault, 6 August 1755, Manigault Family Papers, SCL.

45. William Drayton to Peter Manigault, 31 May 1755; Andrew Rutledge to Peter Manigault, 16 December 1750, Manigault Family Papers, SCL.

46. Cicirelli, *Sibling Relationships across the Life Span;* Victor Cicirelli, "Sibling Influence throughout the Life Span," in Lamb and Sutton-Smith, *Sibling Relationships;* Brenda Bryant, "Sibling Caretaking," in Boer and Dunn, *Children's Sibling Relationships;* Paula Avioli, "The Social Support Functions of Siblings in Later Life," in Bedford and Gold, "Siblings in Later Life," 45–57; Dunn, *Sisters and Brothers;* Dunn and Kendrick, *Siblings: Love Envy, and Understanding.*

47. Alice Izard was reluctant to part with her youngest son, Ralph Jr., and asked her friend Charles Cotesworth Pinckney to check out the schools in Carolina. He assured her they were "much improved," and that she would not be irresponsible if she decided to "keep him near." Alice Izard to Ralph Izard, 8 January 1795, Ralph Izard Papers, SCL.

48. Ralph Izard to Charles Cotesworth Pinckney, date unknown; Ralph Izard to unknown correspondent, 22 October 1794, Ralph Izard Papers, SCL; John Drayton to James Glen, 5 April 1768, James Glen Papers, SCL.

49. Joseph Barnwell, ed., "The Diary of Timothy Ford, 1785-1786," *South Carolina Historical and Genealogical Magazine* 13 (1912), 192.

50. Edmund Brailsford to Edmund Brailsford, 7 February, 1726/27, *South Carolina Historical and Genealogical Magazine* 8 (1907), 156-59.

51. Alice Izard to Ralph Izard, 4 November 1794, Ralph Izard Papers, SCL.

52. Richard Hutson to Isaac Hayne, 9 October 1773, Isaac Hayne Letterbook, SCHS; Maurice Crouse, ed., "Papers of Gabriel Manigault, 1771-1784," *South Carolina Historical Magazine* 64 (1963); Ralph Izard to Edward Rutledge, 16 May 1789, Ralph Izard Papers, SCL.

53. By and large, Chesapeake settlers did not migrate with as many siblings and kin, so it took a generation or two for kin networks to develop there. Breen, *Puritans and Adventurers;* Edmund Morgan, *American Slavery, American Freedom: The Ordeal of Colonial Virginia* (New York: Norton, 1975); Kulikoff, *Tobacco and Slaves;* Smith, *Inside the Great House;* Lois Carr, Philip Morgan, and Jean Russo, eds., *Colonial Chesapeake Society* (Chapel Hill: University of North Carolina Press, 1988); Tate and Ammerman, *Chesapeake in the Seventeenth Century.* One exception to this interpretation is Darrett and Anita Rutman, *A Place in Time,* in which the authors argue that early Virginians cobbled together a fairly stable society based on neighbors, friends, and kin. Still, the Rutmans largely ignored siblings in their study.

54. Psychologists and anthropologists insist that parental death deepens the attachments between siblings and transforms their responsibilities to one another. Dunn, *Sis-*

ters and Brothers; Bank and Kahn, "Intense Sibling Loyalty," in Lamb and Sutton-Smith, *Sibling Relationships;* and Bank and Kahn, *Sibling Bond.*

55. Miscellaneous correspondence, Manigault Family Papers, SCL; Miscellaneous correspondence, James Glen and John Drayton, James Glen Papers, SCL; Robinson, *James Glen,* 129; Eliza Pinckney to Charles Cotesworth Pinckney, August 1758, *Letterbook,* 94–95.

56. Similar patterns have been investigated in the nineteenth-century South by Mary Stovall Richards, "All Our Connections: Kinship, Family Structure, and Dynamics among White Families in the Mid-Nineteenth-Century Central South," *Tennessee Historical Quarterly* 50 (Fall 1991), 142–51. Richards argues that taking in kin, either permanently or temporarily, was a frequent occurrence in the lives of early Southerners. Families expected and sometimes encouraged taking in relatives who were between homes, newly married, or recently orphaned. Anne Wilson to Anne Hart, 29 April 1808, Oliver Hart Papers, SCL.

57. For a similar discussion of the early Chesapeake see Rutman and Rutman, *A Place in Time,* 114–20.

58. William E. Hayne to Jeremiah A. Yates, 23 December 1835, William Edward Hayne Papers, SCL.

59. Maurice Crouse, ed., "Papers of Gabriel Manigault, 1771–1784," *South Carolina Historical Magazine* 64 (1963), 1–2.

60. Joseph Manigault to Gabriel Manigault, 20 March 1772; Anne Manigault to Gabriel Manigault, 3 May 1776; Joseph Manigault to Gabriel Manigault, 5 July 1783, Manigault Family Papers, SCL.

61. Miscellaneous correspondence, Manigault Family Papers, SCL; Jonathan Bryan to Elizabeth Bryan, 17 May 1792, Jonathan Bryan Papers, SCL.

62. Pinckney, *Letterbook;* Isaac Motte to William Drayton, 6 August 1780, Isaac Motte Papers, SCL.

63. Sally Rutledge's mother's sister, Sally (Sarah) Middleton Pinckney, was the first wife of Charles Cotesworth Pinckney. After she died, Pinckney married Mary Stead. Edward Rutledge to Sally Rutledge, 30 April 1792, Edward Rutledge Papers, SCL; *Papers of Henry Laurens;* Oliver Hart to Joseph Hart, 10 September 1778, Oliver Hart Papers, SCL; Harriott Pinckney Horry to Daniel Horry, 28 February 1786; Harriott Pinckney Horry Letterbook, Harriet Ravenel Papers, SCHS.

Politically involved fathers in other regions mirrored the behavior of South Carolinians. Thomas Jefferson spent so much time away from his daughter Polly that she did not even recognize him. Abigail Adams reported: "I show her your picture. She cannot know it, how could she when she could not know you." Abigail Adams to Thomas Jefferson, 26 June 1787. Quoted in Joseph Ellis, *American Sphinx: The Character of Thomas Jefferson* (New York: Knopf, 1997), 86.

64. Alice Izard to Ralph Izard, 11 December 1784, Ralph Izard Papers, SCL.

65. For similar interpretations of the nineteenth century, see Cashin, "Structure of

Antebellum Planter Families," 55-70; Osterud, *Bonds of Community;* and Barry Reay, "Kinship and the Neighborhood in Nineteenth-Century Rural England: The Myth of the Autonomous Nuclear Family," *Journal of Family History* 21 (January 1996), 87-104.

66. Merrell, *Accidental Bond,* 15; Dunn, *Sisters and Brothers,* 14. See also Mildred M. Seltzer, "The Three R's of Life Cycle Sibships," in Bedford and Gold, "Siblings in Later Life," 107-15.

67. As Susan Merrell argued, throughout adulthood, siblings remain "yardsticks against whom our own achievements can be measured." Merrell, *Accidental Bond,* 4. Judy Dunn, a preeminent scholar of siblings, concurs. According to Dunn, sibling ties "withstand the separations of time and space, and provide important emotional security for most people in the later stages of life." Dunn, *Sisters and Brothers,* 140.

68. Court cases might reveal more on this subject, but would tend to overemphasize disunity by illustrating only litigious sibling and kin relationships.

69. Deborah Gold, "Generational Solidarity: Conceptual Antecedents and Consequences," in Bedford and Gold, "Siblings in Later Life," 28.

70. Thomas Pinckney to Harriott Pinckney Horry, 7 April 1778, Jack L. Cross, ed., "Letters of Thomas Pinckney, 1775-1780," *South Carolina Historical Magazine* 58 (1957), 148; William Hasell Gibbes to Peter Manigault, 12 April [year unknown], Manigault Family Papers, SCL; Thomas Pinckney, Jr., to Harriott Pinckney, miscellaneous letters, in Anna Wells Rutledge, ed., "Letters from Thomas Pinckney Jr. to Harriott Pinckney," *South Carolina Historical and Genealogical Magazine* 41 (1940), 99-116; Frances Moore Bayard to Stephen Moore, 12 May 1769, Stephen Moore Papers, SCL.

71. Alice Izard to Ralph Izard, 30 December 1794, Ralph Izard Papers, SCL.

72. This pattern typified family relations among siblings and kin. In her theoretical model of sibling support networks, sociologist Paula Avioli argued that adult sibling interaction could best be characterized by balanced reciprocity, exchanges of support, and maintenance of personal autonomy. That is, siblings cooperate equally and willingly while embracing individual rights. Avioli, "The Social Support Functions of Siblings in Later Life." Similar findings have been uncovered by Kenneth Minkema, whose study of the Edwards sisters demonstrated that sororal connections and cooperation shaped when, why, and who they married. Minkema, "Hannah and Her Sisters."

73. Most studies of incest are done by psychologists and social scientists who view incest as a pathology or focus on treatment and recovery for incest survivors. Examples include Blair Justice, *The Broken Taboo: Sex in the Family* (New York: Human Sciences Press, 1979); James Maddox and Noel Larson, *Incestuous Families: An Ecological Approach to Understanding and Treatment* (New York: Norton, 1995); and Karin Meiselman, *Incest: A Psychological Study of Causes and Effects with Treatment Recommendations* (San Francisco: Jossey-Bass, 1978).

Anthropologists have completed a few works studying incest from a cultural, definitional perspective—how it changes over time and differs across cultures. See Fox, *Kinship and Marriage,* chap. 2; Fox, *Red Lamp of Incest;* Holy, *Anthropological Perspectives in Kin-*

ship; Pasternak, Ember, and Ember, *Sex, Gender, and Kinship,* chaps. 5 and 6; and Wolfram, *In-Laws and Outlaws.* Historians have yet to tackle the subject in a comprehensive manner.

The incest taboo in western culture is based in part on biblical standards presented in Leviticus. In the nineteenth century, scholars like Claude Lévi-Strauss and Lewis Henry Morgan added to this biblical standard new theories about inbreeding and genetic mutations. Still, marital prohibitions within America have varied sharply from region to region and over time. For a brief explanation of the prohibitive degrees of marriage and sexuality, see Ottenheimer, *Forbidden Relatives,* chap. 1. See also Bank and Kahn, *Sibling Bond,* 157–96; Bell, *Interrogating Incest;* Polly Morris, "Incest or Survival Strategy?: Plebeian Marriage within the Prohibited Degrees in Somerset, 1730–1835," *Journal of the History of Sexuality* 2 (October 1991), 235–65; and James Twitchell, *Forbidden Partners: The Incest Taboo in Modern Culture* (New York: Columbia University Press, 1987).

74. Until the mid-nineteenth century, cousin marriages occurred often and with no state restrictions. After mid-century the number of cousin marriages declined dramatically in most parts of the country as state prohibition laws increased. South Carolina, however, never outlawed such unions. For further discussions of cousin marriages see Martin Ottenheimer, "Lewis Henry Morgan and the Prohibition of Cousin Marriage in the United States," *Journal of Family History* 15 (1990), 325–34; Ottenheimer, *Forbidden Relatives;* Bernard Farber, *Comparative Kinship Systems* (New York: John Wiley and Sons, 1968); and Fox, *Kinship and Marriage.* For a comparison to the colonial Chesapeake see Kulikoff, *Tobacco and Slaves.*

75. Edgar, *Letterbook of Robert Pringle;* Izard Family Papers, SCL; Gallay, *The Formation of a Planter Elite.*

76. Farber, *Comparative Kinship Systems.*

77. Anthropologists Bernard Farber and Robin Fox have both concluded that close kin marriages foster homogeneity and conservatism. For further theoretical discussion see Farber, *Comparative Kinship Systems* and Fox, *Kinship and Marriage.*

78. Several scholars have studied the pervasiveness and meaning of visiting in the eighteenth and nineteenth centuries. Examples include Cashin, "The Ties That Bound Us"; Osterud, *Bonds of Community;* Cynthia Kierner, "Hospitality, Sociability, and Gender in the Southern Colonies," *Journal of Southern History* 62 (August 1996), 449–80; Richards, "All Our Connections"; Smith, *Inside the Great House;* Nancy Tomes, "The Quaker Connection: Visiting Patterns among Women in the Philadelphia Society of Friends, 1750–1800," in Michael Zuckerman, ed., *Friends and Neighbors: Group Life in America's First Plural Society* (Philadelphia: Temple University Press, 1982); Ulrich, *A Midwife's Tale;* and Michael Zuckerman, "William Byrd's Family," *Perspectives in American History* 12 (1979), 255–311.

79. Anne Hart to Oliver Hart, 20 February 1785, Oliver Hart Papers, SCL; Henry Laurens to Augustus Johnson, 13 July 1770, *Papers of Henry Laurens,* vol. 7, 312.

80. Ralph Izard to unknown correspondent, 15 July 1796, Ralph Izard Papers, SCL;

Eliza Pinckney to Mrs. Evance, August 1758, *Letterbook,* 99; Anne Hart to Oliver Hart, 20 February 1785, Oliver Hart Papers, SCL.

81. Alice Izard to Ralph Izard, 8 January 1795, Ralph Izard Papers, SCL.

82. In her study of Quaker women's visiting patterns, Nancy Tomes made similar findings. The women in her study, like their neighbors to the south, defined family broadly and derived emotional support from their kinswomen. Visiting was a reflection of these emotional connections. The world of kin-based visiting often resonated more among women than men. Tomes, "The Quaker Connection," 184–85. See also Kulikoff, *Tobacco and Slaves,* 230.

83. Alice Izard to Ralph Izard, 6 December 1794; Alice Izard to Ralph Izard, 4 December 1794, Ralph Izard Papers, SCL.

84. Anne Deas to Ralph Izard, Jr., 9 May 1802, Ralph Izard Papers, SCL.

85. Eliza Lucas to Mary Bartlett, ca. April 1742, *Letterbook,* 34.

86. Daniel Blake Smith explored the idea of female "kin guardians" in *Inside the Great House,* 226–28.

87. Joseph Manigault to Gabriel Manigault, 20 August 1789, Manigault Family Papers, SCL; Rogers, *Charleston in the Age of the Pinckneys,* 124; Joseph Manigault to Gabriel Manigault, 5 January 1787; Joseph Manigault to Gabriel Manigault, 20 August 1789; Joseph Manigault to Gabriel Manigault, 4 January 1790, Manigault Family Papers, SCL; Miscellaneous Correspondence, Pinckney Family Papers, SCL; Barnwell, "The Diary of Timothy Ford," 181–82.

88. Robert Pringle to Andrew Pringle, 20 May 1740, Edgar, *Letterbook of Robert Pringle,* vol. 1; miscellaneous letters, Pinckney Family Papers, SCL.

89. Henry Izard to Margaret Izard Manigault, 28 March 1799, Ralph Izard Papers, SCL; Frances Moore Bayard to Stephen Moore, 24 November 1763; Stephen Moore to Frances Moore Bayard, 28 September 1769, Stephen Moore Papers, SCL; Thomas Pinckney, Jr., to Harriott Pinckney, 23 December 1801; Thomas Pinckney, Jr., to Harriott Pinckney, 2 January 1802, in Rutledge, "Letters from Thomas Pinckney Jr. to Harriott Pinckney," 99–116. Harriott Pinckney was the daughter of Charles Cotesworth Pinckney and Thomas was the son of Thomas Pinckney, Charles Cotesworth Pinckney's brother.

90. By the late eighteenth century, Lord Chesterfield's *Letters to his Son* had become a bestseller in America. Along with Benjamin Franklin's *Ways to Wealth* and George Washington's "110 Precepts," Chesterfield helped codify the ideals of genteel society and encourage a self-conscious attention to the publicly represented self. It was often reprinted, including in R. K. Root, ed., *Lord Chesterfield's Letters to His Son* (London: J. M. Dent, 1929). For further analysis of advice literature in this period see Sarah Newton, *Learning to Behave: A Guide to American Conduct Books before 1900* (Westport, Conn.: Greenwood, 1994); C. Dallett Hemphill, "Class, Gender, and the Regulation of Emotional Expression in Revolutionary Era Conduct Literature," in Jan Lewis and Peter Stearns, eds., *An Emotional History of the United States* (New York: New York University

Press, 1998), 33–51; Bushman, *Refinement of America*, chap. 2; and Arthur Schlesinger, *Learning How to Behave: A Historical Study of American Etiquette Books* (New York: Macmillan, 1946).

91. Bushman, *Refinement of America*. For analysis of letter writing between elites in the old South, see Steven Stowe, *Intimacy and Power in the Old South: Ritual in the Lives of the Planters* (Baltimore: Johns Hopkins University Press, 1987), 88–96. And to see how this influenced the behavior of South Carolina's most famous female planter, see Darcy Fryer, "The Mind of Eliza Pinckney: An Eighteenth-Century Woman's Construction of Herself," *South Carolina Historical Magazine* 99 (July 1998), 215–37.

92. Mary Pinckney to Margaret Manigault, 30 March 1797, Manigault Family Papers, SCL.

93. Eliza Lucas to George Lucas, ca. 1742, *Letterbook*, 52.

94. Again one must turn to developmental psychologists to explain the effects of sibling sickness and death. Recent analyses include Bank and Kahn, *Sibling Bond;* Joanna Fanos, *Sibling Loss* (Hillsdale, N.J.: Lawrence Erlbaum Associates, 1996); and Sidney Moss and Miriam Moss, "The Impact of the Death of an Elderly Sibling," in Bedford and Gold, "Siblings in Later Life," 94–106.

95. Mary Pinckney to Mary Manigault, 30 March 1797, Manigault Family Papers, SCL; Eliza Lucas to Mrs. Boddicott, 29 June 1742, *Letterbook*, 42.

96. Henry Laurens to Joseph Brown, 29 October 1764, *Papers of Henry Laurens*, vol. 4, 483; Alice Izard to Mrs. DeLancey, 12 February 1776, Ralph Izard Papers, SCL; Margaret Manigault to Mrs. Lewis Morris, Jr., 3 January 1813, Manigault-Morris-Grimball Papers, Southern Historical Collection, University of North Carolina, Chapel Hill (hereafter SHC).

97. Alice Izard to Gabriel Manigault, 8 September 1792, Ralph Izard Papers, SCL.

98. James Glen to Henry Drayton, undated letter, James Glen Papers, SCL.

99. Henry Laurens to James Penman, 13 October 1767, *Papers of Henry Laurens*, vol. 5, 355; Alice Izard to Ralph Izard, 30 December 1794, Ralph Izard Papers, SCL.

100. Margaret Manigault to Gabriel Manigault, 20 March 1778, Manigault Family Papers, SCL.

101. Jonathan Bryan to Elizabeth Bryan, 17 May 1792; Jonathan Bryan to Elizabeth Bryan, 20 June 1794, Jonathan Bryan Papers, SCL; Thomas Reaston to Nathaniel Broughton, 20 October 1753, D. E. Huger Smith, ed., "Broughton Letters," *South Carolina Historical and Genealogical Magazine* 15 (1914), 193.

102. Joseph Manigault to Gabriel Manigault, 18 March 1784, Manigault Family Papers, SCL.

103. Charles Izard Manigault, Family Reminiscence, Charles Izard Manigault Papers, SCL.

104. Catherine Read to Elizabeth Ludlow, 9 December 1785, Read Family Papers, SCL; Joseph Manigault to Gabriel Manigault, 4 August 1785, Manigault Family Papers, SCL; Edward Rutledge to Charles Rutledge, ca. 1784, Edward Rutledge Papers, SCL.

105. Ingrid Connidis, "Siblings as Friends in Later Life," in Bedford and Gold, "Siblings in Later Life"; Cicirelli, *Sibling Relationships across the Life Span;* Avioli, "The Social Support Functions of Siblings in Later Life"; and Thomas Weisner, "Sibling Interdependence and Child Caretaking," in Lamb and Sutton-Smith, *Sibling Relationships,* 305–27.

CHAPTER THREE

1. Eliza Wilkinson to Mary P——, 20 September 1782, Eliza Wilkinson to Mary P——, 30 July 1782, Eliza Wilkinson Papers, SCL.
2. Examples include Kathleen M. Brown, *Good Wives, Nasty Wenches, and Anxious Patriarchs: Gender, Race, and Power in Colonial Virginia* (Chapel Hill: University of North Carolina Press, 1996); Kulikoff, *Tobacco and Slaves;* Smith, *Inside the Great House;* and Ulrich, *Good Wives.* See also Linda Kerber, "Separate Spheres, Female Worlds, Women's Place: The Rhetoric of Women's History," *Journal of American History* 75 (1988), 9–39. One of the best and most recent general works on women in colonial America is Carol Berkin, *First Generations: Women in Colonial America* (New York: Hill and Wang, 1996).
3. Mary Beth Norton has recently complicated these categories in her study of gender in seventeenth-century British America. See her excellent *Founding Mothers and Fathers: Gendered Power and the Forming of American Society* (New York: Knopf, 1996) for an analysis of the complex interweaving of public and private life in the early colonies. See also Cynthia Kierner, *Beyond the Household: Women's Place in the Early South, 1700–1835* (Ithaca: Cornell University Press, 1998).
4. Brown, *Good Wives,* 304; Smith, *Inside the Great House,* 71–73.
5. The quote comes from Brown, *Good Wives,* 306. See also Carroll Smith-Rosenberg, "The Female World of Love and Ritual: Relations Between Women in Nineteenth-Century America," *Signs* 1 (Autumn 1979), 1–29; Kerber, "Separate Spheres"; and Mary Beth Norton, "The Evolution of White Women's Experience in Early America," *American Historical Review* 71 (June 1984), 593–619.
6. Several recent works by historians and anthropologists have begun to move beyond looking only at women's status and roles and instead place gender at the center of society and culture. However, they still rely heavily on the traditional framework of power within the patriarchal family. Brown, *Good Wives;* Stephanie McCurry, *Masters of Small Worlds: Yeoman Households, Gender Relations, and the Political Culture of the Antebellum South Carolina Low Country* (New York: Oxford University Press, 1995); Norton, *Founding Mothers and Fathers;* Jane Collier and Sylvia Yanagisako, eds., *Gender and Kinship: Essays toward a Unified Analysis* (Stanford: Stanford University Press, 1987); and Pasternak, Ember, and Ember, *Sex, Gender, and Kinship.*
7. Similar patterns have been uncovered by clinical psychologists working with siblings. Judy Dunn found that the affectionate quality of sibling connections mattered far

more in shaping their patterns of interaction than either gender or birth order. Dunn, *Sisters and Brothers*, 137.

8. A number of scholars have weighed in on the status of women in early America, including Lois Carr and Lorena Walsh, "The Planter's Wife: The Experience of White Women in Seventeenth-Century Maryland," *William and Mary Quarterly* 34 (October 1977), 542–71; Nancy Cott, *The Bonds of Womanhood: Women's Sphere in New England, 1780–1835* (New Haven: Yale University Press, 1977); Cornelia Dayton, *Women before the Bar: Gender, Law and Society in Connecticut, 1639–1789* (Chapel Hill: University of North Carolina Press, 1995); Edith Gelles, *Portia: The World of Abigail Adams* (Bloomington: Indiana University Press, 1992); Kerber, "Separate Spheres"; Norton, "The Evolution of White Women's Experience in Early America"; Marylynn Salmon, "Women and Property Ownership in South Carolina: The Evidence from Marriage Settlements," *William and Mary Quarterly* 39 (October 1982), 655–85; and Brown, *Good Wives*.

9. Eliza Lucas to George Lucas, 2 May 1744, in Harriott Horry Ravenel, *Eliza Pinckney* (New York: Scribners, 1896), 69.

10. Eliza Lucas to George Lucas, undated letter, *Eliza Pinckney*, 56–57.

11. See, for example, Smith, *Inside the Great House;* and Lewis, *The Pursuit of Happiness.*

12. William Read to Jacob Read, 18 December 1795; William Read to Jacob Read, 26 February 1796; William Read to Jacob Read, 29 December 1795, Jacob Read Papers, SCL.

13. Edward Rutledge to Sarah Rutledge, 8 October 1792, Edward Rutledge Papers, SCL; Gabriel Manigault to Margaret Izard Manigault, Miscellaneous Correspondence, Manigault Family Papers, SCL; Eliza Pinckney to Charles and Thomas Pinckney, August 1758, Pinckney, *Letterbook*, 94; Henry Laurens to Lachlan McIntosh, 7 March 1763, *Papers of Henry Laurens*, vol. 3, 362.

14. Ralph Izard to Alice Izard, 28 December 1782, Ralph Izard Papers, SCL.

15. Ralph Izard to Dr. Johnson, 20 December 1787, ibid.

16. Ralph Izard to Alice Izard, 7 November 1775, Ralph Izard to Alice Izard, 28 December 1782, ibid.

17. Samuel Wragg to Peter Manigault, 17 September 1756, Manigault Family Papers, SCL.

18. Henry Laurens to Matthew Robinson, 19 October 1768, *Papers of Henry Laurens*, vol. 6, 139–41.

19. Henry Laurens to Henry Humphreys, 19 May 1770, *Papers of Henry Laurens*, vol. 7, 296–98.

20. Eliza Pinckney to Daniel Horry, Jr., 16 April 1782, *South Carolina Historical Magazine* 76 (1975), 167.

21. John Drayton to James Glen, 6 February 1773, James Glen Papers, SCL.

22. Edward Rutledge to Sarah Rutledge, 8 October 1792, Edward Rutledge Papers, SCL.

23. Henry Laurens to James Habersham, 4 June 1768, *Papers of Henry Laurens*, vol. 5, 717; William Read to Jacob Read, 18 December 1795, Jacob Read Papers, SCL; Edward Rutledge to "Dear Friend," 26 August 1792, Edward Rutledge Papers, SCL.

24. Henry Laurens to Mathias Holmes, 20 May 1763, *Papers of Henry Laurens*, vol. 3, 461; Henry Laurens to Mary Gittens, 18 September 1747, *Papers of Henry Laurens*, vol. 1, 56–58.

25. Joseph Barnwell, ed., "The Diary of Timothy Ford, 1785-1786," *South Carolina Historical and Genealogical Magazine* 13 (1912), 190–91.

26. Joseph Manigault to Gabriel Manigault, 18 December 1786, Manigault Family Papers, SCL.

27. The rise of the affectionate family and the increasing presence of marriages based on love and personal choice has been investigated by a number of scholars. Among the first and most influential works on this topic are Edward Shorter, *The Making of the Modern Family* (New York: Norton, 1975); Lawrence Stone, *The Family, Sex and Marriage in England, 1500-1800* (New York: Harper and Row, 1977); and Smith, *Inside the Great House*.

28. Pinckney, *Letterbook*, xxi.

29. White women also frequently endured their husbands' sexual exploitation of slave women. Much more has been done on this topic by nineteenth-century historians than by early Americanists. See Catherine Clinton, *The Plantation Mistress: Women's World in the Old South* (New York: Pantheon, 1982); Elizabeth Fox-Genovese, *Within the Plantation Household: Black and White Women of the Old South* (Chapel Hill: University of North Carolina Press, 1988); Jacqueline Jones, *Labor of Love, Labor of Sorrow: Black Women, Work, and the Family from Slavery to the Present* (New York: Basic Books, 1985); Winthrop Jordan, *White over Black: American Attitudes toward the Negro, 1550-1812* (Chapel Hill: University of North Carolina Press, 1968); and Deborah Gray White, *'Ar'n't I a Woman': Female Slaves in the Plantation South* (New York: Norton, 1985).

30. Thomas Dale to Thomas Birch, 17 November 1732, Thomas Dale Papers, SCL.

31. George Lucas to Charles Pinckney, 23 December 1745, Harriet Ravenel Papers, SCHS.

32. Part of the happiness no doubt came from continued immersion in the broader family network. In her study of kinship in nineteenth-century New York, Nancy Osterud argued that women married neighbors not only because of proximity and parental approval, but because it allowed them to remain near their kin. Osterud, *Bonds of Community*, 69.

33. Henry Laurens to Matthew Robinson, 30 May 1764, *Papers of Henry Laurens*, vol. 4, 295. (Laurens married Eleanor Ball in 1750.)

34. Oliver Hart to Anne Hart, 12 June 1781, Anne Hart to Oliver Hart, 14 May 1785, Oliver Hart Papers, SCL; Margaret Manigault to Gabriel Manigault, 20 November 1792; Gabriel Manigault to Margaret Manigault, 6 December 1791, Manigault Family

Papers, SCL; Catherine Read to Elizabeth Ludlow, undated letter, Read Family Papers, SCL.

35. Charles Pinckney to Peter Manigault, 8 April 1756, Manigault Family Papers, SCL.

36. John Drayton to James Glen, 3 July 1769, James Glen Papers, SCL. Mrs. Drayton never recovered from her illness, and her brother never forgave John Drayton for refusing the offer that Glen thought would have saved his sister's life.

37. Ralph Izard to Alice Izard, 28 December 1782, Ralph Izard Papers, SCL.

38. For fuller exposition, see Brown, *Good Wives;* David Barry Gaspar and Darlene Clark Hine, eds., *More than Chattel: Black Women and Slavery in the Americas* (Bloomington: Indiana University Press, 1996); and Catherine Clinton and Michele Gillespie, eds., *The Devil's Lane: Sex and Race in the Early South* (New York: Oxford University Press, 1997).

39. For a thorough analysis of this pattern among eighteenth-century Chesapeake gentry, see Kulikoff, *Tobacco and Slaves,* 217–31, and Brown, *Good Wives.* Joan Cashin has recently argued that by the early nineteenth century this had contributed to, among southern women, a "culture of resignation." Joan Cashin, "Culture of Resignation," *Our Common Affairs: Texts from Women in the Old South* (Baltimore: Johns Hopkins University Press, 1996), 1–30.

40. Anne Hart to Oliver Hart, 20 February 1785, Oliver Hart Papers, SCL; Eliza Wilkinson to unknown correspondent, 8 January 1781, Eliza Wilkinson Papers, SCL; Eliza Lucas to George Lucas, c. 1742, *Letterbook,* 52; Henry Izard to Margaret Manigault, 20 March 1799, Ralph Izard Papers, SCL.

41. Thomas Dale to Thomas Birch, 25 November 1734, Thomas Dale Papers, SCL; Henry Laurens to Elizabeth Laurens, 26 December 1748, *Papers of Henry Laurens,* vol. 1, 191; Oliver Hart to Joseph Hart, 10 September 1778, Oliver Hart Papers, SCL.

42. Typical of this tendency, Ralph Izard corresponded with his son-in-law Gabriel Manigault and not his daughter Margaret. Sometimes he asked Gabriel to "Give my Love to my Daughter." Ralph Izard to Gabriel Manigault, 9 July 1789, Ralph Izard Papers, SCL.

43. Miscellaneous correspondence, Manigault Family Papers, SCL. The quotation comes from Mary Pinckney to Margaret Manigault, 30 March 1797, Manigault Family Papers, SCL.

44. Eliza Lucas Pinckney to Mrs. Bartlett, 7 March 1745, Pinckney Papers, Duke University Library (hereafter DUL). See also Fryer, "The Mind of Eliza Pinckney."

45. Eliza Wilkinson to Ms. Brewton, 30 July 1782, Eliza Wilkinson Papers, SCL; Elizabeth Hassell to Gabriel Manigault, 6 June 1775, Manigault Family Papers, SCL.

46. John Lloyd to Julia Campion, 3 June 1794, John Lloyd Letterbook, SCL; Rebecca Moore to Stephen Moore, 13 December 1772, Stephen Moore Papers, SCL.

47. Anne Deas to Ralph Izard, Jr., 9 May 1802, Ralph Izard Papers, SCL; Eliza Lucas to Tommy Lucas, July 1741, *Letterbook,* 17.

48. Margaret Manigault to Gabriel Manigault, 20 November 1792, Manigault Family papers, SCL; Thomas Pinckney to Harriott Pinckney Horry, 20 June 1777, Cross, "Letters of Thomas Pinckney, 1775-1780," 82; Harriott Pinckney to Mrs. Blake, 10 December 1766, Harriott Pinckney Horry Letterbook, SCHS; Margaret Manigault to Gabriel Manigault, 20 November 1792, Manigault Family Papers, SCL.

49. Alice Izard to Ralph Izard, 25 December 1794, Ralph Izard Papers, SCL.

50. Henry Laurens and Henry Smith, miscellaneous correspondence, August 1766, *Papers of Henry Laurens*, vol. 5.

51. Jacob Read to Anne Edgar, 25 January 1795, Read Family Papers, SCL.

52. Henry Laurens to Mary Gittens, 18 September 1747, *Papers of Henry Laurens*, vol. 1, 56-58.

53. David Hunter to Elizabeth Dunlap and Margaret McDermitt, 25 November 1755, David Hunter Papers, SCL.

54. For further analysis see Anne Firor Scott, "Self-Portraits: Three Women," in Richard Bushman et al., eds., *Uprooted Americans: Essays to Honor Oscar Handlin* (Boston: Little, Brown, 1979), 76.

55. Elizabeth Massingbred Hyrne to Burrell Massingbred, 19 January 1701/2, in Schmidt, "Hyrne Family Letters," 63, 154.

56. Thomas Pinckney to Harriott Pinckney Horry, undated letter; Thomas Pinckney to Harriott Pinckney Horry, various letters, in Cross, "Thomas Pinckney Letters"; Henry Izard to Margaret Izard Manigault, 28 March 1799, Ralph Izard Papers, SCL.

57. Thomas Pinckney, Jr., was the son of Thomas and Elizabeth Motte Pinckney. Harriott's father, Charles Cotesworth Pinckney, was Thomas Pinckney, Sr., and Harriott Pinckney Horry's brother. The younger Harriott was born in 1776, Thomas Jr. in 1780. Anna Wells Rutledge, ed., "Letters from Thomas Pinckney Jr. to Harriott Pinckney," *South Carolina Historical and Genealogical Magazine* 41 (1940), 99-116.

58. Thomas Pinckney to Harriott Pinckney, 21 September 1801; Thomas Pinckney to Harriott Pinckney, 2 October 1801; Thomas Pinckney to Harriott Pinckney, 2 January 1802; Thomas Pinckney to Harriott Pinckney, 9 January 1802, Thomas Pinckney to Harriott Pinckney, 10 January 1802, Rutledge, "Letters from Thomas Pinckney Jr. to Harriott Pinckney," 109-10. Elizabeth Izard married Thomas Pinckney in 1803. Harriott's sister Eliza Lucas Pinckney (1776-1866) married Ralph Izard, a relative of Elizabeth Izard.

59. Anne Broughton to Nathaniel Broughton, 5 December 1716, D. E. Huger Smith, ed., "Broughton Letters," *South Carolina Historical and Genealogical Magazine* 15 (1914), 176.

60. Staats Morris to "My dear Sister," undated letter, Morris and Rutherford Family Papers, SCL; Stephen Moore to Frances Moore Bayard, 28 September 1769, Stephen Moore Papers, SCL. Men were particularly concerned that their sisters approve of their wives because their marriage added a new member to the female kin group.

61. Eliza Lucas to Tommy Lucas, July 1741, *Letterbook*, 17.

62. Eliza Lucas to George Lucas, ca. 1742, ibid., 45.

63. Anne Manigault, 23 March 1778, Manigault Family Papers, SCL.

64. For theoretical explanations of the interplay between parent-child relations and sibling connections, see Dunn and Kendrick, *Siblings;* Lamb and Sutton-Smith, *Sibling Relationships;* Bank and Kahn, *Sibling Bond;* and Bedford and Gold, "Siblings in Later Life."

65. Henry Laurens to Mathias Holmes, 20 May 1763, *Papers of Henry Laurens,* vol. 3, 460–61.

66. Richard Hutson to Isaac Hayne, 27 May 1776; Richard Hutson to Isaac Hayne, 24 June 1776; Richard Hutson to Isaac Hayne, 2 September 1776, Letterbook of Richard Hutson, Papers of Langdon Cheves III, SCHS.

67. Cynthia Kierner's recent synthesis of women's lives in the early south reaffirms this. Cynthia Kierner, *Beyond the Household: Women's Place in the Early South, 1700–1835* (Ithaca: Cornell University Press, 1998). See also Kierner, "Hospitality, Sociability, and Gender in the Southern Colonies," and Anzilotti, "Autonomy and the Female Planter in Colonial South Carolina."

68. Brown, *Good Wives;* Kulikoff, *Tobacco and Slaves;* Smith-Rosenberg, "The Female World of Love and Ritual." Similar analyses are undertaken in Cott, *The Bonds of Womanhood;* Linda Kerber, *Women of the Republic: Intellect and Ideology in Revolutionary America* (Chapel Hill: University of North Carolina Press, 1980); Mary Beth Norton, *Liberty's Daughters: The Revolutionary Experience of American Women, 1750–1800* (New York: Little, Brown, 1980); and Smith, *Inside the Great House.*

69. In both *A Midwife's Tale* and *Good Wives,* Laurel Ulrich clearly demonstrated how women's connections with other female kin and neighbors held important meaning and power not only for the women but also for economic, religious, and social activities within the community. By breaking down the artificial barrier between public and private life, we see clearly the relevance of women's networks within the family and community. Cynthia Kierner's recent analysis of early southern women reached a similar conclusion. Ulrich, *Good Wives;* Ulrich, *A Midwife's Tale;* Kierner, *Beyond the Household.*

70. While few scholars pay any attention to sisters, important exceptions have recently appeared. In a 1988 essay in *Signs,* Carol Lasser explored the importance of both real and "elective" sisters to nineteenth-century women, concluding that sisterhood offered a fundamentally important experience and provided an important model for building other female relationships. Carol Lasser, "'Let Us Be Sisters Forever': The Sororal Model of Nineteenth-Century Female Friendships," *Signs* 14 (1988), 158–81. Other recent, yet unfortunately rare, exceptions include Joan Cashin, "'Decidedly Opposed to *the Union*': Women's Culture, Marriage, and Politics in Antebellum South Carolina," *Georgia Historical Quarterly* 78 (Winter 1994), 735–59; Gelles, *Portia,* 104–32; Minkema, "Hannah and Her Sisters," 35–56; Marilyn Ferris Motz, *True Sisterhood; Michigan Women and Their Kin, 1820–1900* (Albany: State University of New York Press, 1983); and John Cashmere, "Sisters Together," *Journal of Family History* 21 (January

1996), 44–62. Clinical psychologists and other social scientists have studied sororal connections far more than historians. Dale Atkins, *Sisters* (New York: Arbor House, 1984); Dunn, *Sisters and Brothers;* Dunn and Kendrick, *Siblings;* Collier and Yanagisako, *Gender and Kinship;* and Cicirelli, *Sibling Relationships across the Life Span.*

71. Despite general agreement that this is so, social scientists disagree over why. See Dale Atkins, *Sisters* (New York: Arbor House, 1984); Cicirelli, *Sibling Relationships across the Life Span,* 73–75; and Cicirelli, "Sibling Influence across the Life Span," in Lamb and Sutton-Smith, *Sibling Relationships,* 267–84. There are, however, dissenting voices. A few scholars argue that much of this interpretation about sisterly bonds is predicated on an ignorance of brothers' connections. Sarah Matthews, Paula Delaney, and Margaret Adamek, "Male Kinship Ties: Bonds Between Adult Brothers," and Ingrid Connidis, "Siblings as Friends in Later Life," in Bedford and Gold, "Siblings in Later Life." This final point is presented in Atkins, *Sisters,* 16–17.

72. This idea is supported by sibling scholars such as Judy Dunn, who argued that sisters provide key emotional support within the family and "play a major role in keeping family relationships together over time." Dunn, *Sisters and Brothers,* 139. Further, this interpretation parallels Carol Lasser's study of nineteenth-century women. According to Lasser, "Sisters saw themselves involved in a connection that required demonstrative affection, emotional mutuality, and the fulfillment of obligations." Lasser, "Let Us Be Sisters Forever," 169.

73. Catherine Read to Elizabeth Ludlow, undated letter, Read Family Papers, SCL; Alice Izard to Mrs. DeLancey, 12 February 1776, Ralph Izard Papers, SCL.

74. Family Reminiscence of Charles Izard Manigault, Charles Izard Manigault Papers, SCL. See also Lasser, "Let Us Be Sisters Forever."

75. Eliza Lucas to George Lucas, March 1740, *Letterbook,* 5; Sophia Penn to Charlotte Izard, 30 November 1784, Ralph Izard Papers, SCL; Mary Pinckney to Margaret Manigault, 16 September 1796, Manigault Family Papers, SCL.

76. Miscellaneous correspondence, Ralph Izard Papers, SCL.

77. Alice Izard to Gabriel Manigault, 8 September 1792, Ralph Izard Papers, SCL; Margaret Manigault to Gabriel Manigault, 20 November 1792, Manigault Family Papers, SCL.

78. William Moultrie to Hannah Moultrie, 29 November 1782, William Moultrie Papers, SCL.

79. Alice Izard to Mrs. DeLancey, 12 February 1776, Ralph Izard Papers, SCL.

80. Catherine Read to Elizabeth Ludlow, undated letter, Read Family Papers, SCL.

81. Nancy Osterud has made similar arguments about nineteenth-century New York, where she found that "women shaped the kinship system to their own purposes, strengthening their position within their households." Osterud, *Bonds of Community,* 11.

82. Cynthia Kierner made a similar conclusion in her work on southern women: "Gentility and its social and civic rituals accentuated the elites' cultural preeminence while affording women, as part of a culturally distinct governing class, unprecedented

access to and influence in the world beyond their households." Kierner, *Beyond the Household*, 5. See also Bushman, *The Refinement of America*.

CHAPTER FOUR

1. Deas, *Recollections of the Ball Family of South Carolina and the Comingtee Plantation*, 157.
2. The next generation of Balls—two of Affra's nephews—fared much better. They immigrated to South Carolina after her death and founded a powerful family dynasty that lasted well into the nineteenth century. For further discussion of the Ball family see Edward Ball, *Slaves in the Family* (New York: Hill and Wang, 1998).
3. Important works exploring the connection between family life and economic activity in the eighteenth century include Anzilotti, "In the Affairs of the World"; Hall, "Family Structure and Economic Organization"; David Hancock, *Citizens of the World: London Merchants and the Integration of the British Atlantic Community, 1735-1785* (Cambridge: Cambridge University Press, 1995); James Henretta, "Families and Farms: Mentalité in Pre-Industrial America," *William and Mary Quarterly* 38 (1978), 3-32; Johnson, *A Shopkeepers Millennium*; Kierner, *Traders and Gentlefolk*; Kulikoff, *Tobacco and Slaves*; Cathy Matson, *Merchants and Empire: Trading in Colonial New York* (Baltimore: Johns Hopkins University Press, 1998); Price, *Perry of London*; and J. M. Sosin, *English America and the Restoration Monarchy of Charles II: Transatlantic Politics, Commerce and Kin* (Lincoln: University of Nebraska Press, 1980).
4. Despite the tremendous wealth of the lowcountry, few early American scholars study the economy of South Carolina. Historians Russell Menard and John McCusker conceded, "We simply know less about the economy of the Lower South than of any other region of British America." Russell Menard and John McCusker, "The Economy of British America, 1607-1790: Needs and Opportunities for Study," 1980 Conference on the Economy of British America, Williamsburg, Virginia, quoted in Richard B. Sheridan, "The Domestic Economy," in Greene and Pole, *Colonial British America*, 43-85. See also Russell Menard, "Financing the Lowcountry Export Boom: Capital and Growth in Early South Carolina," *William and Mary Quarterly* 51 (October 1994), 659-76. For more general information on colonial South Carolina's economy, see Peter Coclanis, *The Shadow of a Dream: Economic Life and Death in the South Carolina Lowcountry, 1670-1920* (New York: Oxford University Press, 1988); Converse Clowse, *Economic Beginnings in Colonial South Carolina, 1670-1730* (Columbia: University of South Carolina Press, 1971); Alice Hanson Jones, *Wealth of a Nation to Be: The American Colonies on the Eve of the Revolution* (New York: Columbia University Press, 1980); Stuart Owen Stumpf, "The Merchants of Colonial Charleston, 1680-1756" (Ph.D. diss., Michigan State University, 1971); Weir, *Colonial South Carolina*, chap. 7.
5. The Perry family of London and Virginia paralleled this pattern of family-based firms. In his study of the Perrys, Jacob Price found that the primary instrument "for the

pursuit of overseas opportunities was most commonly the family firm." Family members provided connections, jobs, status, and, perhaps most importantly, capital. Two brothers originally ran the Perry firm, and their and their sister's marital behavior was predicated on financial considerations. Price, *Perry of London*. For the connections between commerce and kinship (and religion) in the late seventeenth century, see Sosin, *English America and the Restoration Monarchy of Charles II;* chapter 11 focuses specifically on the southern proprietary colonies.

6. Stumpf, "Merchants of Colonial Charleston," 14, 145; Sirmans, *Colonial South Carolina*, 228; Waterhouse, "South Carolina Colonial Elites," 75–80; Bull, *Oligarchs of Colonial and Revolutionary Charleston;* Arthur Hirsch, *The Huguenots of Colonial South Carolina* (Durham, N.C.: Duke University Press, 1928).

Most of South Carolina's merchants centered in Charleston, although a few operated out of Georgetown and Beaufort. Charleston's preeminent merchants imported diverse products including slaves, rum, and English goods. The three largest exports were rice, indigo, and deerskins. Throughout the eighteenth century merchants continued exporting timber, pitch, foodstuffs, and livestock, but these never held more than incidental interest for most elites. For a further discussion of the emergence of Charleston as the center of Carolina commerce, see R. C. Nash, "Urbanization in the Colonial South: Charleston, South Carolina as a Case Study," *Journal of Urban History* 19 (November 1992), 3–29.

7. W. O. Moore, Jr., "The Largest Exporters of Deerskins from Charles Town, 1735–1775," *South Carolina Historical Magazine* 73 (1972), 144. See also Braund, *Deerskins and Duffels;* Tom Hatley, *The Dividing Paths: Cherokees and South Carolinians through the Revolutionary Era* (New York: Oxford University Press, 1995); and Wright, *Only Land They Knew*.

8. Moore, "Largest Exporters of Deerskins from Charles Town," 147. Only one of the top five exporters, John Gordon, appears to have traded skins without officially forming partnerships with relatives. Gordon shipped fewer cargoes and paid less duty than the others, although he traded for more years than three of the largest exporters. Through their family firms, Gordon's fellow deerskin traders oversaw more and larger shipments than did Gordon, who acted alone.

9. Stumpf, "Merchants of Colonial South Carolina," 77; Weir, *Colonial South Carolina*, 145.

10. The cultivation and export of indigo followed the patterns of rice. Established planters quickly entered the indigo trade in large part because it was practical and efficient to grow rice and indigo on the same plantations. Indigo seeds were sown in the early spring and the first cutting of indigo usually occurred in July and the second in August. Rice was planted in April and May and harvested in early September. Thus, no significant overlap in production of the crops occurred. Lelia Sellers, *Charleston Business on the Eve of the American Revolution* (Chapel Hill: University of North Carolina

Press, 1934), 148–63; Clowse, *Economic Beginnings in Colonial South Carolina*, 256–58, 234. Quotation from Clowse, 237.

11. Charleston merchants largely monopolized the slave trade in South Carolina. Between 1735 and 1775, eleven cargoes of slaves arrived in Beaufort, Port Royal, and Georgetown combined. In that same forty-year period, Charleston merchants brought in 1,108 shipments of slaves. W. Robert Higgins, "Charles Town Merchants and Factors Dealing in the External Negro Trade, 1735–1775," *South Carolina Historical Magazine* 65 (1964), 205–17. In 1690, just over 1500 slaves had been brought to South Carolina. By 1730 that number had expanded to 20,000. In the next ten years it almost doubled, so that by 1740, over 39,000 Africans lived in Carolina. The increase occurred in large part because of demands brought on by rice production. Stumpf, "Merchants of Colonial Charleston," 163.

12. Higgins, "Charles Town Merchants and Factors Dealing in the External Negro Trade."

13. A number of scholars, including Jack Greene, have made similar arguments. According to Greene, "Relations between merchants and planters were unusually harmonious . . . and together they dominated South Carolina society." Greene, *Quest for Power*, 32. See also Robert Weir, "'The Harmony We Were Famous For': An Interpretation of Pre-Revolutionary South Carolina Politics," *William and Mary Quarterly* 26 (October 1969), 473–501.

14. Waterhouse, "South Carolina Colonial Elites," 184.

15. See Coclanis, *Shadow of a Dream*; quotation from Carl Bridenbaugh, *Myths and Realities: Societies in the Colonial South* (New York: Atheneum Press, 1974), 58.

16. Waterhouse, "South Carolina Colonial Elites," 160; Sirmans, *Colonial South Carolina*, 227–28. In 1935–36 Wragg and his family firm imported 6,230 gallons of rum and 341 slaves, and exported 6,095 deerskins. Manigault did not trade in slaves but chose instead to concentrate on rum. In 1735–36 he imported 11,333 gallons of rum.

17. Henry Laurens to John Knight, 23 October 1769, *Papers of Henry Laurens*, vol. 7, 170.

18. Robert Pringle to Andrew Pringle, 11 August 1740, in Walter Edgar, ed., *The Letterbook of Robert Pringle*, vol. 1 (Columbia: University of South Carolina Press, 1972).

19. Ralph Izard to Peter Manigault, 23 April 1769, Ralph Izard Papers, SCL; George Lucas to Charles Pinckney, 23 December 1745, Harriett Ravenel Papers, SCHS; miscellaneous letters, Richard Hutson Letterbook, Langdon Cheves III Papers, SCHS.

20. Ralph Izard to Peter Manigault, 23 April 1769, Ralph Izard Papers, SCL; John Drayton to James Glen, 1 March 1767, James Glen Papers, SCL; miscellaneous letters, Manigault Family Papers, SCL. This Gabriel Manigault (1758–1809) was the grandson and namesake of the aforementioned Gabriel Manigault (1704–81).

21. For further discussion of female planters see Anzilotti, "Autonomy and the Female Planter in Colonial South Carolina." Detailed analysis of Eliza Pinckney can be

found in the July 1998 issue of the *South Carolina Historical Magazine*, and in Scott, "Self-Portraits," in Bushman et al., *Uprooted Americans*, 43–76. Cynthia Kierner's *Southern Women in Revolution, 1776–1800: Personal and Political Narratives* (Columbia: University of South Carolina Press, 1998) provides excellent commentary on the public activities and the private motives on southern women during the Revolutionary era.

22. C. C. Harris, *Kinship* (Buckingham: Open University Press, 1990), 95. See also Pasternak, Ember, and Ember, *Sex, Gender, and Kinship*, chap. 7; and Farber, *Comparative Kinship Systems*.

23. Edgar, *The Letterbook of Robert Pringle*; Barnwell, "The Diary of Timothy Ford, 1785–1786," 132–33.

24. Webber, "Dr. John Rutledge and His Descendants," 7–25, 93–106; Cheves, "Blake Family Genealogy," *South Carolina Historical and Genealogical Magazine* 1 (1900), 153–66. The Ralph Izard discussed here was a relative of the more well-known Ralph Izard, husband of Alice DeLancey.

25. Henry Smith, comp., "Wragg of South Carolina," *South Carolina Historical and Genealogical Magazine* 19 (1918), 121.

26. Edgar, *Letterbook of Robert Pringle*; *Papers of Henry Laurens*; Bull, *Oligarchs of Colonial and Revolutionary Charleston*.

27. Barnwell, "The Diary of Timothy Ford," 191–92.

28. Thomas Dale to Thomas Birch, 17 November 1732; Thomas Dale to Thomas Birch, 25 November 1734, Thomas Dale Papers, SCL; Sarah Rhett to Thomas Amory, 20 November 1707, Middleton Family Papers, SCL.

29. "The Bond Family of Hobcaw Plantation," *South Carolina Historical and Genealogical Magazine* 25 (1924), 1–22; Rogers, *Charleston in the Age of the Pinckneys*, 24.

30. John Lloyd to Richard Campion, 22 April 1794; John Lloyd to Richard Campion, 9 May 1794, John Lloyd Letterbook, SCL.

31. Anzilotti, "In the Affairs of the World," 65.

32. Barnwell, "The Diary of Timothy Ford," 137–38.

33. Hall, "Family Structure and Economic Organization," 44–46, 53; Bernard Farber, *Guardians of Virtue: Salem Families in 1800* (New York: Basic Books, 1972), 66–110; Kulikoff, *Tobacco and Slaves*, 252–56; Waters, "Family, Inheritance, and Migration in Colonial New England," 65; Hanger, *Bounded Lives, Bounded Places*, 90. See also Matson, *Merchants and Empire*, and Hancock, *Citizens of the World*.

34. Gough, "Close-Kin Marriage and Upper-Class Formation in Late Eighteenth-Century Philadelphia," 119–36; Farber, *Guardians of Virtue*, 197; Smith, *Inside the Great House*.

35. For further discussion of the effect of marriage on intergroup alliances and class identity, see Martin Ottenheimer, *Forbidden Relatives: The American Myth of Cousin Marriage* (Urbana: University of Illinois Press, 1996), chap. 7; Fox, *Kinship and Marriage*; and Farber, *Comparative Kinship Systems*.

36. Barnwell, "The Diary of Timothy Ford," 145–46.

37. John Crowley, "The Importance of Kinship: Testamentary Evidence from South Carolina," *Journal of Interdisciplinary History* 16 (Spring 1986), 565.

38. Crowley's analysis depended on the identification of individuals in the wills, rather than genealogical reconstitution. In other words, he counted people as brothers or sisters-in-law, cousins, aunts, or uncles only if the deceased specifically noted their relationship in the will. Therefore, he cannot adequately account for those instances in which a member of the kin group was named without the precise familial connections explained. Despite this methodological deficiency, his analysis provides important insight into the familial uniqueness of lowcountry elites. Crowley, "The Importance of Kinship," 571, 576.

39. See Appendix 1. My analysis is based on the wills of members of eleven prominent Charleston families between 1700 and 1800. I analyzed wills from all the families (Ball, Blake, Bull, Drayton, Izard, Laurens, Manigault, Middleton, Pinckney, Rutledge, and Wragg) that fit the following criteria: (1) they were included in Charleston's ruling class; (2) they produced three or more wills over the course of the eighteenth-century; (3) they left personal papers used in this study as anecdotal evidence; and (4) they offer reliable genealogical work. The study yielded seventy-five wills, from seventeen women and fifty-eight men. Wills of Charleston County, South Carolina, microfilm copies of WPA typescript, Reels 1–27 cover the period 1671–1800. (Hereafter cited as Charleston Wills.) The original typescripts are held by the South Carolina Department of Archives and History; the original wills have been destroyed.

40. Crowley, "The Importance of Kinship." Another study of lowcountry wills demonstrated that estate dispersal patterns did not benefit one heir at the expense of other siblings. In an analysis of 502 wills of politically active colonists, Richard Waterhouse found only fourteen that granted land to only one son when other children survived. Waterhouse, "South Carolina Colonial Elites," 194.

41. Crowley, "The Importance of Kinship," 570.

42. Charleston Wills, South Carolina Department of Archives and History.

43. Will of John Izard, probated 10 November 1780, Charleston Wills; A. S. Salley, Jr., ed., "Miles Brewton and Some of His Descendants," *South Carolina Historical and Genealogical Magazine* 2 (1901), 128–52; Will of Elizabeth Izard, probated 23 November 1784, Charleston Wills.

44. Will of Joseph Wragg, probated 16 August 1751, Charleston Wills, vol. 6, 527.

45. Charleston Wills, South Carolina Department of Archives and History.

46. Will of Elias Ball, probated 1 September 1758, Charleston Wills, vol. 8, 200.

47. Charleston Wills, South Carolina Department of Archives and History. In contrast, Crowley found only 29 percent of his subjects naming kin as executors. Crowley, "The Importance of Kinship," 568.

48. Will of Elizabeth Blake, probated 18 October 1792, Charleston Wills, vol. 24,

113; will of Hannah Bull, probated 2 February 1797, Charleston Wills, vol. 26, 612; will of Joseph Blake, probate unknown (died 1700), Charleston Wills, vol. 1, 18; will of William Wragg, probated 9 August 1780, Charleston Wills, vol. 19, 3.

49. Will of James Laurens, probated 21 May 1784, Charleston Wills, vol. 21, 663; will of William Bull, probated 31 January 1792, Charleston Wills, vol. 24, 984.

50. Charleston Wills, South Carolina Department of Archives and History.

51. Thomas Dale to Thomas Birch, 2 October 1735, Thomas Dale Papers, SCL.

52. Bull, *The Oligarchs of Colonial and Revolutionary Charleston*, 26.

53. Henry Laurens to William Fisher, 11 July 1768, *Papers of Henry Laurens*, vol. 5, 735–36; Henry Laurens to William Cowles & Co., 13 July 1768, *Papers of Henry Laurens*, vol. 5, 749.

54. Francis Leigh Williams, *A Founding Family: The Pinckney's of South Carolina* (New York: Harcourt, Brace, Jovanovich, 1978), 9; Joseph Manigault to Gabriel Manigault, 10 September 1784; Joseph Manigault to Gabriel Manigault, 28 August 1789, Manigualt Family Papers, SCL.

55. William Drayton to Peter Manigault, 16 August 1755, Manigault Family Papers, SCL.

56. Robert Calhoon and Robert Weir, "The Scandalous History of Sir Egerton Leigh," *William and Mary Quarterly* 26 (January 1969), 36–38, 64.

57. Bull, *Oligarchs of Colonial and Revolutionary Charleston*, 253–56, 306–16.

58. Webber, "Dr. John Rutledge and His Descendants," 16; Edward Rutledge to Mr. Miller, 22 December 1797, Edward Rutledge Papers, SCL; "The Last Advice of John Rutledge to His Children," 9 September 1799, John Rutledge Papers, SCL. For more on the long, distinguished political careers of John and Edward, see James Haw, *John and Edward Rutledge of South Carolina* (Athens: University of Georgia Press, 1997).

59. William Vernon to Samuel Vernon, 17 January 1746, William Vernon Papers, SCL; Margaret Kennett to Thomas Brett, undated letter, Brett Papers, Bodleian Library, Oxford, reprinted in Brian J. Enright, ed., "An Account of Charles Town in 1725," *South Carolina Historical Magazine* 61 (January 1960), 13–18; Henry Laurens to James Habersham, 25 January 1768, *The Papers of Henry Laurens*, vol. 5, 565; James Habersham to Henry Laurens, 22 February 1768, *Papers of Henry Laurens*, vol. 5, 602. Habersham was a businessman and planter living in Savannah, Georgia.

60. Coclanis, *Shadow of a Dream*, 121–24; Jones, *Wealth of a Nation to Be*.

61. Moses Lopez to Aaron Lopez, 3 May 1764, Thomas J. Tobias, ed., "Charles Town in 1764," *South Carolina Historical Magazine* 67 (April 1966), 63–74, 67; 23 September 1783, letter of Lewis Thibou, SCL; Walter L. Robins, ed., "John Toblers Description of South Carolina," *South Carolina Historical Magazine* 71 (1970), 144; Frederick P. Bowes, *The Culture of Early Charleston* (Chapel Hill: University of North Carolina Press, 1942), 11.

62. Mark Anthony DeWolfe Howe, ed., "Journal of Josiah Quincy, Jr., 1773," *Massachusetts Historical Society Proceedings* 49 (1916), 444; Fraser, *Charleston! Charleston!* 129;

Barnwell, "The Diary of Timothy Ford," 143. Richard Bushman's excellent *Refinement of America* investigates this conscious construction of genteel culture throughout America.

63. For further discussion see Bushman, *Refinement of America;* Kierner, *Beyond the Household;* and Patricia Cleary, "Making Men and Women in the 1770s: Culture, Class, and Commerce in the Anglo-American World," in Laura McCall and Donald Yacovone, eds., *A Shared Experience: Men, Women, and the History of Gender* (New York: New York University Press, 1998), 98-116.

64. The growing control of the colonial economy (and government and society) by interrelated elites occurred in the Chesapeake as well. According to Allan Kulikoff, "During the eighteenth century, gentlemen in the tidewater Chesapeake became a self-conscious ruling class that not only increasingly monopolized power and wealth, but formed their own culture as well." Kulikoff, *Tobacco and Slaves,* 263.

65. George Milligan, *A Short Description of the Province of South Carolina,* in Chapman J. Milling, ed., *Colonial South Carolina: Two Descriptions* (Columbia: University of South Carolina Press, 1951); Sirmans, *Colonial South Carolina,* 228; Howe, "The Journal of Josiah Quincy," 454.

66. Morgan, *Slave Counterpoint.* See also Ira Berlin, *Many Thousands Gone: The First Two Centuries of Slavery in North America* (Cambridge: Harvard University Press, 1998), and Robert Olwell, *Masters, Slaves, and Subjects: The Culture of Power in the South Carolina Lowcountry, 1740-1790* (Ithaca: Cornell University Press, 1998).

67. T. P. Harrison, ed., "Journal of a Voyage to Charlestown in So. Carolina by Pelatiah Webster in 1765," 5, Trinity College Library, DUL; Barnwell, "The Diary of Timothy Ford," 203; Robins, "John Toblers Description of South Carolina," 144.

68. Barnwell, "The Diary of Timothy Ford," 143, 203; Fraser, *Charleston! Charleston!* 134; Bridenbaugh, *Myths and Realities,* 76; Barnwell, "The Diary of Timothy Ford," 143.

69. Thomas Thompson to Reverend Humphries, 1 May 1736, *South Carolina Historical and Genealogical Magazine* 50 (1949), 178; Reverend Gadsden Johnson, 20 September 1708, quoted in Stumpf, "The Merchants of Colonial Charleston," 67.

70. Anzilotti, "In the Affairs of the World," 20; Eliza Lucas to Thomas Lucas, 22 May 1742, *Letterbook,* 39-40; Joseph Manigault to Gabriel Manigault, 30 December 1786, Manigault Family Papers, SCL; Margaret Kennett to Thomas Brett, undated letter; Margaret Brett to Mrs. Brett, 20 January 1725, in Enright, ed., "An Account of Charles Town in 1725," 13-18. See also Michael Byrd, "'Ye have of poor always with you': Attitudes Toward Relief of the Poor in Colonial Charleston" (M. A. Thesis, University of South Carolina, 1973); and Barbara Bellows, "'My Children, Gentlemen Are My Own': Poor Women, the Urban Elite, and the Bonds of Obligation in Antebellum Charleston," in Walter J. Fraser, R. Frank Saunders, Jr., and Jon Wakelyn, eds., *The Web of Southern Social Relations: Women, Family, and Education* (Athens: University of Georgia Press, 1985).

71. H. Roy Merrens, ed., "A View of Coastal South Carolina in 1778: The Journal of Ebenezer Hazard," *South Carolina Historical Magazine* 73 (1972), 190; Barnwell, "The Diary of Timothy Ford," 143.

72. Richard Hutson to Sam Smith, 12 March 1766; Richard Hutson to Joel Benedict, 14 March 1766; Richard Hutson to Ebenezer Pemberton, 24 June 1766, Letterbook of Richard Hutson, Langdon Cheves III Papers, SCHS.

CHAPTER FIVE

1. Edward Rutledge to Henry Rutledge, 2 August 1796, Edward Rutledge Papers, SCHS; Edward Rutledge to Henry Rutledge, 28 July 1796, Edward Rutledge Papers, SCL.

2. Weir, *Colonial South Carolina;* Greene, *Quest for Power;* Rachel Klein, *Unification of a Slave State: The Rise of the Planter Class in the South Carolina Backcountry, 1760–1808* (Chapel Hill: University of North Carolina Press, 1990). See also Weir, "The Harmony We Were Famous For," 473–501.

3. *Colleton Family Papers,* SCL; Easterby, *Wadboo Barony;* Bull, *Oligarchs of Colonial and Revolutionary Charleston;* Geraldine M. Meroney, *Inseparable Loyalty: A Biography of William Bull* (Norcross, Ga.: The Harrison Company, 1991).

4. Weir, *Colonial South Carolina;* Waterhouse, "South Carolina's Colonial Elites."

5. Nairne was eventually exonerated. Eirlys M. Barker, "Pryce Hughes, Colony Planner, of Charles Town and Wales," *South Carolina Historical Magazine* 95 (October 1994), 302–13; Weir, *Colonial South Carolina,* 82–83.

6. During the first twenty years of settlement, the Goose Creek men controlled much of the colony's resident political power. Ultimately in 1719 the Goose Creek men and their successors brought about the collapse of proprietary government. Weir, *Colonial South Carolina.* For more on this topic, see Waterhouse, "South Carolina's Colonial Elites"; Wright, *Only Land They Knew;* and particularly Sirmans, *Colonial South Carolina.*

7. The establishment of the Church of England in South Carolina in 1706 essentially ended the dissenters' political challenges. For more on the growing power of the Goose Creek men, see Wright, *The Only Land They Knew,* chap. 4.

8. For further analysis of the Fundamental Constitutions, see Sirmans, *Colonial South Carolina;* Clarence L. Ver Steeg, *Origins of a Southern Mosaic: Studies of Early Carolina and Georgia* (Athens: University of Georgia Press, 1975); and Waring, *First Voyage and Settlement of Charles Town.*

9. Weir, *Colonial South Carolina,* 70.

10. Middleton Family Papers, SCL; George Lane, "The Middletons of Eighteenth Century South Carolina: A Colonial Dynasty, 1678–1787" (Ph.D. diss., Emory University, 1990); Cheves, "Middleton of South Carolina," 228–62; Rogers, *Charleston in the Age of the Pinckneys.*

11. Vipperman, *Rise of Rawlins Lowndes*.

12. Bull, *Oligarchs of Colonial and Revolutionary South Carolina*, 25–26.

13. In the colonial period, governors of South Carolina were usually Britons. Consequently, the highest office Carolinians held was lieutenant governor. But because governors frequently traveled or resided abroad, the lieutenant governor often served as acting governor. Bull, *Oligarchs in Colonial and Revolutionary Charleston*, 14.

14. James Wright Papers, SCL. The Wright siblings' father, Robert Wright, served as chief justice of South Carolina before his son-in-law.

15. Miscellaneous correspondence, Pinckney Family Paper, SCL. For more information on the Pinckneys see Rogers, *Charleston in the Age of the Pinckneys*, 116–40; and Marvin R. Zahniser, *Charles Cotesworth Pinckney, Founding Father* (Chapel Hill: University of North Carolina Press, 1967).

16. After Rutledge's term as "president," the state renamed that position "governor." Webber, "Dr. John Rutledge and His Descendants," 7–25. For more on the Rutledge brothers, see Haw, *John and Edward Rutledge of South Carolina*.

17. For analyses of the interconnections between marriage and politics in Massachusetts and Maryland, see Farber, *Guardians of Virtue*, chap. 4, and Jordan, "Political Stability and the Emergence of a Native Elite in Maryland," in Tate and Ammerman, *Chesapeake in the Seventeenth Century*, 243–73.

18. James Glen Papers, SCL; Harrison, "Journal of a Voyage to Charlestown in South Carolina by Pelatiah Webster in 1765"; Bull, *Oligarchs of Colonial and Revolutionary Charleston*.

19. Ralph Izard to Gabriel Manigault, 19 December 1789, Ralph Izard Papers, SCL.

20. County courts existed only briefly in South Carolina. Although several were established in 1721, within ten years "the assembly passed a law which allowed the plaintiff in any civil suit to choose the site of the trial; because most of South Carolina's creditors were merchants they invariably preferred the Charles Town court of common pleas." The legal statutes supporting the county courts remained on the books, but the courts ceased to exist. Waterhouse, "South Carolina's Colonial Elites," 206. See also Sirmans, *Colonial South Carolina*.

In neighboring Virginia these courts held far greater prominence, operated as important avenues to attaining political power, and provided valuable experience for the House of Burgesses. For more on the importance of county courts and the impact of familial connections upon them, see Greene, *Quest for Power;* and I. Ferguson, "County Courts in Virginia, 1700–1830," *North Carolina Historical Review* 8 (1931), 14–40.

21. Barnwell, "The Diary of Timothy Ford," 199.

22. Waterhouse, "South Carolina's Colonial Elites," 217.

23. For a detailed analysis of the Royal Council see M. Eugene Sirmans, "The South Carolina Royal Council, 1720–1763," *William and Mary Quarterly* 18 (July 1961), 373–92.

24. A group of interconnected merchants provided ten of the remaining appointments.

25. Sirmans, "South Carolina Royal Council, 1720–1763," 378–79; Sirmans, *Colonial South Carolina*, 285–88.

26. Waterhouse, "South Carolina's Colonial Elite," 306.

27. Ibid., 291.

28. The Charleston area is defined as St. Philip's, St. Michael's (carved out of St. Philip's in 1751), St. Andrew's (just across the Ashley river), and Christ Church.

29. The positions of power are based on Jack Greene's analysis of committee appointments within the assembly. Greene, *Quest for Power*, 475–88; Waterhouse, "South Carolina's Colonial Elites," 306–12.

30. In the early eighteenth century, the South Carolina Royal Council carried far more prestige and membership was very exclusive. Members of the planter-merchant class satisfied their political ambitions in the assembly. Over the course of the eighteenth-century, both the power and the prestige of the assembly rose at the expense of the council and governor. For more on this transformation of the power structure, see Greene, *Quest for Power*.

31. Mark Anthony DeWolfe Howe, ed., "Journal of Josiah Quincy, Jr., 1773," *Massachusetts Historical Society Proceedings* 49 (1916), 452.

32. Greene, "Foundations of Political Power in the Virginia House of Burgesses."

33. According to Jack Greene, "Over half the leaders [in the House of Burgesses] were connected either through blood or marriage to one of the great eighteenth-century families, and only a conspicuous few reached the top level of power without such connections." Greene, "Foundations of Political Power in the Virginia House of Burgesses," 489. See also Charles S. Sydnor, *American Revolutionaries in the Making: Political Practice in Washington's Virginia* (New York: Free Press, 1965). For comparison studies, see Jordan, "Political Stability and the Emergence of a Native Elite in Maryland"; Jack Greene, "Society, Ideology, and Politics: An Analysis of the Political Culture of Mid-Eighteenth-Century Virginia," in Richard M. Jellison, ed., *Society, Freedom, and Conscience: The Coming of the Revolution in Virginia, Massachusetts, and New York* (New York: W. W. Norton, 1976), 14–76; and Kurtz, *Kinship and Politics*.

34. Gary Nash, "The Transformation of Urban Politics, 1700–1740," *Journal of American History* 60 (December 1973), 605–32.

35. Gough, "Close-Kin Marriage and Upper-Class Formation in Late Eighteenth-Century Philadelphia," 119–36.

36. Members of the planter-elite could easily sidestep the land requirement. For example, in 1756 Gabriel Manigault transferred 2,476 acres of land to his son Peter so he could take his seat in the assembly. By 1768 Peter had advanced to Speaker of the assembly. Land Deed, 10 January 1756; Peter Manigault letter, 28 July 1768, Manigault Family Papers, SCL. In the end, the royal government disallowed this expansion of the property qualification.

37. This analysis is based on Jack Greene's data concerning members of the southern colonial assemblies in *Quest for Power*, 475–88. "Significant positions of power" is

defined as more than one term in the most prominent and powerful committees. Those who held only one appointment in the first-rank committees or only appointments in the secondary or second-rank committees are not included here.

38. See Appendix 2. Henry Hyrne, William Drake, and Paul Trapier each served only two terms in the first rank. Although they represented outlying areas, Rawlins Lowndes, Henry Middleton, Charles Cotesworth Pinckney, William Wragg, and Thomas Lynch all lived primarily in Charleston. None can be considered appropriate representatives of backcountry interests.

39. Outlying parishes actually elected thirteen men to the assembly who served extended periods. However, included in those thirteen were Thomas Lynch, Peter Taylor, and Rawlins Lowndes, each of whom resided in Charleston and identified strongly with the elites there. For that reason, they are not included as actual representatives of the outlying parishes.

40. See Appendix 3. Years of service are cumulative rather than consecutive.

41. Thomas Middleton did not serve in the highest capacity, but he certainly had the familial support to do so if he desired.

42. Myriad works debate the power of deference in early America. See Gordon Wood, *The Radicalism of the American Revolution* (New York: Knopf, 1992), part one; and "Deference or Defiance in Eighteenth-Century America? A Roundtable," *Journal of American History* 85 (June 1998), 13–97, particularly Michael Zuckerman's essay, "Tocqueville, Turner, and Turds: Four Stories of Manners in Early America," 13–42.

43. The clause is first found in section XXI of the 19 March 1778 constitution and subsequently in the constitutions of 1790 and 1865. "And whereas the ministers of the gospel are by their profession dedicated to the service of God and the cure of souls, and ought not to be diverted from the great duties of their function—therefore no minister of the gospel or public teacher of any religious persuasion, while he continues in the exercise of his pastoral function, and for two years after, shall be elligible either as Governor, Lieutenant-Governor, an member of the Senate, House of Representatives, or Privy Council in this State."

44. Barnwell, "The Diary of Timothy Ford," 197.

45. Henry Laurens to James Grant, 1 October 1768, *Papers of Henry Laurens*, vol. 6, 119. For further discussion of mechanics and artisans in Revolutionary South Carolina see Richard Walsh, *Charleston's Sons of Liberty: A Study of Artisans, 1763–1789* (Columbia: University of South Carolina Press, 1959).

46. Weir, *Colonial South Carolina*, 275; Klein, *Unification of a Slave State*, 9. For more on the disparity of wealth and influence between the lowcountry and backcountry on the eve of the American Revolution, see Klein, *Unification of a Slave State*.

47. Richard Brown, *The South Carolina Regulators* (New York: Belknap, 1963); and Klein, *Unification of a Slave State*.

48. Weir, *Colonial South Carolina*, 275–77.

49. In her influential study of the Carolina backcountry in this era, Rachel Klein

conceded that the 1790 Constitutional Convention "was the culmination of a successful effort by the coast-dominated government to legitimate its own authority in the midst of mounting challenges." Klein, *Unification of a Slave State*, 109, 113.

50. For general analysis see Jeffrey Crow and Larry Tise, eds., *The Southern Experience in the American Revolution* (Chapel Hill: University of North Carolina Press, 1978); and Don Higginbotham, *The War of American Independence: Military Attitudes, Policies, and Practice, 1763–1789* (New York: Macmillan, 1971).

51. A. S. Salley, ed., *Journal of the House of Representatives of South Carolina, January 8, 1782 to February 26, 1872* (Columbia: State Company, 1916), 9–10; "Account of Reverend Archibald Simpson, 1783–1784," Katherine M. Jones, ed., *Port Royal under Six Flags* (Indianapolis: Bobbs-Merrill, 1960), 138–39.

52. Other studies on the interplay between war and family include Joy Day Buel and Richard Buel, Jr., *The Way of Duty: A Woman and Her Family in Revolutionary America* (New York: Norton, 1984); Reid Mitchell, *The Vacant Chair: The Northern Soldier Leaves Home* (New York: Oxford University Press, 1993); and Melvin Yazawa, *From Colonies to Commonwealth: Familial Ideology and the Beginnings of the American Republic* (Baltimore: Johns Hopkins University Press, 1985).

53. Salley, *Journal of the House of Representatives of South Carolina, January 8, 1782 to February 26, 1872*, 13; Francis Kinloch to Thomas Boone, 1 October 1782, in Felix Gilbert, ed., "Letters of Francis Kinloch to Thomas Boone, 1782–1788," *Journal of Southern History* 8 (1942), 91–92; Oliver Hart to Joseph Hart, 24 March 1778, Oliver Hart Papers, SCL.

54. South Carolinians were not unique in this regard. Massachusetts men also joined the patriot cause with their brothers, and family was a vital tool in the mobilization of Massachusetts forces. As Robert Gross explained, "The muster was almost a family reunion" in Concord. Robert Gross, *The Minutemen and Their World* (New York: Hill and Wang, 1976); and Bill Boller, "Kinship and Culture in the Mobilization of Colonial Massachusetts," *The Historian* 57 (Winter 1995), 291–302.

55. Weir, *Colonial South Carolina*, 324–25; Miscellaneous letters, Manigault Family Papers, SCL; miscellaneous letters, Pinckney Family Papers, SCL; Bull, *Oligarchs in Colonial and Revolutionary Charleston*, 242–43.

56. Many attending the Continental Congress perceived John Rutledge as one of the most conservative delegates, while Edward Rutledge appeared more radical. The Rutledge brothers surprised the other states' delegates, however, by agreeing to support one another in Congress. Despite his less conservative leanings, Edward followed John's lead, and the desires of the planter-merchants of Charleston was the main impetus for their political behavior. James Haw, "The Rutledges, the Continental Congress, and Independence," *South Carolina Historical Magazine* 94 (October 1993), 232–51; Cheves, "Middleton of South Carolina"; Webber, "Dr. John Rutledge and His Descendants," 7–25, 93–106; and George C. Rogers, Jr., "Four Who Went to Philadelphia," *South Caro-*

liniana Society Annual Program, 1989. John Rutledge, Thomas Lynch, and Christopher Gadsden had also attended the Stamp Act Congress together. Weir, *Colonial South Carolina*, 294.

57. Maurice A. Crouse, ed., "Papers of Gabriel Manigault, 1771–1784," *South Carolina Historical Magazine* 64 (1963), 6–7; Gabriel Manigault to Gabriel Manigault, 4 April 1778, Manigault Family Papers, SCL. For more on the loyalist exodus from South Carolina, see Robert Barnwell, "The Migration of Loyalists from South Carolina," *Proceedings of the South Carolina Historical Association*, 1937.

58. John Laurens to Gabriel Manigault, 5 April 1776, Manigault Family Papers, SCL.

59. Bull, *Oligarchs in Colonial and Revolutionary Charleston*, 222–23.

60. Richard Hutson to Isaac Hayne, 22 March 1777, Letterbook of Richard Hutson, Langdon Cheves III Papers, SCHS.

61. Robert Stansbury Lambert, *South Carolina Loyalists in the American Revolution* (Columbia: University of South Carolina Press, 1987); Ronald Hoffman et al., eds., *An Uncivil War: The Southern Backcountry during the American Revolution* (Charlottesville: University of Virginia Press, 1985).

62. Oliver Hart Diary, 12 August 1775 and 13 August 1775, Oliver Hart Papers, SCL.

63. Nisbet Balfour to Lt. McPherson, 21 January 1781, Nisbet Balfour Papers, SCL.

64. For a fuller analysis of slavery during the Revolutionary War, see Olwell, *Masters, Slaves and Subjects*, 226–70.

65. The best overviews of women in the Revolutionary era are Norton, *Liberty's Daughters;* and Kerber, *Women of the Republic.*

66. For similar analyses see Kierner, *Southern Women in Revolution;* and Mary Beth Norton, "'What an Alarming Crisis is This': Southern Women and the American Revolution," in Crow and Tise, *The Southern Experience in the American Revolution*, 203–34. Psychologists argue that trauma, whether the death of parents or social turmoil, heightens bonds between siblings. As siblings face life crises, they intensify their dependence on one another. Bank and Kahn, *Sibling Bond;* Dunn and Kendrick, *Siblings;* Cicirelli, *Sibling Relationships across the Life Span.*

67. Anzilotti, "In the Affairs of the World," 189; Harriott Pinckney Horry Letterbook, SCHS; Eliza Pinckney to Thomas Pinckney, 17 May 1779, *South Carolina Historical Magazine* 76 (1975), 158; Anne Manigault to Gabriel Manigault, 6 June 1775, Manigault Family Papers, SCL; Richard Hutson to Isaac Hayne, 24 June 1776, Letterbook of Isaac Hayne, Langdon Cheves III Papers, SCHS; William Hayne to Jeremiah Yates, 23 December 1835, William Edward Hayne Papers, SCL. See also David K. Bowden, *The Execution of Isaac Hayne* (Lexington, S.C.: Sandlapper Store, 1977).

68. Kierner, *Southern Women in Revolution*, 99. See also Linda Kerber, *No Constitutional Right to Be Ladies: Women and the Obligations of Citizenship* (New York: Hill and Wang, 1998), chap. 1, concerning the case of Anna Gordon Martin of Massachusetts.

69. Eliza Pinckney to Dr. Garden, 14 May 1782, *South Carolina Historical Magazine* 76 (1975), 168–70.

70. Isaac Motte to William Drayton, 6 August 1780, Isaac Motte Papers, SCL.

71. Kierner, *Southern Women in Revolution;* Lambert, *South Carolina Loyalists.*

72. The best synthesis of the Revolutionary era is Wood, *Radicalism of the American Revolution.*

73. Carol Pateman, *The Disorder of Women: Democracy, Feminism, and Political Theory* (Cambridge: Polity Press, 1989); Kierner, *Beyond the Household;* and Wood, *Radicalism of the American Revolution.*

74. For an extensive analysis of South Carolina political culture in the early national era, see Thomas S. Price, "Palmettos and Property: Historical Memory and Political Culture in Early National South Carolina" (Ph.D. diss., University of Illinois at Chicago, 1994).

75. Henry Laurens was also selected, but he could not attend the convention. When the delegation was selected, his daughter Eleanor was courting Charles Pinckney. Eleanor Laurens and Charles Pinckney married in 1788. Rogers, "Four Who Went to Philadelphia."

76. In his extensive study of the Pinckney family, George Rogers argued, "The Rutledge-Pinckney faction was a key group in a crucial state. . . . Without the city [Charleston], the state would not have been for ratification. Without South Carolina, there would have been no United States." Rogers, *Charleston in the Age of the Pinckneys,* 130. Historian Mark Kaplanoff argued that ratification was predicated on a lowcountry planter-merchant agenda. According to Kaplanoff, "South Carolina's was a nationalism of a very qualified sort." Despite their purported advocacy of the Federalist agenda, during the Constitutional debates of 1787–88, the lowcountry really seemed most concerned with advancing its own political and economic agenda. Even in the 1780s, "Carolinians had a clear perception of their own separate interests." Kaplanoff insisted that "South Carolina's nationalism was always conditional—not a commitment to abstract principles, but an expedient to protect and promote perceived economic interests." Mark Kaplanoff, "How Federalist was South Carolina in 1787–1788?" in *The Meaning of South Carolina History* 67, 89.

77. Charles Pinckney married Frances Brewton, Miles Brewton's sister. Frances and Miles were Charles's cousins—the children of his mother's (Ruth Brewton) brother. Rogers, *Charleston in the Age of the Pinckneys,* 127; Bull, *Oligarchs in Colonial and Revolutionary Charleston.*

78. Rogers, *Charleston in the Age of the Pinckneys,* 117–18.

79. William Read to Jacob Read, 18 December 1795, Jacob Read Papers, SCL; Ralph Izard to Jacob Read, 17 November 1795; Ralph Izard to Charles Cotesworth Pinckney, 18 January 1795, Ralph Izard Papers, SCL.

CONCLUSION

1. Eliza Lucas to George Lucas, 1 June 1742, *Letterbook*, 49.
2. Allan Kulikoff found that Virginia's gentry used education in a similar manner. Kulikoff, *Tobacco and Slaves*. In the early nineteenth century some Carolinians did urge a revitalization of education, but they remained in the minority. The majority focused attention (or paranoia) on white power and protecting themselves against slave rebellions and threats of abolition. George Rogers argued that "what was developing was a certain reverence for the past, a living to protect that past, a rigidity, an inflexibility." Rogers, *Charleston in the Age of the Pinckneys*, 154. See also Michael O'Brien and David Moltke-Hansen, eds., *Intellectual Life in Antebellum Charleston* (Knoxville: University of Tennessee Press, 1986). For an extensive analysis of political developments, see Price, "Palmettos and Property."
3. Morgan, *Slave Counterpoint*, 664.
4. Coclanis, *Shadow of a Dream*, 139.
5. For a comprehensive explanation of the economic decline of the lowcountry in the nineteenth century, see ibid., 111-58. And for an excellent analysis of yeoman families in that era, see McCurry, *Masters of Small Worlds*.
6. Coclanis, *Shadow of a Dream*, 136-37. For more on the rise of the backcountry see Klein, *Unification of a Slave State*.
7. Rogers, *Charleston in the Age of the Pinckneys*, 161.
8. Klein, *Unification of a Slave State*; Orville Vernon Burton, *In My Father's House Are Many Mansions: Family and Community in Edgefield, South Carolina* (Chapel Hill: University of North Carolina Press, 1985).
9. For regional comparisons see Farber, *Guardians of Virtue*, 111-55; Kurtz, *Kinship and Politics*; Kulikoff, *Tobacco and Slaves*; Nash, "Transformation of Urban Politics," 605-32; Jordan, "Political Stability and the Emergence of a Native Elite in Maryland," in Tate and Ammerman, *The Chesapeake in the Seventeenth Century*, 243-73; Gough, "Close-Kin Marriage and Upper-Class Formation in Late Eighteenth-Century Philadelphia," 119-36. See also Wood, *Radicalism of the American Revolution*, 11-92.
10. Hall, "Family Structure and Economic Organization." In his work on New England merchants, Bernard Bailyn also demonstrated the importance of family in developing business contacts, acquiring capital, and creating a merchant class. Bailyn, *The New England Merchants in the Seventeenth Century*.
11. Hall, "Family Structure and Economic Organization"; Gough, "Close-Kin Marriage and Upper-Class Formation"; and Kulikoff, *Tobacco and Slaves*.
12. See also Mary Beth Norton's recent analysis of these terms in Norton, *Founding Mothers and Fathers*, 20-24.
13. The *Journal of American History* recently published a provocative roundtable on the power of deference in early America: "Deference or Defiance in Eighteenth-

Century America?: A Roundtable," *Journal of American History* 85 (June 1998), 13–97. See especially Zuckerman's essay, "Tocqueville, Turner, and Turds," 13–42.

14. Examples include Smith, *Inside the Great House,* and Lewis, *The Pursuit of Happiness.* See also Wood's excellent synthesis of colonial social history in part 1 of *Radicalism of the American Revolution.*

INDEX

advice literature, 53, 176–7n. 90
African Americans, xi, 6, 100, 142, 162n. 5; kinship, xiv–xv. *See also* slavery
American Revolution, xiii; destruction in, 130; and family displacement, 44, 80–1, 132–4; ideology in, 133, 135–6; kin and allegiance, 130–2; kin divisions, 105–6, 131–2; reliance on kin, 43, 130, 134–5, 136
Amory, Sarah, 6, 98
Assembly, South Carolina, 114, 117, 118–9, 123–7; apportionment, 123–4, 128–9; gentry control, 123–7, 128, 151–4; growing power of, 114, 124, 125–6, 194n. 30
Austin, Eleanor, 65, 80
Austin, George, 65, 80, 89, 97, 103, 155
Austin & Laurens, 89, 91, 92, 93

backcountry: growth of, 128–9, 143; *vs.* lowcountry and estate settlement, 101; *vs.* lowcountry and family, 129, 143; *vs.* lowcountry and politics, xiii, 114, 123–4, 126–7, 128–30, 132, 135–6; surpasses lowcountry, 143–4
Ball, Elias (1676–1751), 7, 155
Ball, Elias (1709–86), 103, 155
Ball, John Coming, 55, 75, 97, 155
Ball family, 7, 16, 75, 185n. 2
Barbados, and South Carolina, xii, 3–5, 14, 90. *See also* West Indies
Bayard, Francis Moore, 34
birth order, xiii, 28, 160–1n. 9
Blake, Daniel, 29, 32
Blake family, 29, 32–3, 88, 96, 122
blended families, 8, 28, 99
boarding relatives, 25, 35, 39, 44–6, 50, 173n. 56; in Revolutionary War, 133, 134–5, 136
Bond sisters, 98
Boston, 3; gentry and kinship, xv, 99, 100, 145; politics, 125
Brailsford, Edmund, 18, 40–1, 170–1n. 33
Brailsford, Edward, 18, 40–1
Brett, Thomas, 21

Brewton, Miles, 91, 94, 102, 108, 137–8
Britain, influences on Carolina gentry, 23
British families: and extended kin, 11–2; and relatives in South Carolina, 10–1, 12, 13, 18–20, 21; *vs.* South Carolina families, 7–12
brothers: and American Revolution, 131; business partnerships, 15–6, 88–9, 94, 104–5; and colonization, 14–5; conflict between, 106; detachment from siblings, 74; emotional ties among, 42–3, 51; and politics, 118, 119–20, 137, 138; psychological analyses, 184n. 71; relationships with sisters, 35, 52, 59–62, 70–81, 85
Bryan, Arthur, 44
Bryan, Jonathan, 29, 44
Bryan brothers, 49, 56–7
Bull, Stephen (1635–1706), 1–2, 15, 88, 115
Bull, Stephen (1708–50), 104, 119
Bull, Stephen (1734–95), 105–6, 132
Bull, William, II, 104, 105–6, 118–9, 120, 132, 138
Bull family, 1–2, 15, 88, 104, 105–6, 115, 118, 120, 122, 132
businesses: Atlantic context, xii, 3, 12–3, 15–6, 21, 88–93; and initial colonization, xii, 2, 8, 9–12; and kin, x, 3–5, 12, 15–6, 21, 29, 87–95; in 19th century, 143
Butler, Pierce, 136–7

Charleston: as center of politics, 114, 116–7, 121–30, 137; economic marginalization in 19th century, 143; founding, 1; travelers accounts, 107–11
Chesapeake Bay, 42; planters, xv, 144–5, 168n. 8; slavery, 109
childbirth, 26–7
childlessness, xv
child rearing, 30–47, 74; and class, 63; and filial duty, 64–5; and gender, 60, 62–6; in late 18th century, 63; maternal presence, 44–5

Christ Church parish, 6
Civil War, 142-3
class: and child rearing, 63; divisions, xi, xiv, 108-9, 141, 144; and education, 32, 36, 141; and estate settlement, 101-2; and marriage, x, 8, 9-10, 33, 47-9, 67-8, 95-101, 120, 125; women's role in, 85-6, 95, 108. *See also* gentry
Colleton, John, 5, 115
Colleton family, 3-4, 14, 16-7, 20, 88, 115
Coming, Affra Harleston, 7, 13, 87, 88, 112
Coming, John, 7
conjugal family, xi, 48, 49, 66, 85, 159n. 2; and estate settlement, 10-1, 102-4, 149-50. *See also* patriarchal family
Constitution, U.S., 109, 119, 136-7, 198n. 76
Council, South Carolina, 114, 119; gentry control of, 122, 194n. 30
courtship, 47, 59, 60, 64, 78; awkwardness in, 66-7; kin involvement, 47-8, 78, 98-9
cousin marriage, x, 9-10, 48, 96, 175n. 74
Crowley, John, 101-2

Dale, Thomas, 9, 15, 98
Deas, Anne Izard, 51, 73, 155
deerskin trade, 88, 89-90; gentry control of, 89-90
deference, x-xi, 31, 36-7, 58, 62, 66, 70, 74, 76, 109, 146-7; in kin groups, 78, 79-80; in politics, 127-8, 135-6
demographic instability: in early colonization, 5-6, 9, 42, 54; England *vs.* South Carolina, 8-9; and family structure, xii, 5-6, 23-4, 42
Drayton, John, 37-8, 40, 55-6, 65, 69, 94-5, 104, 120, 122
Drayton, Margaret Glen, 55-6, 120
Drayton, William, 38-9
Drayton brothers, 37-8, 40, 42-3, 55-6
Dyssli, Samuel, 17-8

Edgar, Anne, 75
education, 30-42, 64; and class, 32, 36, 141; dearth in Charleston, 110, 141; travel abroad, 28, 32, 39, 40
elites. *See* gentry
estate settlement, 10-1, 76, 87, 101-4, 149-50, 189nn. 38-40; in England, 10-1; and family conflict, 40, 75
exchange marriage, 9-10, 48-9, 96

family: as economic entity, xv, 12, 36, 47, 87, 93; empires, ix, 4, 5, 14-5, 17, 20, 21-2, 88-93, 95, 98, 120, 127; historians, xi-xii, 47, 59-60, 62, 140, 145-7
fatherhood, 27, 63-6; and emotional bonds, 63-4; and political careers, 44-5, 74
Ford, Timothy, 40, 96, 97, 100, 108, 110, 111
friendship, 59-60, 64, 83; *vs.* parental authority, 38-9
Fundamental Constitutions, 116-7

gender: and family duties, 65-6; relations, among siblings and kin, 59-62, 70-86, 146; relations, in patriarchal family, xi, 59-70, 80-1; roles, in early colonization, 13-4; segregation, 60, 70, 82. *See also* men's culture; women
gentry: *vs.* backcountry, 114, 123-4, 126-7, 128-30; challenges to, 127-30, 133, 135-6; conservatism, 110, 136, 139, 141-4; conspicuous consumption, 107-9; control of economy, 87-95, 107, 111-2, 140-1, 144-5; "dissipation," 110-1; and education, 32, 36; expulsion from, 105-6; identity, and kinship, ix, 31-2, 35, 49, 58, 85-6, 93, 95, 106-7, 108-9, 110-2, 114, 121, 126-7, 129, 135-6, 139, 140-1, 144-7; and letter writing, xiii, 53-4, 85-6; lifestyles, 48, 107-11, 141; marriage practices, x, 8-10, 33, 47-9, 67-8, 95-101, 120, 125; in 19th century, 140-4; *vs.* outsiders, 21, 49, 58; *vs.* outsiders, and economics, 87-8, 90-3, 95, 107, 108-9, 110-2; *vs.* outsiders, and politics, 114, 121, 125-6, 127-8, 136, 139, 143-4; and politics, 65, 113-39, 140-1, 144-5; religious indifference of, 10, 100, 110, 116, 122, 145; and revolutionary ideology, 133-4; and slavery, 90-1, 92, 94, 109-11, 142
Gittens, Mary Laurens, 66, 75-6
Gittens, Nathaniel, 66, 75-6
Glen, James, 37-8, 40, 43, 55-6, 69, 94-5, 120, 122
Gondy, Anthony, 17
"Goose Creek" men, 5, 12, 116, 120
grandparents, 41, 43-4, 64
Greene, Jack P., 4, 152, 154

Habersham, James, 107
Harleston, John, 7
Hart, Anne, 50, 68, 70

Index

Hart, Oliver, 45, 68, 130, 132
Hayne, Elizabeth Hutson, 80-1, 133
Hayne, Isaac (ca. 1738-81), 36-7, 41, 43, 80-1, 94, 133
Hayne, Isaac (1766-1802), 36-7, 41
Hazard, Ebenezer, 111
"hidden family," xii, xvi, 140, 146
Horry, Daniel (alias Charles Lucas Pinckney Horry), 34, 36, 45, 171n. 34
Horry, Harriott Pinckney (1748-1830), 34, 36, 45, 47, 52, 74, 77, 95, 113, 133, 155, 156
Huguenots, 7
Hutson, Richard, 36-7, 38, 41, 43, 80-1, 94, 111, 133
Hyrne, Edward, 1-2, 18-9, 20, 77
Hyrne, Elizabeth Massingberd, 1-2, 13, 18-9, 20, 77

illness, 5, 49-50, 54-5, 89; and pregnancy, 26-7
incest, x, 9-10, 48, 174-5n. 73
indigo, ix, 91, 186n. 10
inheritance strategies. *See* estate settlement
intragenerational family, ix-x, 24, 42, 57-8, 85, 147; focus in early colonial era, 5-6, 8-12, 21-2, 23-4; and gender, 60-1; and gentry culture, 30, 147; *vs.* patriarchal family, 25, 46-7, 49, 56, 57-8, 61-2, 76, 79-81, 85, 103-4, 146. *See also* kin
Izard, Alice DeLancey, 34, 39, 41, 50, 55, 69, 74, 83-4, 155, 157, 172n. 47
Izard, George, 34, 39-40, 41, 74
Izard, Henry, 33-4, 39, 41, 52, 77-8, 155
Izard, Ralph (ca. 1741-1804), 32-4, 39-40, 41, 63-4, 69, 74, 83-4, 94, 121, 138, 155, 157
Izard, Ralph, Jr., 41, 73, 155
Izard family, 32-3, 55, 96, 122, 155, 157

judicial system, 118, 119, 121-2, 128, 193n. 20

Kennett, Margaret Brett, 21, 107
kin: absence in colonization, 1-2, 17-9, 21, 87-8; and affection, 17, 25, 35, 41, 57; in American Revolution, 130-5; and Atlantic businesses, 12-3, 88-93; and businesses, xii, 2, 8, 12-3, 15-6, 87-95; and childbirth, 26-7; and child rearing, 30-47, 74; correspondence, xiii-xiv, 71, 72-3, 85; and courtship, 47-8, 78, 98-9; difficulty investigating, xi-xii, 20, 53-4; duty *vs.* individual desires, 33-4, 36, 45-6, 47-9, 99, 106, 113-4, 146-7; in early colonization, 1-3, 12-22, 87-9, 115-7; and economic aid, 37, 50, 104-7; and economic power, 15-6, 87-112; and education, 28, 30-42; and estate settlement, 74-5, 101-4, 149-50; and gentry conservatism, 136, 139, 141-4; and gentry identity, ix, 31-2, 35, 49, 58, 85-6, 93, 95, 106-7, 108-9, 110-2, 114, 121, 126-7, 129, 135-6, 139, 140-1, 144-7; and marriage, x, 9-10, 47-9, 96, 175n. 74; and naming practices, 29-30; necessity for education, 34, 35, 41; necessity in politics, 118-21, 125, 126, 138-9; ostracism, 105-6; *vs.* patriarchal family, 36-9, 41-2, 56, 57-8, 146-7; and plantation management, 94-5; and political culture, 114, 121, 125, 135-6, 138-9; and political networks, 5, 16-7, 115, 117, 118-21, 122-3, 124, 136-9; residential proximity, 12-3, 100, 125, 145; scholarly disinterest in, xi, xii, 147; sickness and death, 54-5; as surrogate parents, 32, 40, 41, 42-6, 75; and travel, 32-3, 39-40, 50. *See also* brothers; intragenerational family; siblings; sisters
kin conflict: in American Revolution, 105-6, 131-2; and estrangement, xiv, 18-20, 21, 38, 40-1, 55-7, 58, 75, 80-1, 84, 105-6; and literary sources, 20, 53-4; over marriage, 98-9

land: availability in South Carolina, 7, 8, 10-1; and inheritance, 10-1; ownership and gentry, 91-2
Laurens, Eleanor Ball, 29, 80, 97, 155
Laurens, Henry, 29, 38, 76, 80, 110, 128, 155; and Ball family, 50, 55, 75, 97, 103; business interests, 89, 93, 94, 105, 107; and children, 45, 63, 64, 65; and educational networks, 32, 37
Laurens, James, 103
Laurens, John, 65-6, 75-6
Laurens family, 155
Leigh, Egerton, 105
letter writing: and gentry identity, xiii, 53-4, 85-6; between siblings and kin, xiii-xiv, 20, 44, 52-4, 58, 70-3, 77-8
Lloyd, John, 73, 98
Lopez, Moses, 107
Lowndes, Charles, 17, 118

Lowndes, Rawlins, 17, 118
loyalism, 131, 132, 134, 135
Lucas, Eliza (later Eliza Lucas Pinckney), ix-x, 12, 13, 17, 35, 44, 54, 55, 62, 68, 70, 72, 79, 83, 94, 110, 140, 156. *See also* Pinckney, Eliza Lucas
Lucas, George (?-1747), ix, 5, 62, 68, 94, 156
Lucas, George (ca. 1725-1756), ix, 156
Lucas, Polly, ix, 35, 156
Lucas, Thomas, ix, 79, 156
Lucas family, ix, 44, 156

Manigault, Anne (1762-1811), 53-4, 79-80, 133, 155-6
Manigault, Anne Ashby (1705-82), 12, 43-4, 155-6
Manigault, Charles Izard, 83
Manigault, Elizabeth Wragg, 26, 93, 97, 155-6
Manigault, Gabriel (1704-81), 12, 38-9, 41, 43-4, 88, 92-3, 122, 131, 155-6, 194n. 36
Manigault, Gabriel (1758-1809), 34, 39, 111, 155-6; and brother, Joseph, 42-3, 44, 51, 57, 95, 105; and politics, 121, 131, 138; and sister Anne, 53-4, 79-80, 133; and wife, Margaret Izard, 63, 68, 73, 84
Manigault, Harry, 34, 57
Manigault, Joseph, 29, 42-3, 44, 51, 53-4, 57, 67, 73, 95, 105, 111, 131, 155-6
Manigault, Margaret Izard, 26, 29, 34, 52, 55, 56, 64, 68, 72, 74, 77-8, 83-4, 155, 157
Manigault, Peter, 12-3, 29, 38-9, 43-4, 64, 93, 94, 97, 155-6, 194n. 36
Manigault family, 42-3, 88, 131, 155-6
manufacturing, dearth in lowcountry of, 110, 143
marriage, 47-9, 60-1, 67-70; and affection, 8, 47, 67-8; conflict in, 97-9, 134; and economic interests, 8, 9-10, 47-9, 65-6, 67-8, 75, 87, 95-101; in England, 8-10; and gentry, x, 8-10, 33, 47-9, 67-8, 95-101, 120, 125; inequality in, x, 67-70; instability in early colonization, 23; parental oversight, 65-6; and personal choice, 47-9, 68, 99-100; and political power, 47, 67, 120, 125; prohibitions, 48; theoretical analyses, 96. *See also* cousin marriage; exchange marriage
Maryland, 2-3. *See also* Chesapeake Bay
Massingberd, Burrell, 2, 19, 77
men's culture, 70, 72, 73, 85, 86

merchants: cooperation between, 88-90, 91, 92-5; diversification, 92-3; intermarriage, 96-7; outside Charleston, 186n. 6, 187n. 11; relations with planters, 91-2
Middleton, Arthur, 5, 28, 118
Middleton, Edward, 5
Middleton, Henry, 118-9, 131
Middleton family, 14, 28, 29, 88, 118, 122
migration: into backcountry, 128, 129; into lowcountry, 6, 7; regional comparisons, 2-3, 162-3n. 6, 163n. 8
Moore, Stephen, 34
Moore siblings, 73
Morgan, Philip, 109
mortality, xii, 5-6; and family strategies, 8-10, 142; infant, 26; and naming patterns, 30
motherhood, 26-9, 65

Nairne, Thomas, 15, 115
naming practices, 29-30, 169-70n. 24; necronymic, 30
Native Americans, xi, xiv; Cherokee, 89; Creeks, 89; Yamassee, 10
New England, 2-3; marriages in, 100; and patriarchal families, 23
New York, 2-3; gentry, 100, 145; politics, 125
non-elites, xi, 15, 141, 162n. 5; and estate settlement, 101-2; exclusion from businesses and wealth, 87-8, 91, 92, 93, 95, 107, 108-9, 110-2; exclusion from politics, 114, 121, 125-6, 127-8, 136, 139; and kinship, xiv; political activities of, 128, 135-6

only children, xv, 43
orphans, 23-4, 25, 29, 41, 42-6, 102-3; reliance on siblings and kin, 6, 42-3

parental death, 23-4, 32, 42-6; effects on children, 6; and intensification of sibling bonds, 42-3, 172-3n. 54
parent-child relations, x-xi, 31, 40-1, 62-6, 75-6; conditional affection, 64-5; conflict, 37-8; and demographic instability, 23-4; *vs.* kin ties, 36-42; loss of parental authority, 39-40; psychological analyses, 25. *See also* patriarchal family
partible inheritance, 10-1
patriarchal family, x, 23-4, 25-7; child rearing in, 31, 37, 62-5; and demographic

instability, xii, 5-6, 23-4, 42; in England, 11-2; ostracism, 65-6, 75-6, 80, 99; and sibling and kin influences, x-xi, 24-5, 46-7, 49, 56, 57-8, 61-2, 76, 79-81, 85, 103-4, 146; women within, 51, 60-86
patriarchy, x-xi, 25, 36-9, 47, 159n. 3; female challenges to, 66, 85; *vs.* revolutionary ideology, 134, 135; and sexual power, 69; *vs.* sibling values, xi, 80-1, 146; and women, 60-1, 62, 81, 85
Peronneau, Arthur, 94, 132
Peronneau, Mary Hutson, 43, 80, 132, 133
Philadelphia, 2-3; gentry and kinship, xv, 100, 145; politics, 125
Pinckney, Charles (ca. 1699-1758), 9, 68, 94, 156
Pinckney, Charles (1732-82), 137
Pinckney, Charles (1757-1824), 119, 136-7, 156, 198n. 75
Pinckney, Charles Cotesworth, 45, 63, 155, 156, 157; and educational networks, 32, 39-40; and politics, 113, 119, 131, 136-7, 138; and siblings, 34, 51, 52, 76-7; in youth, 35, 43
Pinckney, Eliza Lucas, 9, 35, 36, 43, 50, 63, 72, 95, 133, 134, 155, 156. *See also* Lucas, Eliza
Pinckney, Harriott (1748-1830). *See* Horry, Harriott Pinckney
Pinckney, Harriott (1776-1866), 47, 52, 78, 156
Pinckney, Mary, 26-7, 54, 72, 83
Pinckney, Sally (Sarah) Middleton, 133, 156, 157
Pinckney, Thomas (1750-1828), 63, 155, 156; and politics, 119, 131, 137; and siblings, 34, 47, 51, 52, 73-4, 76-7; in youth, 35, 43
Pinckney, Thomas, Jr. (1780-1842), 47, 52, 78, 156
Pinckney family, 14, 88, 155, 156, 171n. 34
planters: cooperation between, 88, 92, 94; leisured lifestyle, 111; relations with merchants, 91-2
politics: in early national era, 113, 119-20, 121, 128-9, 136-9, 141, 143-4, 198n. 76; and kinship, 5, 16-7, 113-39; in proprietary era, 5, 114, 115-7, 120; in revolutionary era, 130-6; in royal colonial era, 117-26, 128, 138
pregnancy, 26-7
primogeniture, 10-1

Prince Frederick's parish, 123-4
Pringle, Andrew, 52, 94
Pringle, Robert, 52, 94, 96, 97
Pringle family, 48, 52, 96
proprietary era, 1-5, 114, 115-7, 120; collapse of, 117
proprietors, 1, 5; population programs, 7, 116; *vs.* resident gentry, 116-7, 120
provost marshal, 118, 128
public/private dichotomy, x, xv, 60, 81, 86, 145-7

Quincy, Josiah, 108, 109

Read, Catherine, 57, 68, 84
Read, Jacob, 63, 75, 138
Read, William, 27, 29, 63, 64, 65, 138
Read family, 27, 63
regional comparisons: kin and class, xv, 144-5; kin and migration, 2-3, 21-2, 162-3n. 6, 163n. 8; kinship, 2-3, 23, 25, 168n. 8; marriage, 67, 99-100; naming practices, 29-30; parenting, 62-3; politics, 124-5; slavery, 109; wealth, 107-8
regulators, 127, 128
religion: dissenters, 7, 116; gentry indifference to, 10, 100, 110, 116, 122, 145
remarriage, 8-9; and blended families, 28; in England, 8-9; and estate settlement, 99
Rhett, Sarah, 6, 98
rice trade, 90-2
Rutledge, Andrew, 15, 156
Rutledge, Edward, 45, 57, 63, 65, 106, 156-7; and educational networks, 33-4, 35, 39, 41; and politics, 113, 119-20, 131, 137, 138, 196n. 56
Rutledge, Henrietta Middleton, 133, 157
Rutledge, Henry, 33, 34, 113
Rutledge, Hugh, 119-20, 156-7
Rutledge, John (?-1750), 15, 96, 156
Rutledge, John (1739-1800), 106, 119-20, 130, 131, 136-7, 156-7, 196n. 56
Rutledge family, 15, 88, 156-7
Rutledge-Pinckney coalition, 113, 137, 138

ship-building, 88, 98
siblings: affection, ix, 59, 71, 77-8, 81, 83-5; age differences, xiii, 27-8, 71, 79-80; birth order, xiii, 28, 160-1n. 9; and child rearing, 30-47; conflict, xiii, 10-1, 28-9, 45-6, 57, 77, 102; conflict, and literary

siblings (cont.)
  sources, 45–6, 53–4; and courtship, 47–8; detachment, 28–9, 56–7, 74, 80, 102, 104; and education, 30–42; emotional ties, 23–58; equality between, x, 24, 28, 31, 39, 47, 58, 60–2, 70–8, 81–6, 146–7, 174n. 72; and estate settlement, 10–1, 101–4, 149–50; idealizations, 53–4; and identity, 25, 31, 46; in later life, 46–57; letter writing, 44, 52–4, 70–3, 77–8; limits of equality, 79–81; longevity of bonds, 31, 46, 71, 82; and naming practices, 29–30; psychological analyses, 24–5, 30–1, 39, 160n. 8, 174n. 72; sickness and death, 30, 54–5, 84; values, and gentry culture, ix, 25–6, 31, 58, 86, 93, 95, 109, 112, 114, 121, 135–6, 139, 140, 144, 147; values, *vs.* patriarchal family, x–xi, 24–5, 31, 36–7, 39, 41–2, 57–8, 60–2, 70–7, 80–1, 83, 85, 146–7; values, in "women's world," 71–2, 82, 86. *See also* brothers; kin; sisters
sisters: and brothers, 35, 52, 59–62, 70–81, 85; and childbirth, 27; criticism of brothers, 73–4, 77; death of, 84; emotional ties among, 61–2, 81–5; estrangement, 84; and identity, 82–3; as model of female ties, 83, 183–4n. 70; psychological analyses, 82, 184nn. 71–2; scholarly inattention to, 82; visiting, 84
slaveholding, 4, 92, 94, 107, 109–10, 111; and gentry identity, 109–11, 142
slavery, xi, xiv, 4, 90; in antebellum era, 142–3; and lowcountry economy, 90–1; in revolutionary era, 133, 135–6, 137; and women, 69, 180n. 29
slave trade, 88, 91; gentry control of, 91
Smith, Charlotte Georgina Izard, 48, 155, 157
Smith, Charlotte Izard, 55, 83–4, 155, 157
Smith, Joseph Allen, 48–9, 157
Smith, William Loughton, 34, 39, 49, 55, 74, 84, 138, 155, 157
St. George's parish, 123

St. John's parish, 5–6
Stead family, 89, 90, 94
stratification of wealth, 88, 90–1, 92, 93, 108–11
surrogate parents, 71, 98; kin as, 32, 40, 41, 42–6, 75; reluctance of, 45–6

Tennent, William, 127
Thibou, Lewis, 108
Toblers, John, 108, 110
travelers, accounts of Charleston by, 107–11

Virginia, 2–3; gentry, xv, 100; House of Burgesses, 124–5. *See also* Chesapeake Bay
virtual representation, 123–4
visiting, 25, 27, 44, 49–52, 84

wealth, in Charleston, 107–11
Webster, Pelatiah, 110
West Indies: family in, 4; and South Carolina, 2–5, 13, 88, 89, 90, 92
widows/widowers, 8–9, 134
Wilkinson, Eliza, 59–60, 66, 70, 72–3
wills. *See* estate settlement
women: in American Revolution, 133–4; and class identity, 85–6, 95, 108; culture of, 60, 70, 71–2, 81–2, 85, 86, 146; education, 32, 34–5; and female kin, 27, 35, 60, 61–2, 79, 81–5; friendships, 59–60, 83; kin supervision, 51, 72–4, 75, 85–6, 133; legal status, 67, 81; managing estates, 77, 81, 86, 95; in patriarchal family, x–xi, 51, 60–70, 75, 134, 135; and political ideology, 134, 135; in "public" life, 60, 70, 82, 85–6, 95, 146; status with siblings and kin, 60–2, 70–8, 81–6; surrogate mothers, 44–46; visiting, 50–1
Woodmason, Charles, 128
Wragg, Joseph, 16, 88, 91, 92–3, 96–7, 102
Wragg, Samuel, 16, 64, 88, 96–7, 102
Wragg family, 15–6, 92, 96–7
Wright siblings, 119

Library of Congress Cataloging-in-Publication Data
Glover, Lorri, 1967–
All our relations : blood ties and emotional bonds among the early
South Carolina gentry / Lorri Glover.
p.   cm. — (Gender relations in the American experience)
Includes bibliographical references and index.
ISBN 0-8018-6474-7 (acid-free paper)
1. Family—South Carolina—History.   2. Kinship—South
Carolina—History.   3. Upper classes—South Carolina—History.
4. Women—South Carolina—Family relationships.   5. Siblings—
South Carolina—Family relationships.   6. South Carolina—
History.   7. South Carolina—Social life and customs.   I. Title.
II. Series.

HQ536.15.S6 G56   2000
306.85'09757—dc21   00-030152